THE ANTHROPOLOGY OF CHINA

China as Ethnographic and Theoretical Critique

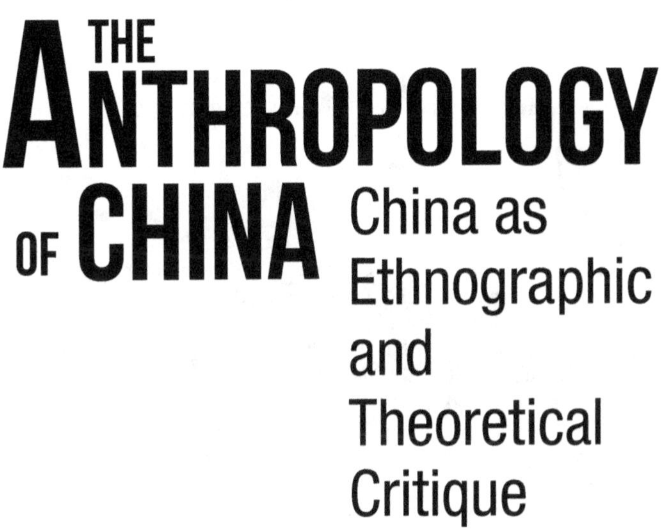

Charlotte Bruckermann
Stephan Feuchtwang

London School of Economics, UK

Imperial College Press
ICP

Published by

Imperial College Press
57 Shelton Street
Covent Garden
London WC2H 9HE

Distributed by

World Scientific Publishing Co. Pte. Ltd.

5 Toh Tuck Link, Singapore 596224

USA office: 27 Warren Street, Suite 401-402, Hackensack, NJ 07601

UK office: 57 Shelton Street, Covent Garden, London WC2H 9HE

Library of Congress Cataloging-in-Publication Data
Names: Feuchtwang, Stephan, author. | Bruckermann, Charlotte, 1984– author.
Title: The anthropology of China : China as ethnographic and theoretical critique /
Stephan Feuchtwang (London School of Economics, UK) &
Charlotte Bruckermann (London School of Economics, UK).
Description: New Jersey : Imperial College Press, 2016.
Identifiers: LCCN 2016002960| ISBN 9781783269822 (hc : alk. paper) |
ISBN 9781783269839 (pbk : alk. paper)
Subjects: LCSH: Families--China. | China--Social life and customs. |
Food--China. | Ethnology--China.
Classification: LCC HQ503 .F48 2016 | DDC 306.850951--dc23
LC record available at http://lccn.loc.gov/2016002960

British Library Cataloguing-in-Publication Data
A catalogue record for this book is available from the British Library.

Desk Editors: Herbert Moses/Mary Simpson

Typeset by Stallion Press
Email: enquiries@stallionpress.com

About the Authors

Professor Stephan Feuchtwang is an emeritus professor of the Anthropology Department at the London School of Economics. He has been engaged in research on popular religion and politics in mainland China and Taiwan since 1966, resulting in publications on charisma, place, temples and festivals, and civil society. He has recently been engaged in a comparative project exploring the theme of the recognition of catastrophic loss. In 2015, he completed the coordination of research on planning and community formation in urban neighborhoods of four cities as part of a European Commission project on sustainable urbanization in China. He has also been pursuing a project on the comparison of civilizations and empires.

Dr. Charlotte Bruckermann is a research fellow at the Max Planck Institute for Social Anthropology in Halle, Germany. Since completing her PhD in Anthropology at the University of Oxford in 2013, she has worked at the London School of Economics, Humboldt University and the University of Basel. Her areas of expertise include the anthropology of China, ritual, work, gender, economic transformation, and post-socialism. Based on fieldwork in rural Shanxi Province, her research has explored how villagers make themselves at home despite economic inequality, political rupture, and ecological degradation. She is about to embark on research investigating the role of finance in driving environmental projects.

Contents

About the Authors v

Chapter 1 Introduction 1
1.1 Outline of the Contents 2

Chapter 2 Anthropology of China: History, Regionalism, and Comparison 9
2.1 Anthropology's Crisis of Representation 11
2.2 Ethnographic Authority and the Regionalization of Anthropology 14
2.3 Revolution and Reform in the Anthropology of China 17
2.4 Regionalization from a Chinese Perspective 21
2.5 Fei and the Study of Chinese Society 24
2.6 Fei's Non-western Sociological Theory of China 26
2.7 Moral Crisis and Individual Ethics 31
2.8 China in a Changing World 35

Chapter 3 Kinship as Ideology and as Corporation 39
3.1 Developing Cognition between Individual and Ideology 40
3.2 Chinese Kinship from Family to Lineage 47
3.3 Changes from above: The Role of Neo-Confucian Ideologues 53
3.4 Bottom–up Rites as Drivers of Change 56

	3.5 The State, Laws, and Taxes in Kinship as Patricorporation	61
	3.6 Development of Historical Consciousness	65
	3.7 Conclusion	68
Chapter 4	Relatedness and Gender	71
	4.1 From Kinship to Relatedness	72
	4.2 Nurturing Reciprocity	78
	4.3 Engendering Desire	82
	4.4 Families Women Create	85
	4.5 Migration and Gendered Spaces	88
	4.6 Family Planning	90
	4.7 From Holism to Partial Processes	95
Chapter 5	Love, Emotion and Sentiment	99
	5.1 Love as Transcendence of the Self	100
	5.2 Love as Knowledge Revealed and Concealed	101
	5.3 How Structural is Love in China?	103
	5.4 Expressing Emotion through Action and Words	105
	5.5 Love between Passion and Affection	107
	5.6 The Romantic Revolution	108
	5.7 Romantic Scripts, Sex, and the City	110
	5.8 Affection and Dependence between Parents and Children	113
	5.9 Patriotism as Love Extended	115
	5.10 Love and Emotion in China	116
Chapter 6	The Exchange of Money, Gifts, and Favors	119
	6.1 Money and the Morality of Exchange	120
	6.2 Money in Chinese History	123
	6.3 Rural Relationships	130
	6.4 Urban Connections	132
	6.5 Status, Merit, and Self-Interest	133
	6.6 Elite Networks	135
	6.7 Kinship and Property	137
	6.8 Conclusion	139

Chapter 7	The Localization and Globalization of Food	143
	7.1 Chinese Cooking and Cuisines in Comparison	144
	7.2 National Cuisines on a Global Stage	146
	7.3 Chinese Food as World Cuisine	150
	7.4 The Generation Gap at the Table	153
	7.5 Inside and Outside Culinary Principles	156
	7.6 Localism from Cooking to Cuisine	158
	7.7 Consumer Culture and Corporate Food	160
	7.8 Faith, Food, and Identity	164
	7.9 Eating Modernity and Consuming Exoticism	166
Chapter 8	Nature, Environment, and Activism	171
	8.1 The Dualism of Nature and Culture	173
	8.2 Globalizing Nature in China and Taiwan	176
	8.3 Social Justice in Environmental Protest	180
	8.4 Compensation for Industrial Pollution	183
	8.5 Reason and Law in Rural Resource Management	184
	8.6 Global Environmentalism and *fengshui*	186
	8.7 Social Harmony Beyond Nature–Culture Dualism	188
Chapter 9	Ritual and Belief	191
	9.1 Government by Rite	192
	9.2 Ritual and Ideology	193
	9.3 Belief and Ritual Practice: Orthodoxy and Orthopraxy	198
	9.4 So, are We Actually Talking about the Influence of Writing and a State?	200
	9.5 Liberal Modernity, Ritual and the Cult of Sincerity	203
	9.6 Maoist Political Ritual	204
	9.7 Funerals Post-Mao	207
Chapter 10	Hospitality	213
	10.1 The Constraint to Share and Be Generous: The Basis of Civilization	213
	10.2 Altruism: The Impossible Gift on the Ultimate Scale of Humanity	215

10.3 An Anthropological Study of Hospitality 216
10.4 Imperial Chinese Guest Ritual 217
10.5 Chinese Anthropologies of Hospitality 220
10.6 Guest as a Parasite; Host as a Poisoner 222
10.7 Hosting Gods, Ghosts and Other Guests 223

Chapter 11 The Stranger-King and the Outside of an Imperial Civilization 227
11.1 The Theme of the Stranger-King 228
11.2 Heteronomy 230
11.3 The Outside of Tianxia — All Under Heaven 232
11.4 Ethnography of a Border Region 235
11.5 The Wild: Another View of the Center from the Margin 239
11.6 Conclusion 241

Chapter 12 The Anthropology of the Modern State in China 243
12.1 Some Benchmark Characteristics of Modern States 246
12.2 China's Formation as an East Asian State 247
12.3 Not Fleeing but Keeping a Negotiable Distance: Local Cultures in the PRC 249
12.4 Further Cases of Cultural Distancing and Cultural Incorporation 252
12.5 The Bai of Dali and their Culture in the New Dispensation 254
12.6 The Villages of Bashan in Enshi 257
12.7 An Indisputably Han Local Study 260
12.8 Conclusion 261

Chapter 13 Conclusion 263

Index 269

Chapter 1

Introduction

"The Anthropology of China" that we offer here works in two complementary directions. It offers students, teachers, and other readers a number of *anthropological topics* that we introduce in each chapter. In each case, we show many ways that the anthropology of China finds its inclusion in these mainstream topics and at the same time challenges the ways they have been construed. In the other direction, it offers students, teachers, and other readers primarily interested *in China*, the insights that anthropological studies gives to aspects of the social, economic and political history, and contemporary life of China.

Teachers of undergraduate and postgraduate courses can use this as a textbook for a full course. We have tested the course, teaching it at the level of final year undergraduates in anthropology. But readers will see that many of the topics are appropriate for sociology, politics, and history courses as well.

Each chapter introduces a general topic and conceptual frameworks for tackling it, with some empirical illustrations or sources from elsewhere than China. There are often substantial theoretical differences to be found in the conceptual treatments of these topics. The chapter then expounds a number of anthropological studies of China, many of them recently completed, showing how each one in turn illuminates the theoretical discussion by questioning, modifying, and extending the debate. Usually, these texts have not been juxtaposed as we have done, with each study exposed to the others thereby showing how each contribution takes the topic in a further or just another direction. Chapters conclude with a short review of how these studies add up in their contribution to the general theory. Appended to each chapter is a list of readings, including both the general theories and the China studies expounded in the chapter, and a list of further references made in our expositions. Questions that students could be asked in class or seminar are an important part of each chapter's ending because from their reading of the studies we have recommended they might well come to different conclusions and expositions than the ones we offer. Teachers and students may indeed have added other readings, or extended the topic in their own ways to reach different conclusions.

The texts of anthropologists of China, including those of native Chinese anthropologists, are all in English, either translated from Chinese or written originally in English. We did consider including Chinese-language text for Chinese readers, however, as the book is intended for readers both within and outside of China, we have chosen only English-language texts.

The book can with benefit be read as a whole consecutively, since each chapter follows the previous one in that their themes are quite closely linked. But it can also be read selectively.

1.1 Outline of the Contents

The next chapter (Chapter 2) is an extended discussion of the whole project of a comparative anthropology, a discussion conducted not only in general anthropology but also by anthropologists of and from China. It covers issues of how possible and necessary it is to rely on concepts developed within a particular society to understand that society, how much of the comparison is confined to the region in which that society is embedded, and how far insights can be extended to more general principles, applicable to any region, whether derived from the West or from China. It sets up the basic parameters for the whole book and introduces discussions of the constitution of the self and morality in agrarian China and how these have changed.

Chapter 3 takes up what has been a central topic, possibly the one most elaborated in anthropology: kinship. For a long time, the designation of different systems of descent, forms of address and conduct, and systems of alliance were the defining glory of both functional and structural anthropology. Then, challenges to these conceptions were mounted on several grounds and they are covered not only in this but also in the next chapter. In this chapter, the central argument covered is that a kinship system is an ideology, just as rituals, particularly death rituals and those of the worship of ancestors, are ideological. They establish the authors and authority over the sources of life and fate. In the Chinese case, the hierarchy of authority has to be historicized and placed in context, first the history of the dynastic state and of patrilineal descent as a way of governing, locally through lineages, but also through a central state authority, and then in the modernizing project of the state and the changes it has affected. All this is mediated through the way children learn their place in a family and in a history.

Chapter 4 follows on this critique of kinship studies with another that focuses on the practices of forming relationships of care and sociality designated as "relatedness." This focus brings to the fore the roles not only of children, but even more of women. Further, it stresses the materiality of making and maintaining close and more distant relations through everyday practices. Women in China not only sustain relations with their husbands' kin but also with their own natal kin, as well as with neighbors and friends. The Chinese case offers insights into the effects of government policy and of the economy on practical relations and bureaucratic abstraction. This becomes particularly apparent with the population policy, which brings together birth registration, fertility planning and civilizational quality, and further channels flows of migration and mobility to find waged work. All have a direct impact on gender relations and intergenerational responsibilities. Even while male lines of descent and women's marital migration to their husbands' households are upheld, the processes of choosing which relations to maintain reveal radically different experiences of relations of kinship by women from men in China. This opens up questions about the unity and the continuity of a kinship "system" in China, as relatedness does elsewhere.

Chapter 5 follows up the subject of making and maintenance of personal relations with the broader topic of exchange and reciprocity, another central theme of anthropology. It examines the possibility of differentiating between the exchange of commodities, the use of money, and interpersonal gifts in China. Here, the distinction between lasting social relationships and the short-term temporality of immediate exchange raises the question of the socially corrosive effect of pervasive capitalism and its money economy, posing a larger question of the reproduction of social life and moral cohesion. Chinese moral discourse is rich in judgmental descriptions of banqueting and other gift exchanges, and how instrumental and enduring the resulting relations are. As for other topics, an historical and political-economic anthropology is fruitful and indeed necessary in China, starting with the history of money and the status of commerce under the imperial courts, but including the socialism of collective responsibility and the market era of the People's Republic, in which interpersonal exchanges continue to thrive. This historical and political-economic anthropology of exchange in China offers new perspectives on the interleaving of monetary and gift exchanges and the hierarchy of value, status, and contentious moral judgment these entail.

Chapter 6 tracks another extension from kinship, after relatedness and interpersonal exchange, namely the anthropology of love and affection, particularly in sexual relations and in marriage. The anthropological issue is where to draw the line between humans and culture, especially as historical specificities meet the effects of modernizing projects advancing global capitalist relations, including wage labor, migration, and popular culture. How has romantic love and its related choice of sexual and marital partners changed in the Chinese tradition with the flow of global popular cultures? Anthropological studies in China might indicate a peculiar retention of intergenerational binding sentiments of support in work and affection, transformative, but continuous with a tradition of filial duty, since the family is still held responsible for much welfare by the contemporary state and conversely that state invokes patriotic affection.

Relatedness, interpersonal gifts, and care and affection are largely substantiated through sharing of food and the ritual exchange of special kinds of meals. Chapter 7 now takes up the question of how food separates as well as binds, in the same way and as how "cultures" distinguish themselves from others. Ostensibly delineated "cultures" with identifiable characteristics, including culinary practices or formalized cuisines, spread into each other and borrow from each other, yet consider themselves distinctive if not unique. People often have strong senses of belonging to a given "food culture," particularly since it is intimately transmitted down generations in families. At the same time, food as a knowledge system and as a habit, marks local and class identities at different scales of inclusion and exclusion, such as high and low cuisines. Comparing Chinese culinary practices with regional, foreign and diasporic cuisines, this chapter explores the attraction of the exotic and of the modern in food consumption on both local and global scales. It follows Chinese case studies, as they have contributed to the relatively new anthropology of food.

Chapter 8 moves from food to the environment and to conceptions of nature and ecology. The anthropological question is, whether the modernist cosmology that pits human society into a controlling and exploitative relation to nature, and into suffering the unpredicted environmental consequences of that relation, is shared in contemporary China. Anthropological studies of resistance to industrial pollution, the management of environmental resources, and the mobilization of *fengshui* elements in environmental discourse in contemporary China suggest that they are similar to global activism in their insistence on social justice. However, grass-roots Chinese activists tend to emphasize human-centered harm, demand economic compensation rather than ecological restoration, and incorporate a state-promoted value of social harmony that only recently became infected with the alleged Western opposition of nature and culture.

Closely following from food and all the previous chapters in another direction, Chapter 9 is about ritual and belief. Here we ask what and how is a changing, but traditional view of the world transmitted in the performance of rituals of greeting and separation, of marking and dealing with death, of addressing deities, ancestors, ghosts and demons, in the invisible world that encompasses the living world as its past but in the present. A transmitted cosmology may inform religious groups, such as redemptive societies that join in environmental movements even though they are incompatible with the conception of nature these modern movements involve. But the main anthropological issue in this chapter is whether rituals convey beliefs, in the sense of propositional truths, and what does the inclusion of written texts in rituals say about this. Is the cosmology they convey a "belief?" Chinese rituals do include the recital of written texts, but that is part of what all rituals are: a prescribed performance that is a sequence of actions. How does the ritual of professing faith in an ultimate truth that may be in a revealed text, such as the Bible and the Quran, differ from the recital of revelations of spirit writing or written dreams and visions? In either case, we are back with the transmission of ideals in ritual and in myth as an ideology of authority. In the present day, when the science of nature has replaced the transmitted cosmology, do these restored and reinvented rituals convey a counter-hegemonic ideology, in China and elsewhere? And how do the political rituals of the Mao era compare with religious rituals, apart from both doing and teaching what ritual does: leave a lasting lesson of how things could be?

Chapter 10 extends and expands the anthropology of gift to the more recently revived anthropology of hospitality. Hospitality, is the key virtue of civility or civilization. As an ultimate ideal, it is altruistic, a readiness to sacrifice oneself for another. But in practice, anthropologists have found hospitality to be an assertion of sovereignty in a contest of sovereignty that is enacted at several scales from household up to imperial or national sovereignty. In the anthropology of relations between guests and hosts, there has been an emphasis on the fraught acceptance of being a guest and the fear of the host as a poisoning threat. Here Chinese history offers an extreme paradox, in which a guest has to be treated as a host, when the guest is a representative of an order that encompasses the host, occurring in instances of an imperial representative's visit, or of a deity protecting and representing a territory that includes the host community.

Chapter 11 expands the anthropological study of sovereignty through the paradigm of the stranger king, the sovereign who comes from outside to claim legitimate, but also fearsome authority. It was typical of the first emperors of Chinese imperial dynasties to come from outside by conquest and other means. But do Chinese imperial conceptions of an imperial center and the rituals of centering and belonging at lower scales of "all under heaven" (tianxia) conceive of an outside, whose spiritual powers, life-giving and -destroying, fit the paradigm of the stranger king and the state derived from other civilizations? Studies of tributary kingdoms and egalitarian societies keeping a sovereign distance on the fringes of rule by the imperial son of heaven (tian) indicate the paradigm's applicability, but at the same time show that it needs modification.

Chapter 12 brings this anthropology of Chinese sovereignty and its states up to date. A number of studies of localities show how they hold their own distance, despite dependence on state agencies under the

People's Republic. They also reveal that one characteristic of all nation-state formation, especially multinational states, is the proliferation of cultural self-consciousness and its performance for others, such as local tourists or media and foreign tourists and global media, behind which some older civilizations and traditions are preserved. This chapter also asks from the bottom up, what can ethnographic studies add to conceptions of a state, administrations of rule, including forceful coercion, and in the case of China the extraordinary institution of the ruling Party and its extension beyond the lowest levels of state administration.

Chapter 13 brings us to a conclusion that offers an appraisal of what the anthropology of China adds, not just to the study of China, but also to anthropology in general, following the themes and topics to which readers of this book have been introduced. But readers are encouraged to form their own conclusions after reading the other texts.

Chapter 2

Anthropology of China: History, Regionalism, and Comparison

Anthropology, as the study of humankind, traces both the commonalities and specificities of humanity across time and space. In order to accomplish this, anthropological projects often focus their attention on particular people and represent their lives through a type of writing called ethnography. In doing so, anthropologists usually engage in more or less explicit forms of comparison, often within the constructed boundaries of a group of people at various spatial scales (e.g. local, national, regional) or across different periods of time (e.g. lifetimes, decades, epochs). Making comparisons necessitates a level of abstraction that simplifies, even distorts, the complexity of a particular situation. There is a long-standing and unresolved debate about how far anthropological comparisons should reach across particular ethnographic specificities. In addition, any form of textual representation involves the author making a selection process from the vast complexity of everyday life as experienced in order to create an account of events that persuades the reader of its validity. These issues of comparability and representation have been linked to a 'crisis in anthropology' in the wake of the crumbling of anthropology's scientific paradigm.

When this discussion came to head in the late 1980s, two broad camps emerged. On the one hand, cultural relativists advocated abandoning comparison in favor of evaluating each ethnographic endeavor on its own terms. On the other, anthropologists supporting comparative projects argued that the particular experience of a specific ethnographer could not form the basis for evaluating the quality of a given ethnography and that comparison was intrinsic and necessary to the anthropological endeavor. One solution posited by Fardon (1990) was that anthropologists explicitly analyze the regionalization of ethnographic accounts. Political contexts, disciplinary practices and institutional factors often shape the formation of anthropological specialization into particular, but often, arbitrarily bounded regions. In addition, through cross-referencing between texts, regions often become exemplars of anthropological interests, and their societies are held up as instances of particular types, features or problems.

This chapter takes up questions surrounding the regionalization of ethnographic accounts in relation to China. The chapter introduces the anthropology of China in relation to key themes and provides background knowledge about the political and institutional context for the study of Chinese society.

By taking up Fardon's appeal for more attention to the regionalization of ethnographic accounts, the chapter looks at both political and institutional factors affecting the production of ethnography and analyzes how regions become paradigms of particular anthropological topics. In order to put this into dialogue with the anthropology of China, the chapter charts ethnographic research and its absence through factors that affected Chinese society and the study of Chinese people in recent history. A general overview accounts for the fate of anthropology and social science through various epochs and eras in the 20th century and ends with a short survey of issues and interests concerning anthropologists of China today.

Turning to the life and work of China's most prominent anthropologist and sociologist, Fei Xiaotong, offers insights into both the political and institutional challenges, but also academic understandings of Chinese society and the opportunities for policy-oriented improvement to Chinese lives throughout the 20th century. One of Fei's initial pre-revolutionary thematic areas of interest, morality in China, will then be placed into comparison with recent debates on the subject. Morality is a topic on which Chinese ethnography has contributed a wealth of insights to general anthropological theory, and is therefore well placed to offer perspectives onto the regional questions that open the chapter. In particular, Yan Yunxiang's research into the shaping of discourses and shifting perspectives on morality may indicate where the anthropology of China has come from and is heading. In conclusion, Chinese anthropological debates about morality are shown to chime with contemporary ethnography that is political, historical, and contingent.

2.1 Anthropology's Crisis of Representation

Fardon looks at the production of anthropological knowledge through time, with a particular focus on the "new critics" of scientific paradigms in anthropology. Fardon argues that this is not a novel "movement," but that this critique had gathered pace and amplified in volume in the 1980s. This debate culminated in the publication of Writing Culture in 1986, to which Fardon's 1990 piece on the regionalization of ethnographic accounts can be seen as a rebuttal. To Fardon, the basis for this crisis lies at the very foundation on which anthropology as an academic discipline has been built, both intellectually and institutionally.

Franz Boas and Bronisław Malinowski, two great ancestors and founding fathers of modern anthropology in the USA and UK, respectively, established three key elements among their students: 'fieldwork, shorthand for participant observation, theoretical argument, and monograph writing' (p. 1). Although, all three ingredients were considered essential to anthropological success, these three components did not receive the same attention in terms of intellectual complexity, critical rigor, and temporal reach. Fieldwork was seen as relatively self-evident "data collection" followed by a straightforward process of "writing up" that did not require much methodological, let alone epistemological, soul-searching (pp. 3–4). By contrast, anthropological theory had to be couched in an illustrious genealogical heritage with credible precedents and notable advances to be taken seriously. Nonetheless, while theory could be overtaken and overturned with time, ethnography was considered timeless, and the value of any good piece of ethnographic writing could be redeemed by subsequent reanalysis, regardless of its original theoretical framework. Fardon argues, that this rests on an unexamined faith in "experiential positivism," where theory is assumed to leave the primacy and immediacy of the fieldworkers' experiences untainted (p. 3).

If anthropology rests on the three pillars of fieldwork, ethnography and theory, what happens when only the last leg of the tripod, theory, moves? The whole project is off kilter. Theory may have breakthroughs, but fieldwork is only thought to make tiny incremental advances in an already established ethnographic canon, 'building upon pioneer researches, "filling in gaps" in the record, perhaps correcting misconceptions (even serious ones), but not entirely overturning the terms of all previous writing on the area' (p. 3). In fact, ethnographic validity has only been overhauled completely once, when anthropologists stood up from their armchair and descended (*via* the veranda) to the field, with subsequent ethnography deemed a task of fine-tuning (p. 3). This leaves no place for the seismic shifts associated with Thomas Kuhn's paradigmatic breaks and scientific revolutions necessary in the advance of knowledge (p. 3). Anthropology needs "a new vision of the past [that] relocates our present standing and, in turn, revises our assessments of where we should be heading" (p. 4).

At this point, Fardon takes what he calls the "new critics" of the 1980s to task. He separates them into two camps, both of whom critically reflect on the production of texts: first, the Foucauldian and Marxist camp calling for "the critique from power" (pp. 6, 10); second, the literary school borrowing postmodern techniques of deconstruction and rhetoric to push an agenda of "the critique of representation" (pp. 7, 10). Both push the Geertzian analogy between culture and texts into new directions, while remaining skeptical of authority and authorship.

The critique from power interrogates the colonial framework enabling anthropology, positing anthropology as imperialism's twin in terms of power and knowledge. Here predatory European culture cloaked in the mantle of anthropology paraded around as "the inversion of a self-image [that] was generalized to some fictive collectivity based on geography, skin color, tribe, or whatever" (p. 6). Now the wool has been stripped from our eyes and 'we pride ourselves that we see through the mirrors we set up, no longer dazzled by the pleasing images of ourselves they reflected. The temporal transpositions have been rendered transparent for what they were: artifices of imagination in the service of power' (p. 6). Fardon remains unconvinced that scratching away at the surface of the machinery of power and knowledge will change its course. Furthermore, these accounts must take an absolute stance and privilege a particular vision of power over others, thereby rendering them incompatible with the second line of criticism.

The second, literary deconstruction of representation posits ethnographies as fictions, in the sense of accounts created or made (rather than false). As Clifford points out in his chapter of *Writing Culture*, the use of the term fiction is not opposed to truth, but highlights what is left out and how authority is asserted by examining how the poetics and politics of ethnography hinges on representation (Clifford, 1986). In Clifford's (1986: p. 2) words, ethnography 'makes the familiar strange, the exotic quotidian' and therefore, anthropology 'is actively situated *between* powerful systems of meaning.' Clifford and his co-authors in *Writing Culture* therefore, turn their gaze on how these narratives are composed and contested.

The literary turn criticizes ethnography as a kind of writing with telltale patterns of rhetorical tropes and stylistic devices to convince readers that the generalizations presented are valid and true (Fardon, 1990: p. 7). These include the omnipotent third person account where the author recedes from voicing her or his presence, opinion, and subjective involvement in creating anthropological knowledge. Occasionally, the ethnographer pops up on the scene in clichéd assertions that "I was there" such as arrival narratives in the field. Interlocutors are only allowed to express their perspective in free indirect speech, rather than speaking subjects. By highlighting these literary devices, the authors of *Writing Culture* attempt to break down authorship as a stabilizing feature of ethnographic writing.

But how to solve this dilemma of authorship and representation? Clifford notes with approval the increasing openness and clarity with which ethnographers elaborate on the situation in which ethnographic knowledge was created: 'who speaks? who writes? when and where? with or to whom? under what institutional and historical constraints?' (Clifford, 1986: p. 13). But Clifford wants people to go further, to bring the many voices, perspectives, opinions, and disagreements into the ethnographic record through advocating what he calls polyphony. Through giving voice to many voices, oscillating between harmonies and discord, Clifford believes the new ethnography would chime with the complexity of fieldwork.

However, as Fardon points out, there is a kind of utopian impossibility lurking in this idea, as polyphony just leads to a more elaborate orchestration of many voices by the author as master conductor. Fardon also highlights the incompatibility of the political and poetic approaches as, 'they start form different premises (one from power, the other internal to the text)' and that, 'improvement in terms of one criterion can be attacked as back-sliding in terms of another. Intransigent espousal of a particular view of power relations presupposes textual authority; an open text may be deemed politically uncommitted, even collusive' (p. 8).

In short, Fardon engages with question of interpretation and what makes good ethnography, and argues that this cannot just be a relativistic analysis of a single author and her or his text. He critiques the reflexive turn more broadly for relying on the trope of the lone anthropologist discovering the "Other" and representing them through ethnography. To Fardon, a good ethnography is not just about the production of texts, but the process of fieldwork, and the relationship between various ethnographic texts penned by different authors working on shared or related concepts.

2.2 Ethnographic Authority and the Regionalization of Anthropology

Like the "new critics" Fardon also addresses the question, where does the authority of ethnography come from? However, Fardon argues that authority does not come from an ethnographic author alone, but inter-textuality between ethnographies, as they are constantly cross-referenced, especially in describing particular regions, which adds to their validity and authority. Fardon thereby develops an argument of how ethnographic accounts are regionalized through two interrelated processes: first, through institutional and political conditions; and second, through the academic process of writing about particular ethnographic regions in particular ways.

Fardon outlines how anthropological research has long been influenced by political and institutional conditions. Politically, the phrase that anthropology "follows the flag" has a long history of imperialism and relations of dominance between countries where anthropologists come from and the countries they study. For instance, many British and French anthropologists work in post-colonial Africa, and many North American anthropologists specialize in central and south America. These political conditions lead to a regionalization of academic interest and exchanges. Academic departments are frequently set up with an interest in a particular region, sometimes under the umbrella of anthropology or social science, but frequently also very explicitly, as departments of Southeast Asia or Latin America and so forth. This regional specialism is further enshrined through regional titled posts, conferences, journals, and professional bodies dedicated to particular places (p. 24). This further contributes to an institutional academic interest and boundary-making of (often relatively arbitrary) regions.

The second and related process of regionalization, can be pithily summarized by the statement that anthropologists do not just write, they read. Here Fardon refers to how anthropologists read, write and reference between texts of a particular region, and thereby establish '[r]egion, problem and descriptive values…intertextually' (p. 22). Fardon points out that 'Devoid of mastery of regional literature, within and outside the range of accepted "anthropology" texts, the "ethnographers magic" can easily fail to charm' (p. 24). Cutting-edge cross-referencing within and between texts is the name of the game. Regional expectations and conditions do not just influence entry into a field and how fieldwork is carried out, but what and how it is written about (p. 24). Issues of audience emerge as ethnographers refer to academic heavyweights to bolster their regional narrative. In the process, regionalization 'reproduces, refines or alters the image of areas' (p. 24). Simultaneously, regionalization creates cliques around what are often historically arbitrary delimitations, and this very important phenomenon deserves more critical attention.

By taking a relational view of locality and theoretical focus, we see how this cross-referencing also leads certain regions to become paradigms of particular ethnographic concepts and issues, such that entire regions become exemplars of type features and problems. The lineage is considered prototypically African, exchange must be taken into account in Melanesia, and caste systems are a unique characteristic of India. Notably, the contributions in Fardon's volume look at these processes and outcomes of regionalization all over the world, with three sections focused on: first, hunting and gathering societies, especially Inuit and Australian Aborigines; second, areas previously part of the British empire in

Sub-Saharan Africa and Melanesia; and third, Asian societies, with a focus on localities with long textual histories and the Great Traditions of religious worship. Each of these sections also illuminates a particular issue around anthropological contributions to wider research.

What anthropologists have to offer a particular region often varies widely, for instance along the dimension of oral and literate societies, where the latter have often been scrutinized by historical, religious, and textual specialists before anthropologists even entered the scene (p. 25). This is a dimension relevant to China, where an older tradition of Sinology has more recently been complemented by a social science perspective in Chinese Studies. Furthermore, as explored later, the study of Chinese society has been somewhat divided between sociological studies of people categorized as Han, while ethnological studies have focused on ethnic minority and peripheral peoples.

As Fardon points out in the wider argument, anthropology is not about a lone researcher encountering an Other, but a 'nuanced continuation and modification of a relation between an approach delineating a region and the people who live within it' (p. 25). In China, the tension between unity and diversity remain a central regional and spatial concern as cleavages between rural and urban, as well as center and periphery, continue to loom large. In fact, the designation of people along rural–urban and even class categories in China has frequently been described as caste-like due to its hereditary nature and ascription of social status. However, Fardon's observation that caste in itself is held to be distinctively Indian is borne out by analysts avoiding the full application of the term in China.

To Fardon, the production of anthropological knowledge is inherently political and awareness and attentiveness to the regionalization of ethnographic accounts is essential to understanding anthropology. As he cuttingly observes: 'If anthropology is permanently in crisis, then the reason may plausibly be sought in the audacity of the ambition to write ethnography at all' (p. 22). In sum, ethnography often relies on an implicit regionalism in anthropology that can be explained in the following two ways: first, political processes and institutional practices; second, cross-referencing between texts, so that certain societies become exemplars of anthropological types, features, and problems. Despite a section on Asia, China is notably absent from Fardon's edited volume on regionalism in anthropology.

How can a volume on the political, institutional, and textual regionalization of ethnographic accounts in 1990 leave out China? Fardon warns readers that 'little significance should be read into our criteria for the inclusion of some areas and exclusion of others' (pp. 28–29). However, it is nonetheless worthwhile to consider why China was not included and trace some of the ways that anthropology has been regionalized in China. Drawing on Fardon's two parallel processes for regionalization in anthropology, the following sections will investigate these in relation to the anthropology of China and the study of Chinese society more generally. First, political and institutional developments that shaped the study of Chinese society in the 20th and 21st centuries will be explored. More specifically, debates surrounding the renewal of Chinese anthropology and the anthropology of China in recent decades will emerge. Second, the chapter turns to the themes and topics that became prominent in the anthropology of China as a region, with particular attention given to debates surrounding morality.

2.3 Revolution and Reform in the Anthropology of China

Harrell (2001) implicitly addresses the question of China's elusive position on the anthropological map by charting ethnographic research, and its absence, in the 20th century within and outside of China. Harrell offers a brief account of the institutional and political factors that hampered, or facilitated social science studies of China. He also provides a bird's eye account of current anthropological approaches to China, and his article can be approached as a good source for further reading on various anthropological topics. As the lion's share of the article is a review of the literature, this chapter does not provide the place to review a review. For further reference, the article falls in three topical sections: the first review on communities begins with a concern with village communities as places of shared identity in contrast to cities as nodes in a rural–urban continuum, particularly before and since the loosening of the household registration policy (see below). The second section on lives in contemporary China takes into account issues of gender, sexuality, kinship, and consumption. The third section traces the nation and its components through unity and diversity, in terms of ethnic, regional, and global identities associated with China.

In the briefest possible way, the following attempts to introduce some of the most important historical shifts and political campaigns both shaping and addressed by anthropologists of China. In terms of the intersection of space and history, one of the most important features that has shaped the entire nation is the separation of rural and urban areas and citizens that emerged during Maoism. This rural–urban dichotomy was not a strict feature of imperial China (Skinner, 1971), but became more acute in Maoist era, particularly as it was formalized through household registration in one's native place (Harrell, 2001). The household registration, or *hukou* system, was first established in urban areas in 1951 and then extended to the countryside in 1955. The system had a dual function: on one hand, it classified and recorded people's residence for the purpose of population statistics and identification of personal status (Chan and Zhang, 1999); on the other, it determined people's social-economic eligibility to live in certain areas, perform certain jobs, and have access to certain resources (such as grain staples) and therefore, regulated population distribution and controlled population mobility (Chan and Zhang, 1999). Although the household registration system and its function as something akin to an internal passport system was a unique feature of Maoist China, this identification has been compared to caste in India due to both its centrality in defining social status in rural and urban areas (e.g. Kleinman *et al.*, 2011; Potter and Potter, 1990). The experiences between rural and urban residents diverged widely during the Maoist Era.

In brief, the countryside in 1950s was subjected to a nationwide Land Reform where ownership of land was transferred to the Chinese state and farming was collectivized. Rural residents were organized into production teams, brigades, and communes. People worked in return for work points in a system that gave them access to resources, but rural consumption mostly continued at the household level. Political campaigns of communist education occurred under the direction of local communist party cadres. Furthermore, families were classified by their pre-revolutionary class status, ranging from landlord to landless peasant. These labels were very important in subsequent political campaigns as "bad class" families were often scapegoats and "good class" families were favored in terms of administrative and bureaucratic processes allocating resources and privileges.

In the cities, the non-agricultural population worked and lived in urban work-units (*danwei*) that organized most aspects of people's lives. Typically, work units were contained in

> 'one or more compounds consisting of part or all of a city block, surrounded by a wall and approached through a gate with a gatehouse, and including in its most developed form workshops, residences, meeting rooms, clinics, bathhouses, childcare centers, and sometimes even schools.'
> (Harrell, 2011: p. 144)

Furthermore, urban residents enjoyed privileges of state-provision food staples, education, health care, child care, and elderly care that their rural counterpoints could only dream of. This was one of the great paradoxes of communist policies that exalted peasants ideologically while depriving them of vital resources and investing developmental resources into cities.

Despite the radical reorganization of economic and social life, the transition to socialism was preceded by decades of national upheaval. The end of the Qing Empire, the shifting relationship between the Republican government and various warlords, the Sino-Japanese War and WWII, and civil war between Communist and Guomindang forces had caused widespread social strife across the country. The early 1950s saw an incremental improvement of most people's lives as the reforms evened out some of the graver inequalities across the population and access to food, medicine, and education improved. Intellectually, an initial clampdown on academic diversity was eased during the "Hundred Flowers" period after Mao Zedong's 1956 call to "let a hundred flowers bloom, let a hundred schools contend." However, the Anti-Rightist campaign initiated the following year in 1957, dashed hopes of intellectual flourishing beyond the doctrine of Marxism.

The Great Leap Forward (1958–1961) initiated a drive towards industrialization and collectivization, in an attempt to "catch up" with Western powers. The campaign included mass infrastructural projects like building dams and roads, and utilized materials that were on occasion even smelted down in back-yard furnaces, as well as the introduction of technology in agriculture, such as combine harvesters. However, the campaign has become notorious due to the mass starvation that occurred in its wake during the famine years of 1959–1961. The factors and ultimate responsibility for the famine that led to the deaths of tens of millions of people continue to be the subject of political debate and contention, as resource allocation policies compounded the strain on agricultural production due to drought and weather. For instance, during these years, many overzealous brigade leaders in charge of meeting targets to feed cities and repay Soviet loans over-inflated their agricultural production numbers and contributions, thereby effectively starving their comrades in the countryside. After the Great Leap Forward was discontinued, the early 1960s experienced nutritional improvement and economic progress.

The Great Proletarian Cultural Revolution (1966–1976) was a traumatic experience for many people throughout the country. Following Mao Zedong thoughts, class struggle from below initiated perpetual revolution against "bad" class elements that then expanded to include any authority figures, including teachers and parents. Denunciations and violence became common place and political ideology was often used to settle personal grievances. In the 1960s and 1970s, there was also one-way urban-to-rural migration during this time that involved sending urbanites to the countryside to "learn from the peasants" by going "up to the mountains and down to the countryside" (*shanshang xiaxiang*). Some of the most insightful anthropological accounts today come from Chinese anthropologists who experienced this movement, although most anthropological research formally halted during Maoism.

After Mao's death in 1976, Deng Xiaoping secured power by 1978, and initiated policies aimed at "Reform and Opening" (*gaige kaifang*). In the countryside, the household responsibility system put families back in charge of agricultural production, as land was reallocated from collective farms to families. Similar processes of privatization also gave rise to new entrepreneurship. The reforms enabled individuals to accumulate wealth on a scale not seen since before the revolution. In cities, these changes became especially visible through the rise in consumption and the growing separation of the private sphere from places of work. The loosening of the household registration system saw mass migration and rural urbanization occur. As a result, migrants have gathered as "floating populations" (*liudong renkou*) in cities, where they are often subject to prejudice, despite their central role in urban construction and service industries (Harrell, 2001: p. 146). Young migrants often send vital remittances to the countryside, where women and elderly people are often left behind, sometimes with children.

Chinese population policy has been characterized by three successive waves, with respective emphasis placed on location, then quantity, and now quality (Greenhalgh and Winckler, 2005). While population management in terms of location began as early as the household registration system since the 1950s, the emphasis on quantity came to prominence with the contested Family Planning Policy beginning in the late 1970s. The most recent, quality dynamic in population governance hinges on the Chinese term of *suzhi*, which can be translated as "human quality" and has become progressively more central to state discourse since the 1980s (Kipnis, 2006). The term condenses values associated with education, health, comportment, class, consumption, and rural–urban background in ways that make the acquisition and cultivation of *suzhi* into a kind of aspirational refinement of the person. Themes that these successive regimes of governance touch upon will recur in the following chapter, such as how hopes for the family and the nation rest on children trained for success. Changes at the level of the family, and the implications for gender more widely, will also be explored as women balance domestic work and outside employment. Due to the sheer scope of population management, Greenhalgh (2010) has deemed this transition as a shift from population policies to human governance, one of the key organizational strategies of the Chinese state in recent decades.

2.4 Regionalization from a Chinese Perspective

Although Harrell's (2001) article mainly focuses on the study of Chinese society in the Reform Era, he also includes an important section on the political and institutional history that shaped anthropology of and in China. We will trace developments parallel to his description through the work and life of prominent anthropologist and sociologist Fei Xiaotong below (see Hamilton and Wang, 1992; Morgan, 2014). Imperial China had a tradition of charting the lives of cultural others through ethnography and cartography (Harrell, 2001: p. 140). But in the 1930s, mostly foreign-trained scholars began social science studies of people in China, importing methodological and theoretical approaches from British functionalism and American historicism. These early sociologists, anthropologists, and ethnologists mostly conducted village studies as well as research into ethnic and linguistic minority communities.

After the establishment of the People's Republic in 1949, anthropological and sociological research was cut short by the transition to revolutionary socialism and its ideological vocation to promote Marxism. During the period of High Socialism dominated by Maoist–Marxist thought from 1949–1976, a process of peripheralization in the study of Chinese society occurred in two parallel ways: first, within the PRC researchers who turned to the study of ethnic minorities rather than the Han majority; second, outside the PRC researchers focused their attention on Chinese people living in Taiwan and Hong Kong, as well as textual sources. The periphery thereby came to stand for the center and Chineseness came to be defined through the margins.

When the PRC banned sociology as a bourgeois pseudoscience in 1952, some scholars studying Chinese society shifted attention to "problems" of ethnic minorities (Hamilton and Wang, 1992: pp. 10–11). Furthermore, under the influence of Russian cooperation, Soviet-style ethnological classification was introduced in the 1950s, where nationality was defined by 'a common language, a common territory, a common economic life, and a common psychological make-up' (Gladney, 2004: p. 9). The paradigm of Lewis Henry Morgan's conception of society, as moving from matriarchy to patriarchy, and a Marxist–Leninist progression of material evolution ending in communism also influenced the way Chinese scholars approached ethnic relations during this period (Gladney, 2004). The Chinese population was classified into 56 ethnicities with the Han ethnic majority dominating numerically and clustering in the central and coastal areas of the PRC. Chinese ethnology often documented minorities and their history in relation to a Han center, as the most civilized, advanced, and modern ethnic group in China.

Studies of Han Chinese life outside the mainland between 1949 and 1979 were often conducted by foreign anthropologists who were denied access to the mainland. In addition to the fieldwork conducted in Taiwan and Hong Kong, a number of influential studies were also based predominantly on textual analyses of material from the mainland, such as journalism and émigré interviews (Harrell, 2001: p. 140). Both Taiwan and Hong Kong experienced a trajectory that diverged significantly from the mainland: Taiwan was actually a Japanese colony from 1895 to 1945 after which it was taken over by the Chinese Nationalist i.e. Guomindang forces that evacuated the mainland; Hong Kong became a British colony after the Opium wars in 1842 and remained a British free port until 1997, so was politically separated from the mainland for 156 years. Harrell summarizes the state of affairs whereby peripheries of Sinic civilization in Hong Kong and Taiwan became surrogates for China itself, laboratories for the study of "Chinese Society and Culture" (p. 140).

This peripheral perspective on Chinese identity refocused onto mainland China after the demise of high socialism in the People's Republic of China and the economic liberalization that ensued from the 1980s onwards. After Mao's death in 1976, Deng progressively consolidated power. Deng began what is referred to as the "reform and opening" (*gaige kaifang*) process of economic liberalization and privatization, which initiated transition to a capitalist economy. In the 1980s, anthropological studies of China increasingly considered this transformation from socialist collectivism to the new era of state-fostered capitalism.

In short, the political upheavals that engulfed China in the 20th century deeply affected the academic possibilities and institutional forms that the anthropological study of Chinese society could take. In addition, these economic forms and social processes have meant that contemporary anthropological studies of China largely concentrate on the period from the early 1980s onwards. Since then, an increasing number of academic institutions in the PRC, particularly universities and academies, have added anthropology to their programs and hired anthropologists to join their faculties. An interesting academic movement that emerged within China in recent years has been the call for "nativization" (*bentuhua*) of academic concepts rather than relying on foreign concepts to understand China (Harrell, 2001: p. 155). On the one hand, this effort has a strong basis in Fei's writing, who explicitly sought frameworks to understand Chinese society from the bottom–up, rather than simply importing models from the West. On the other, Fei's work explicitly seeks comparative mirroring between China and the West through constant juxtaposition.

In the following sections, Fei's life and work will be discussed in order to reveal some of the ways in which a wider political and economic context impacted the study of Chinese society through the experiences of one of its most influential figures. In addition, Fei's writing on morality will provide the foundation for comparison with more recent work on the topic. In particular, Yan addresses the topic of morality in the Market Era, where popular discourse meets academic interest, as Chinese citizens grapple with constituting new moral values after the erosion of the Maoist ideology of social collectivism.

2.5 Fei and the Study of Chinese Society

Fei was a central actor in developing sociology and anthropology in China, despite experiencing significant periods of intellectual sanction, as his research was not aligned with the Maoist–Marxist model of Chinese society. His biography is refracted through the prism of historical transformations of 20th century life in mainland China. Most of the following description of Fei's academic life and career is based on Hamilton and Wang's (1992) insightful introduction to their translation of Fei's classic text, *From the Soil.* After exploring the fate of his life and works, the chapter will take a closer look at the general sociological theories of China Fei developed before the revolution, which have gained new prominence in the reform era. Delving into his exploration of morality in pre-revolutionary China and the resurgence of debate on the topic since the rise of the Market era serves as a great example for how a particular problem may become regionalized and yet link to wider debates in anthropology.

Fei (1910–2005) began his academic career studying medicine at the missionary-sponsored Suzhou University in his native Jiangsu Province before transferring to Yanjing University in Beijing. Shortly thereafter, Fei also changed his field of study to sociology, in his words reasoning that, 'as a medical doctor I might cure the afflictions of a few, but not those of hundreds of millions engendered by an irrational society…to cure society we have to study social theories first' (quoted in Hamilton and Wang, 1992: p. 5). This statement reveals Fei's lifelong social and political commitment to improving the lives of ordinary Chinese citizens.

In his senior year in 1932, at Yanjing University, Fei was taught by the American sociologist Robert Park, an esteemed member of the Chicago School that strongly emphasized field research methods. As a graduate student at Qinghua University in Beijing, Fei trained with the Russian anthropologist S.M. Shirokogoroff whose research on tribal people solidified Fei's basis in empirical research methods and interest in Chinese ethnic minorities. Fei won a scholarship to study abroad at the London School of Economics in 1936 where he wrote his first ethnography under the direction of Malinowski. Like his teachers, Fei was strongly committed to research methods and theoretical practices grounded in an intimate familiarity with a given society. Furthermore, Fei put these methodological commitments into practice by developing a bottom–up understanding of Chinese society.

He undertook his second substantial period of fieldwork during the summer of 1936 in a Jiangsu village, after his first, which was a study of indigenous groups in Guangxi province jointly with his wife, was followed by the tragedy of his first wife's death the previous year. It laid the foundation for the publication of his ethnography, *Peasant Life in China,* in 1939. Upon his return to China from England in 1938, Fei became a rising star among the non-Marxist intellectual *avant-garde* and a leading force in the following decade's effervescence in Chinese sociology. He took up a position in sociology at Yunnan University in Kunming, where he directed a group of young researchers in conducting fieldwork and writing over a dozen ethnographic monographs. Fei also initiated what he called the "second phase" of Chinese sociology, writing two very important works analyzing Chinese social structure. The first, *From the Soil,* established a non-Western social theory for the study of China. The second, *Reconstructing Rural China,* provided a sociological analysis for the countryside and outlined a practical agenda for the improvement of rural life.

To Fei, the stakes in developing Chinese sociology were nothing less than China's future. However, despite a common commitment to improving China, Hamilton and Wang (1992: p. 18) explicate how

> 'Mao's Marxism and Fei's sociology still worked in opposite directions and aimed at different goals. Simply stated, Mao wanted to eradicate the old society and create an entirely new social order; he was the quintessential revolutionary. In contrast, Fei wanted to retain many elements of the old society and use those elements as the foundation on which to build a modernized society; Fei was the quintessential reformist. For this reason, if for no other, Fei's sociology waned as Mao's Marxism dominated the first thirty years of the people's Republic of China.'
>
> (Hamilton and Wang, 1992: p. 18)

Fei's meteoric rise, becoming a full professor and head of department in Sociology at Yunnan University by 1941, was cut short by the aftermath of the revolution in 1949. After this, his career changed course rather radically. In 1952, all sociology departments were closed, and Fei and his colleagues initially dedicated their expertise to issues surrounding ethnic minorities under a Marxist–Leninist framework. The Hundred Flowers campaign offered Fei, a brief glimmer of hope that sociology would be reestablished. However, Fei's appeal was shot down by the subsequent Anti-Rightist Campaign in which Mao Zedong himself singled Fei out by name, and denounced his sociological aspirations as a rightist conspiracy (see Morgan, 2014: p. 19). As a result, Fei was stripped of his positions and forced to abandon academic work, until after Mao's death.

When the reformers in the late 1970s sought rapid modernization, they needed intellectuals to reinvigorate the economy and promoted both natural and social sciences. Under the eyes of the new party leaders, Fei returned to national prominence. His rehabilitation as an intellectual was solidified in 1979 with his appointment as the first president of the newly founded Chinese Society of Sociology. Furthermore, from 1989 Fei also returned to standing as a political figure, working as the vice president of the National People's Congress and president of the Democratic League of China. In the final decades of his life, Fei traveled widely and won international awards, gaining increasing recognition and fame for his sociological contributions both within and outside of China. Fei also taught and directed as a Professor of Sociology at Peking University up until his death in 2005.

2.6 Fei's Non-western Sociological Theory of China

Fei's sociological theory of China was an attempt to break free from Western models dominating the discipline and being unreflexively applied to the Chinese context. Rather than comparing China as a "case study" to a Western model posturing as the universal standard, Fei's approach was to juxtapose and compare Chinese and Western social structures. Through the process of this theoretical mirroring, a clearer, crisper analytic model of Chinese social structures emerged. These comparative theoretical reflections simultaneously systematized and formalized social structures taken for granted within China and carried an implicit criticism of the universalism posited by Western theoreticians. As Hamilton and Wang (1992: p. 34) point out, "what passes in the West for general social theory is often, in fact, local knowledge — particular rules about particular people in particular places. Fei's sociology demands that we in the West rethink ourselves."

In order not to simply turn the tables and set out a folk model for Chinese sociology, Fei subjected social assumptions and commonsense knowledge within China, to social analysis. Fei avails himself of classic anthropological techniques to make the familiar strange and the exotic quotidian (to paraphrase Clifford, above). Fei advanced comparative juxtapositions, evocative analogies, and visual cues, as well as proposing specialist language outside of the ordinary linguistic repertoire. For instance, Fei proposed a model linking personhood, relatedness and morality and labeled it with an "awkward" term, both in the Chinese original of *chaxugeju* and in the English translation as "differential mode of association" (see Hamilton and Wang, 1992: p. 20). By coining a technically descriptive term to encapsulate the model, Fei made Chinese readers pay attention and not write off a characteristic of their own society that they may have found so commonsense that it barely warranted mention: that each person forms the center of hierarchically linked social ties with others, which emanates from the self out into the world.

How does Fei conceptualize *chaxugeju* as a model for understanding personhood, relatedness, and morality as part of a general sociological theory? Fei seeks to illustrate how people draw the line between selves and others, between individuals and groups, in cross-cultural comparison between China and the West (p. 61). In China, the self is linked to others through *chaxugeju*, the "differential mode of association." In the West, by contrast, the individual is linked groups through *tuantigeju*, the "organizational mode of association." To conceptualize the contrasting social structures, Fei illustrates the two modes of relatedness through a lucid comparative analogy: ripples of water in China and stacks of hay in the West.

In Western societies, organizations bundle individuals together like rice straw, first gathered together in small bundles, then bound into larger bundles and eventually piled together as a haystack. 'The separate straws, the separate bundles, and finally the separate stacks all fit together to make up the whole haystack' (p. 61). Each straw is analogous to an individual, each bundle forms separate units as organizations, and each bundle makes up the haystack as an all-encompassing organization, such as the state. These bundle-like organizations clearly demarcate which individuals are included and excluded. Individuals therefore make up organizations as separate units and the aggregated organization as a unifying principle.

In China, the pattern of the self to others,

> 'is like the circles that appear on the surface of a lake when a rock is thrown into it. Everyone stands at the center of the circles produced by his or her own social influence. Everyone's circles are interrelated. One touches different circles at different times and places' (pp. 61–62).

The ripples emanating outwards from the self in the center are relationships, or *lun*, to others (p. 65). Each dyadic relationship between self and other has a hierarchical differentiation, e.g. between father and son, but must also be achieved by living up to the moral expectations of what having that relationship entails in a given situation (see Wang and Hamilton, 1992: pp. 21–22). By cultivating these relationships with others the self emanates outwards through concentric circles.

The self extends itself through cultivating relationships with others further and further from the center like paths into the world (pp. 66–67). Like a perfectly unique spider web, each network identifies a distinctively different person, as do their kinship ties. The self remains at the center of an elastic of web of networks, but the size of the circles produced correlates to the power of social influence (p. 62). The more authority and power a given person has, the greater the ripples from the center, leading to an elasticity of the social circle over time (p. 63). This also holds for Chinese families, where the scope of kin depends on family fortune (p. 64).

Fei clearly differentiates egocentric from individualist self at the root of the differential and organizational mode of association, respectively. He further compares the foundations of each mode in Confucianism and Christianity, and extends their logics to the Chinese emperor and the Western state. In individualism, individuals make up parts of a whole and each part relates to the whole in the same way (p. 67). Therefore, a concept of equality and sameness operates between each individual, and the rights of each individual are externally guaranteed by their substitutable position in relation to the overall organization. The organization transcends the individual and orders individuals' behavior according to universal moral laws guaranteed by its external authority. This is much like Jesus transcends human organization (as the son of God by virtue of the virgin birth) and submits only to the external law of God as father. God evaluates the moral conduct of Christians to each other according to his absolute and universal judgment. Similarly, the Western state regulates the rights of each individual citizen to each other through its unified and codified body of laws.

The egocentric person in the differential mode has the compulsion to submit to the moral expectations demanded by the specific hierarchical relationship, rather than a universal code of values or laws. This is captured by Confucian dictum, that one should *ke ji fu li* (subdue the self and follow what is right). 'From the Son of Heaven down to the ordinary people, all must consider the cultivation of the person as the root of everything' (p. 74). This means that '[e]xtending out from the self are the social spheres formed by one's personal relationships. Each sphere is sustained by a specific type of social ethic' (p. 74). The compulsion to submit to the relationship and to the rituals associated with it are enforced by tradition as education transmitted across generations (p. 99). This means that China appears as a society where neither people nor laws, but rituals, rule (p. 99).

There is no universal normative principle governing the morality of all relationships in China. 'A society with a differential mode of association is composed of webs woven out of countless personal relationships. To each knot in these webs is attached a specific ethical principle. For this reason, the traditional moral system was incapable of producing a comprehensive moral concept. Therefore, all the standards of value in this system were incapable of transcending the differential personal relationships of the Chinese social structure' (p. 78). The lack of a universal principle is the reason Confucius encounters problems defining absolute characteristics and personal behavior exhibiting the ethical concept of *ren* or "benevolence" in the absence of specific contexts and particular relationships (p. 75). The story Mencius told shows how even the emperor cannot serve the concrete relationship to his father and an abstract relationship to the state with equal measure at the same time, and the father must always take precedence (p. 77). The closer the other is to the self, the more important the relationship is. This reveals scales of encompassment, where the boundary between the public and the private is relative. Furthermore, even if one acknowledges the public as *tianxia*, meaning "all under heaven", the state remains the emperor's family (not a state in the Western organizational sense) (pp. 69–70). Moral evaluation is always context- and relationship-dependent, despite the shared logic of hierarchical differentiation.

Fei delineates the boundaries between an egocentric and an individualist conception of selfhood in terms of the Chinese differential and Western organizational mode of association. However, in order to analyze the collectivist ideals held under Maoism, we must consider two problems in light of Fei's theory: first, whether Maoist collectivism can be considered as a continuity of imperial subservience to relationships; second, whether an egocentric or individualist self was dominant under high socialism, both in ethical practice and collectivist ideology. Here the implication that collectivism and collectivist morality implies subservience of the self to a total und universal social order is highly relevant. In Fei's elaboration, the egocentric self does not submit to a universal governing totality in the form of *tianxia*, but only to the specific moral value that ties a person to another through a given relationship. Much like individualism, collectivism would necessitate the substitutability and equality of different parts in making up a whole, but the relational specificity and hierarchical differentiation of *chaxugeju* makes this into a logical and practical impossibility. A contrast between an individualist and a collectivist social order therefore, cannot capture the ego-centric network society that Fei describes.

Another point of confusion that could arise in reading Fei's sociological theory is when he is analyzing social structures arising from the contrast between rural traditional and urban modern societies in general, and when he is describing something distinctly Chinese, such as Confucian morality. For instance, in his chapters, contrasting communication and governance in rural and urban China, Fei addresses the contrast between closed, intimate, and familiar face-to-face social relations and societies where open, frequent, and short-term interactions with strangers are the norm. As Yan points out in his own work on morality in contemporary China, aspects of Fei's work evoke parallels with the later work of Anthony Giddens and other foreign social scientists. However, in contrast to Fei, Yan describes the demise of a collectivist morality, rather than ego-centered networks, in transforming a society based on responsibility to one relying on individual rights.

In sum, Fei posited foundational hierarchical relations within Confucian kinship systems as elaborations of concentric ego-centered models of relationality. This established what could be a hierarchical type that could neither be described as "collectivist" nor "individualist." Historically, however, class-based struggles under Maoism attempted to bring about an egalitarian society. The subsequent demise of Maoism is said to have created a moral crisis of self-serving individualism. The extent to which the old hierarchy has been replaced by a new kind of family and person is a matter of dispute among ethnographies of contemporary China.

2.7 Moral Crisis and Individual Ethics

In the last two decades, Yan (2011) has taken up the debate on morality through the prism of 'selfishness' and accusations of immorality more generally, which has been an understudied area in anthropology. In the 1980s, a Chinese debate was sparked on the meaning of life that can now be viewed as, 'the beginning of a departure from a morality of collective responsibilities to the justification for self-interest' (p. 42). Yan begins his chapter with a puzzling phenomenon: In recent years youngsters across China insist that they are fulfilling their duty of filial piety towards their parents, not through making great sacrifices, but through the pursuit of pleasure and comfort. Their logic is that their own happiness completes their parents' happiness (pp. 36–37). This nonetheless demands a radical departure from an orientation of responsibility towards others to be refocused on taking care of oneself, even if this is ostensibly done for the sake of others. How can this be?

The widespread perception of moral crisis that began in the 1980s coincided with the demise of beliefs and cracking of confidence in communist ideology. Yan argues that this debate was the first departure from a collective ethics in Chinese morality (p. 42). To Yan, this collective morality extends back into history through the values Confucianism places on the family, kinship and the emperor. This form of subjecting the self to the interests of the larger scale was then further enforced through socialist collectives under the governance of the Chinese communist party and Chairman Mao. In a sense, the 1949 revolution emancipated the self from the constraints of family and kinship networks as part of the traditional hierarchy of social status, only to re-subject the self to the control of an all-encompassing system of socialist redistribution and political control.

Yan departs from Fei's elaboration of the traditional imperial state and the emperor as subject to the same processes of relational submission necessitated by the differential mode of association. To Fei, this meant that all relationships were particularistic and there was no universal external guarantor of morality. However, for Yan the Chinese history of ethics was guaranteed by the central moral authority of collectivism through the Confucian empire and the Communist state. Yan also writes that, 'the personified and mystified moral authority, be it Confucius or Mao, no longer exists, and the dominance of a single version of collective ethics has ended. This has led to a national panic about a "moral vacuum"' (p. 51). Yan leaves this collapsing between particularistic morality and universal collectivism guaranteed by an external moral authority unelaborated, thereby creating a blurred area between the two (to him overlapping) forms of morality. Logically, Yan may be suggesting that the personification of moral authority means that those subject to their governance, nonetheless form particularistic ties to Confucius and Mao, despite, or maybe even thereby, perpetuating their universal moral authority.

Writing more than half a century after Fei, Yan not only historicizes, but contextualizes his arguments within broader debates about morality and trust. Following Giddens, Yan argues that there has been a transformation of familiar faces based on personal trust to a world of strangers in need of social trust. Fei (1992: pp. 44, 59) also touched upon this dynamic in elaborations of how rural society's long-term engagements with the same interlocutors made written communication, and even verbal expression, somewhat superfluous in establishing trust. However, with the power of hindsight and comparison in observing these transformations across the globe, Yan elaborates on this transformation in China in far more detail.

Yan argues that Maoism attacked particularistic morality and sought to replace it with universalistic values of socialism, but never succeeded (p. 60). Instead, the separation between in-group and out-group dynamics remained strong until the 1970s. While the West has a guarantee of external moral authority through God and the nation-state, China's moral values were guaranteed through submission to heaven, the family, and community power that was then supplanted by Chairman Mao and communist morality (p. 61). But this was still a particularistic form of trust based on on-going familiarity. The work units and communes of Maoist era formed a localized world of day-to-day engagement with the same people in a fixed location. Therefore, through the particularistic ties with familiar people, personal trust remained paramount.

By contrast, in the increasingly mobile and open society since the Reform Era, engagements with strangers increased so people need what Giddens has termed social trust. Without an 'external and absolute authority' of morality, the 'independent and self-serving individual is more vulnerable than ever to encroachment and aggression by other equally self-serving individuals and must seek protection from social institutions' that Yan argues are not well developed in China (p. 61). When this social trust has not been forthcoming, people since the 1980s experienced a sense of moral crisis. In the1990s, the rush of political and cultural elites to make money turned being poor from a marker of revolutionary force to a disgrace. Nowadays, personal interest is no longer deemed immoral, and a discourse on selfishness as part of human nature has developed in China. Yan sees this as part of a general trend in the Reform Era where a 'shift of moral emphasis from family responsibilities and self-sacrifice to individual rights and self-realization' has occurred (p. 46). Yan flags problems of corruption, but also notes that freedom of speech and independent judiciary are necessary to secure rights within a state-guaranteed system of social trust. In short, an earlier ethics of responsibilities towards others in China has been replaced by a contemporary ethics of rights and self-development towards the self.

Social conditions in post-Mao China have allowed the self to construct a self-identity outside the "caste-like" structure of socialist hierarchy (Yan *et al.*, 2011: pp. 3, 19). The analogous use of caste in this volume echoes Fardon's argument that caste forms a distinct characteristic of South Asia, and yet carries comparative connotations that are transferable to other regions. In any case, the shift towards a state-led market economy and the privatization of formerly collective assets has meant not only the rise of a private sector and growing realm of competition and profit. The transformation towards capitalism has allowed the burgeoning of relative wealth and inequality that manifests and expresses itself through new lifestyle and life choices. Sexual, material, and affective desires come to the fore as the class consciousness of socialist configurations give way to post-socialist sensibilities of personal desire. Yan draws on Lisa Rofel's book on the rise of the new desiring self on the waves of neoliberalism and consumerism, creatively rereading her argument as one about morality in which 'the ethical shift from a collective system of responsibility and self-sacrifice to an individualistic system of rights and self-development' (p. 47).

Yan's chapter also charts the public perception of moral crisis through a number of nation-wide events that would be familiar to any informed Chinese citizen or foreign China watcher. This is part of a wider shift in anthropology that brings macro- and micro-processes together through engaging with how information and opinions surrounding key social, political, and economic events are disseminated and received in various media, including avenues ranging from state-owned television to social media blogging sites. Yan's three main areas of focus are family relations, food safety, and charity.

Building on some of his equally innovative ethnographic fieldwork in rural Heilongjiang, Yan examines how moral evaluations shift along generational and gender fault lines on issues of family dynamics. Here the sexual revolution and the new practices of creating relationships emerge as key to understanding marriage, bride wealth, and filial piety (p. 53). For instance, sex workers as moral family members supporting relatives through remittances may seem counter-intuitive, and yet possible in the emerging ethical landscape (p. 48). While the emotional fall-out from these shifts may be involuntary, Yan also traces processes where deliberate harm is on the rise. Food safety scares, but also the notorious melamine milk scandal that harmed the health of thousands of victims, and even claimed the lives of six infants, receives attention here (p. 56). However, Yan also turns to emergent forms of ethics, the bright side, of the moral transformation. Particularly, the Sichuan earthquake created a monumental sea change in how compassion and caring is channeled in disaster relief (p. 65). Departing from previous emergency responses, monopolized by state resource distribution and hence disaster relief, private individuals volunteered their time, finances, and resources in a mass response to alleviate the suffering of strangers struck by disaster (p. 64). Yan claims this reveals the emergence of a civil society response characterized by empathy towards strangers outside of personal acquaintances that has been staked through individual choice and agency (p. 66). A long history of charity in China that was undermined by the Maoist state's monopoly over resource distribution has thereby found a new dynamic and force in the market era.

In sum, Yan traces the shift from authoritarian, collective ethics of responsibilities towards new, optional, individual ethics based on rights and self-development. Yan thereby, brings together perceptions of moral decline and practices of moral recovery in contemporary China. As a Chinese academic looking at a problematic people in China's face, Yan also makes comparisons to reveal common tendencies when human societies shift from engagement with locales of familiar faces to a world of strangers. By making this non-regional comparison, Yan effectively counterbalances many other accounts that contain China and Asia within a regional focus.

2.8 China in a Changing World

This chapter began with an exploration of the relationship of general anthropology to its main institutional practice, the writing of ethnography as a specific form of representation of particular people. To investigate the tensions between the larger project of anthropology as the study of humankind and the practices involved in producing specific ethnographies, we turned to debates revolving around the "crisis of representation" where this debate has been polarized between "universalists" positing comparability between human groups and "relativists" arguing that unique qualities of particular people cannot be compared without distortion. The critics engaging with the crisis of representation have frequently framed their arguments in terms of ethnographies as fictions, where the literary tropes of ethnographic texts come to the fore, or in terms of the power dynamics that place anthropologists in the field, such that ethnographers frequently follow the flag. However, a third possibility to examine the fault line between anthropological comparison and ethnographic specificity is through the epistemological prism of the regionalization of knowledge.

Following Richard Fardon, a dual carriage emerges that drives this process of constituting regions in anthropology: on one hand, political and institutional factors draw lines around regionalized blocks on the ethnographic world map; on the other hand, regions then become paradigms for particular anthropological problems and debates, and the validity of a given ethnographic argument is weighed up against neighboring and adjacent texts. As such, anthropologists do not just write, they read, both before, after, and during their fieldwork, and their evidence of reading is a key component in making their own ethnography convincing towards others. However, this book is not about coloring in a Chinese area on the ethnographers' map. This book explicitly attempts to uncover regionalized assumptions by putting larger questions in anthropological theory in dialogue with the ethnography of China.

In this vein, China's own history of political upheaval and institutionalized academic endeavors was traced through the study of Chinese society, with particular emphasis on the related fields of anthropology, sociology, and ethnology. As one of the luminaries of China in 20th century of social science, Fei's biography shed light on many of these developments, while his theories revealed an elegant balancing act between creating a Chinese sociological model that could nonetheless offer comparative insights with Western counterparts. In addition to surveying Fei's broader theoretical contributions, the theme of morality was highlighted and compared to more recent anthropological studies on the topic.

Yan Yunxiang's writing on the perception of moral crisis since the 1980s offered important counterpoints for comparison with Fei's work. In particular, the constitution of ego-centered, individualist, and collectivist forms of personhood and morality are pertinent as China moved through various political systems in the 20th century. Narratives of modernity that stipulate predictable patterns of trust and risk, or opportunity and danger, were also compared as Chinese citizens moved from predominantly face-to-face encounters with familiar contacts to increasing engagements with unknown strangers. Thereby, the chapter not only investigated sources of ethnographic authority and anthropological comparison, but wider origins and outcomes of different forms of moral authority in China and beyond.

Seminar Question

How have institutional and political developments framed China as both an *example* of and an *exception* to wider debates in anthropology?

Readings

Fardon, Richard (1990). 'Localizing Strategies: The Regionalization of Ethnographic Accounts', in *Localizing Strategies: Regional Traditions of Ethnographic Writing.* Washington: Smithsonian Institution Press, pp. 1–35.

Fei, Xiaotong (1992). *From the Soil: The Foundations of Chinese Society* (translated by Gary Hamilton and Wang Zheng). Berkeley: University of California Press.

Hamilton, Gary and Wang, Zheng (1992). 'Introduction: Fei Xiaotong and the Beginnings of a Chinese Sociology', in Fei Xiaotong (ed.) *From the Soil: The Foundations of Chinese Society* (translated by Gary Hamilton and Wang Zheng). Berkeley: University of California Press, pp. 1–34.

Harrell, Steven (2001). 'The Anthropology of Reform and the Reform of Anthropology: Anthropological Narratives of Recovery and Progress in China', *Annual Review of Anthropology,* 30(1), pp. 139–161.

Yan, Yunxiang (2011). 'The Changing Moral Landscape', in Kleinman, Arthur; Yan, Yunxiang; Jing, Jun; Lee, Sing; Zhang Everett; Pan, Tianshu; Wu, Fei; Guo, Jinhua (eds.) *Deep China: The moral life of the person.* University of California Press, Berkeley, pp. 36–77.

References

Chan, Kam Wing and Zhang, Li (1999). 'The Hukou System and Rural-Urban Migration in China: Processes and Changes', *The China Quarterly,* 160, pp. 818–855.

Clifford, James (1986). 'Introduction: partial truths' in Clifford, James, and George E. Marcus (eds.) *Writing Culture: The Poetics and Politics of Ethnography,* pp. 1–26.

Gladney, Dru (2004). *Dislocating China: Muslims, Minorities, and other Subaltern Subjects.* University of Chicago Press, Chicago: USA.

Greenhalgh, Susan and Winckler, Edwin (2005). *Governing China's Population: From Leninist to Neoliberal Biopolitics.* Stanford University Press, Stanford: USA.

Greenhalgh, Susan (2010). *Cultivating Global Citizens.* Harvard University Press, Cambridge: UK.

Kipnis, Andrew (2006). 'Suzhi: A keyword approach' in *The China Quarterly,* 186, pp. 295–313.

Kleinman, Arthur; Yan, Yunxiang; Jing, Jun; Lee, Sing; Zhang, Everett; Pan, Tianshu; Wu, Fei; Guo, Jinhua (eds.) 2011 *Deep China: The Moral Life of the Person.* University of California Press, Berkeley: USA.

Morgan, W. John (2014). 'Fei Xiao Tong: A public intellectual in Communist China', *Anthropology Today*, 30, pp. 18–21.

Potter, Sulamith and Potter, Jack (1990). *China's Peasants: The Anthropology of a Revolution.* Cambridge University Press, Cambridge: UK.

Skinner, G. William (1971). 'Chinese peasants and the closed community: An open and shut case', *Comparative Studies in Society and History*, 13(03), pp. 270–281.

Chapter 3

Kinship as Ideology and as Corporation

In anthropology, the study of kinship has a long held pride of place in the disciplinary showcase, not least as the discipline could offer unique insights. The anthropological study of kinship found footing somewhere between the individual focus of psychology and the institutional dynamics traced by sociologists. In many ways, anthropologists of kinship stood on middle ground between the two, while simultaneously offering perspectives well beyond the remit of the Western academy and normative nuclear families associated with modernity.

Anthropological studies of kinship over the course of the last two centuries have provided particularly fertile ground for offering accounts of human diversity, not least due to kinship's universal role in reproduction, both in terms of procreation and political economy. Building on biological and biologistic premises many kinship studies assumed reproductive connection as the self-evident basis for kinship earlier, but more recent research has questioned whether anthropologists were not, after all, relying on Western folk models themselves and exalting them to the level of universal science.

Questioning what has been naturalized through assumptions about kinship also provided ways of investigating political and economic orders that deviated from Western states. In Africa, particularly, anthropologists analyzed lineages as complex kinship systems that provided relatively stable distributions of power and resources in the absence of centralized states. By contrast, in China kinship and the state were interwoven in a long and complex history, despite sharing some institutional similarities with African lineages. This chapter will explore these historical dimensions of kinship in China, and explore what this can tell us about different types of cognition, through which we understand the world.

By taking the lineage in China as an exemplar, this chapter analyzes two dimensions of the historical evolution of kinship in China. The first revolves around continuity, the persistence of this particular institutional formation, the lineage, through time. As we will see, the relative stability of this kinship constellation appears particularly puzzling in view of seismic shifts that occurred in the last 800 years in China. The second and corollary field of enquiry will examine how changes to Chinese kinship occurred historically, not only in terms of slow transformations and creeping changes, but also radical breaks and unexpected turns that deviate from a predictable or expected trajectory. Where did the force for stability and continuity reside, and at what points and how consciously did agents of change intervene to make transformation possible, desirable, or inevitable?

These are, of course, monumental questions that have piqued human interest throughout its history, and here we begin with a theoretical text that engages with both anthropological and psychological approaches to these questions. Bloch ambitiously attempts to bring together anthropological and psychological approaches to cognition through the medium of ritual as a form of communication that both transmits and teaches, so a given individual forms an understanding of the world in interaction with their historically and ideologically permeated environment. From this starting point we will consider kinship, in general, and the lineage, more specifically, as an ideology communicated through ritual and a corporation underwriting the political and economic order in China throughout its history.

3.1 Developing Cognition between Individual and Ideology

Bloch (1989) examines the relationship between cognition and ideology with ritual as a vehicle for transmission between the two realms. The problem he addresses is how particular worldviews are assumed as common sense, not only by a single individual, but a group of people. Furthermore, these assumptions do not just live and die with those people, but are transmitted from one generation to the next, with many of these assumptions being replicated in people's minds, sometimes over long periods of time, even though they must learned anew by each child from care takers, peers, and the wider environment in which they develop. Bloch begins by exploring two disciplines that have explicitly engaged with this problematic: first, developmental psychology; second, social, and cultural anthropologists. However, he finds both approaches insufficient, as psychologists with their Universalist ambitions fail to account for cultural and historical diversity, while anthropologists treat this diversity as something transmitted as a whole without engaging with the cognitive processes needed for an individual to assume these ideas to be natural, true, and everlasting. Through the vivid example of a Merina circumcision ritual in Madagascar, Bloch connects these two theories through a Marxian notion of ideology. Let us now turn to the specifics of this argument on cognition and ideology.

Psychological theories of cognition begin with the individual subject immersed in its environment as the starting point of a developmental process. This environment includes the child's own body, other humans, and the wider non-human environment. Through interaction with that environment over time, a child builds up a cognitive system that is as much constructed as received from experiences of engagement with the world. Language acquisition provides a particularly apposite example because it must be so clearly replicated not just in the individual child's mind, but based on shared assumptions with other people's grasp of language and perception of the world in the child's environment. From studies of language acquisition, but also psychological studies more broadly, Bloch isolates two extra-cultural factors in cognitive development: first, the physical nature of environment partially accounts for variation in human cognition; second, neurological processes structure cognition and thereby delimit infinite variation, e.g. in language acquisition (p. 113). In short, a child is not just taught how to think, but learns how to think through interaction with a given environment that contributes to how a child's mind constructs knowledge over time.

Bloch contrasts this psychological theory of cognition with the second, anthropological approach to cognition, which he feels often fails to truly engage with cognition at all. This is because the anthropologists he cites assume that people receive cognition ready-made from previous generations, often as a holistic and complete entity that is both internally coherent and non-individual. Bloch sees the sources of this flawed understanding in some of the founding fathers of social science, tracing this to Kant's anti-empiricist stance *via* Durkheim's anti-individualist "collective representations." He traces this tendency in a number of anthropological works that show how cognitive systems are frequently equated with culture, cosmology, and even ideology that members of a given society supposedly all absorb in its entirety. To Bloch, this does not do justice to how a particular person acquires bits-and-pieces of knowledge over time, rather swallows a whole worldview in one big gulp. Therefore, this approach also ignores the variation between individual perspectives within a particular context, instead flattening out cognition to what everybody (allegedly) thinks. This simply cannot account for the coexistence of different types of knowledge that can be overlapping, contradictory or even particular to a specific individual within a given context.

Bloch notes with approval the work of Pierre Bourdieu whose analysis of the Berber Kabyle house in Morocco provides a vivid illustration of how practical and ideological knowledge come together through spaces, activities, and time. Nonetheless, Bloch argues that Bourdieu's Kabyle house also reproduces the anthropological problem of thinking of culture as an undivided and systematic whole. In general, a gaping absence in this anthropological literature on cognition is how, exactly, these abstract, elaborate, arbitrary schemes, that some anthropologists call ideology, are constructed in the individuals' mind. Bloch insists on the need to see 'the acquisition of knowledge as the combination of different processes of different nature' (p. 119) and to 'try not to think of knowledge as a whole, either unitary or fragmented, but to see it as the momentary crystallization of different processes which interact on each other, to focus on the processes of formation and their interaction rather than on the finished product' (p. 121).

In order to help them on their way, anthropologists would well remember that even Marx and Engels posited two formative processes in the construction of knowledge: first, experiential knowledge arises 'from processes of cognitive adaptation to the environment' (p. 108); the second, which often subverts the first, is a historical and exploitative system of representation called ideology, that builds on concepts like property and the state. Ideology does not directly derive from experiences in interaction with the environment, but often even negates or hides perception e.g. the inequality of labor exploitation (p. 108). Ideology is transferred from one generation to the next as a historical system that may be arbitrary, and yet convincingly asserts validity as the necessary and only way to think about things. A functional difference between ideology and non-ideological cognition has been recognized by some anthropologists, who distinguish 'between a system of knowledge which organizes perception and a system of knowledge which legitimates the social order by building up schemes about the nature of the world which place authority at the source of all good things' (p. 120). However, to Bloch the relationship between these two forms of cognition are not so clear-cut, and he sets out to reveal the interaction between them and to trace how ideology is created both historically and individually. So, where does ideology come from? Bloch sees ritual as the point of contact between two types of cognition.

The ritual process moves from non-ideological cognition to ideology in a series of stages. The staging of ritual into distinct phases that move between distinct social states is often associated with Victor Turner's work in which ritual moves from a state of social structure to an anarchic, carnevalesque, and chaotic stage of anti-structure before reorienting and restratifying into a familiar social structure. However, in Bloch's conception the ritual process does not simply return its audience to the initial point of departure *via* the tumultuous middle phase, but actually inculcates the cognition of the individual with the outcome of the previous ritual stages.

Bloch offers the example of the Merina circumcision ritual in Madagascar to show how the ritual process moves from non-ideological cognition to ideology and convinces the participant of the validity of ritual's ideological outcome. The first stage of the circumcision ritual involves an exaggerated emphasis on women as being solely responsible for the control of reproduction and nurturing of children. By representing women as holding the supreme power over the creation of people, the ritual creates an intriguing, but one-sided recognition of what has already been learned through interaction with the environment: the fact that women have a central and necessary (though only partial) role to play in procreation. Therefore, the incomplete knowledge presented in the first stage begs to be toppled and overturned in the second stage of the ritual. In this second phase, women are symbolically assaulted. By mocking and attacking women the ritual not only hazes women, but also mounts an onslaught on non-ideological cognition itself. This part of the ritual unfolds in chaotic and anarchic ways that foster a sense of liminal disruption and disorientation amongst participants. Again, the ritual anticipates its own reversal in the following phase, where the frantic disorder gives way to the assertion of authority. In the third and final phase of the ritual the elders as the power holders of the community establish their role as the source of everything by legitimizing their authority as timeless and natural through ideology.

Ideological knowledge asserts its validity over other forms of knowledge through this sequence of ritual stages by acknowledging, overturning and surpassing non-ideological cognition. Instead of building a logical sequence of cause-and-effect to legitimize the authority of the elders, the ritual builds on the participants' disorienting exposure to both exaggerated practical knowledge, tumultuous assault and overturning, before positing an authoritative form of ideological knowledge sustained by the transcendent superiority of the elders. Ideology becomes powerful through ritual process where, 'it is built on the apparent truth of non-ideological cognition both outside and inside, and therefore it cannot simply be denied; it is a construction which seems also to deny this truth [...] it both affirms and denies at the same time, rather in the way that the Christian message of the victory over death affirms by implication the finality of death. This is how ideology can mystify, invert and hide the real conditions of existence. This is never completely successful but it is often submitted to, because it is sanctioned directly or indirectly by force or threat' (p. 123).

This final assertion of ideology derives part of its potency from its elusive evocation of a transcendent and encompassing order that would be difficult to make explicit in any form of communication other than ritual. Bloch sees this as part of 'a mechanical aspect of ritualization which ensures the removal of ritual communication from non-ritual communication so that the one cannot be expressed in terms of the other or only misleadingly' (p. 123). Therefore, variation may occur in how interested people are in their belief, or how explicit they are in expounding them, and how much instituted hierarchy there is, in terms of ritualization of ideology. In short, Bloch posits a correlation between the inability to formulate beliefs explicitly and the degree of ritualization found in a society. Another important insight here is that ideology can persist through rituals that validate authority from power holders even when the particular identity of those power holders may change over time. Thereby, rituals form a recoverable instrument for domination and legitimation.

Bloch points out that the centrality of gender symbolism found in the Merina circumcision ritual is part of a larger cross-cultural repertoire of rituals that use gender as a powerful ideological tool to legitimize hierarchy and inequality. Although Bloch does not explicitly make the link here, this phenomenon of gender symbolism as a naturalizing trope for female subordination was a central feature of debates among 1970s feminist anthropologists. These thinkers sought to analyze how gender symbolism was employed to legitimize inequality through contrasting associations between male and female attributes in relation to nature and culture, production and reproduction, domestic and political spaces, and the creation of perishable and enduring goods. While Bloch's work here reveals how gender becomes entwined with bodily reproduction (and its assault) in favor of social reproduction (and its sacralization), we now turn to how kinship, the very immediate environment in which most children find themselves in their early developmental phases, may be turned into ideology.

To recapitulate, Bloch contrasts practical and experiential knowledge as individual with historical and transmitted knowledge as ideological, with the two forms spanned by ritual. In his view, kinship itself comes from what a person learns in everyday interaction, but may simultaneously become ideological through formalization in ritual.

In Merina kinship, the seniority between generations (e.g. parents and children) and within generations (e.g. between older and younger siblings) is marked in practice through obedience, respect, and rites, but also through language and terminology that specifies very particular ego-centered relationships to each relative. While hierarchy is anchored in the domestic group through an unchallenged hierarchy based on seniority and gender, hierarchy is downplayed between domestic groups in favor of egalitarian principles. Between domestic groups, Merina stress that egalitarian blood ties make them consubstantial and link these to positive values of community, solidarity, and sociability through shared ancestral tombs and rituals.

Through different kin ties and the rituals associated with them contradictory principles of hierarchy and equality are affirmed and countered, evoked and negated in rituals such as marriage. The contradictory tension between hierarchical and egalitarian principles provides potential for oscillating between them when negotiating and expressing marital alliances between domestic groups. This dynamic becomes most apparent when considering Merina kinship stratified across different levels of social class. The same kinship system reinforces equality at the lower strata with increasing hierarchical differentiation as one moves up the social ladder. When looking at Merina kinship from the perspective of social class, the potential to emphasize various elements while abiding by the same principles, allows the system to appear patrilineal in the lower, bilateral in the middle classes, and matrilineal at the social apex of the ruling monarch's family. Merina kinship reveals that anthropological analysis can be misleading if it gets caught up in classificatory and terminological systems without considering "the nature of the social system it operates" (p. 150). Furthermore, by bringing together contradictory principles, kinship may be a powerful vehicle by which 'the hierarchic mode can be easily changed to stress corporateness, the egalitarian mode can also be used to reinforce inequality' (p. 150).

A number of comparisons can be drawn between Bloch's theoretical and ethnographic insights and Chinese social dynamics. Ethnographically, analogies between different forms of kin and submission to authority, particularly how this inculcates subservience to political hierarchy, emerged as themes in the last chapter. Both Fei and Yan explored how Confucian morality emphasized both father–son dyads in parallel with ruler-subject relationships, although filial piety always ties an individual to a very specific relationship. Similar to Merina kinship terminology, Chinese kin terms also follow a very specific ego-centered classification of seniority both within and between generations that further reinforces hierarchies of gender and generation. Note that Fei also pointed out that this positions each person at the center of a web of relationships that are unique to that person and yet overlapping with the webs of others. At the end of this chapter, we will return to how the learning of names and naming develops self-awareness of personhood within a given social environment, thereby establishing who, where, and when one is in the world.

The following sections concentrate on debates that have placed Chinese kinship within larger ideals of order, both politically and economically, by looking at kinship as ideology and/or corporation. Some of the questions that emerge here are how far kinship as something learned through experiences in the everyday, can be part of acquiring ideological knowledge? How does this learning process through family, peers, and relatives emanate into wider spheres of political loyalty and distribution of rule? In order to focus this debate on Chinese kinship, we will examine one of its core features, often framed by anthropological commentators as its most notable characteristic, the Chinese lineage. The following section will consider what the lineage is, before going on to ask how it came into being historically. Here anthropological and historical debates meet in agreement and dispute. By taking up a very specific phenomenon, the tracing of descent from a first ancestor, we will see how debates coalesce around issues of territory and ritual, politics and economics, as different analysts stress various dimensions. To begin, it is worth examining a foundational classic in approaching Chinese kinship, more generally, and the Chinese lineage, more specifically, through Freedman's hotly debated lineage model.

3.2 Chinese Kinship from Family to Lineage

For a long time, Chinese kinship studies assumed the primacy of the corporate patrilineage as the main ordering mechanism of "traditional" Chinese society. This "lineage paradigm" relied heavily on Freedman's structural-functionalist model of Chinese kinship in southeastern China, which was largely based on textual sources from the pre-revolutionary period and fieldwork in the New Territories of Hong Kong (Freedman, 1958, 1966). Theoretically, Freedman attempted to apply the structural-functionalist approaches to lineages developed within the African context to Chinese society.

In general terms, Freedman's approach places lineage at the center of social organization in southeast China. These localized communities are constituted primarily of male agnates and secondarily of their dependent wives and unmarried female agnates (Freedman, 1958: pp. 3, 32). The lineages live in territorial vicinity with other members and trace descent from a shared ancestor who is communally worshipped in the ancestral hall. Echoing Africanists' bifurcation of kinship into the politico-jural and domestic domain, Freedman compartmentalizes kinship into the 'lineage as a whole and its sub-lineages, at one end of the system' and 'the family and the compound, at the other end' (Freedman, 1958: p. 37). On the whole, Freedman presents "the family" as a socio-economic unit resulting from the politico-jural rules of Chinese patriarchy and thereby subordinates the family to the lineage as a corporate agnatic unit ordered by patriarchal authority, filial devotion, and a system of equal inheritance among brothers.

Although Freedman explicitly delimited his study as a *model* rather than any real or existing lineage (Freedman, 1958: p. 7) and stressed that the "corporate" character of the lineage was a geographically restricted phenomenon (Freedman, 1958: p. 11), many of his followers were less careful in their application of his ideas (see Chun, 1996: pp. 429–432). Furthermore, Freedman was clear that there was geographic and temporal variation in lineage formations, which could be shallow or deep in terms of their generational reach, include small or large numbers of members, and be organized in very simple or highly complex ways, waxing and waning over time (Freedman, 1979: p. 335).

To Freedman, local lineages were created through the migration of a group of agnates, who established a common ancestor from whom to trace descent and set aside a portion of land to finance rites to commemorate this (p. 335). Over time, fission and fusion between segments were usually due to financial considerations, especially balancing the relative value of ancestral property and family property, such that the former could not be divided and survived longer (p. 336). Local lineages could also aggregate into higher order lineages (p. 337). However, the lineage crucially went beyond a common surname alliance and involved the permanent establishment of an estate, i.e. served an economic function (p. 337).

In Freedman's analysis, the role of the state is central to the formation and functioning of lineages. He explicitly contrasted his model to the African lineage as an ordering mechanism in the absence of a state, as the Chinese situation revealed an alternative vision in which the state mediated the relationship between the central power and the individual subject through kinship ties. Here the family comes in as 'a group of people owning a common estate and standing responsible for one another in some realms of conduct' (p. 338). Through a combination of the family (or *jia*) and the rule of five mourning grades (or *wu-fu*), double loyalty was institutionalized. Kinship cut across loyalties through analogical obligations to the sovereign, so that 'a man who fulfilled his kinship obligations was by that fact a good and loyal subject' (p. 338). Confucian virtue based around kinship solidarity was also vital to encouraging self-policing and enabling smooth tax-collecting. Effectively, lineages absolved the state of responsibility in managing security and taxes.

Inequality in wealth and power not only occurred between but within lineages (p. 339). When a particular lineage member had achieved exceptional wealth or status, for instance through high officialdom or examination honors, this often resulted in a filial descendant forming a trust in the name of this honored ancestor, thereby dividing his line from the rest of the lineage out of genealogical context. Freedman called this "asymmetrical segmentation," noting how it distinguished lineage organization in China from the African model. More broadly, lineage composition including a heterogeneous membership of rich and poor, strong and weak, bound together despite unequal accumulation of wealth and power between agnates. Moreover, political leaders and ritual elders were often distinct, with the former status based on political and economic management skills, the latter on genealogical position (p. 339). The consequence was that ritual status was often ascribed, while political or economic standing could be achieved, particularly by pooling skills, talent, and labor across the lineage, possibly in opposition or competition with other lineages.

This connects with Skinner's findings on rural–urban continuity through hierarchies of market places and administrative centers across China, such that lineages serve as vehicles for assembling power and privileges in profitable ways for its members. As Freedman pithily observes: 'a poor family in a powerful lineage was inferior and exploitable at home yet in a privileged position against the wider world' (p. 340). However, the state had to keep the lineage in check lest it threaten the political order by becoming too influential by amassing wealth or power. When lineages became too powerful, the state clamped down and reduced its power on the local scene, revealing that 'what had up to then been agnation respectable became at once agnation perilous. In other words, the Chinese state was responsible for creating a stick for beating its own back' (p. 341). In effect, political order was a balancing act between the state and kin ties, though the latter functioned symbolically to support the former, when lineages outstripped the state materially, the state had to reign in its power and autonomy.

To Freedman, this precarious balancing act of political order between state and kin also serves to explain the uneven geographic distribution of deep and large lineages across China. Individuals are part of lineages as corporations, or even a series of corporations, scaling up through descent lines, but they are also part of wider frameworks of other groups and relationships that include villages, marketing communities, townships, secret societies, and the like (p. 347). Furthermore, lineages played a role in mobilizing sizeable forces for local military defense (p. 347). For instance in the middle of the 19th century when central political power weakened, the gentry and local militias gained a foothold in many parts of the country (p. 348). This occurred despite the fact that in contrast to commoners, the gentry's position of privilege and standing largely derived from their potential positions in the bureaucracy (p. 349). The gentry at large shared literary values and skills and therefore formed the core of the potential talent pool for bureaucratic recruitment (p. 349). Freedman concludes: 'As an anthropologist one starts from the Chinese lineage and one finishes up on the grand theme of the disintegration of the traditional Chinese political order' (p. 350).

While Freedman's work on this is strongly political and jural, Skinner (1964) makes an argument for economic market systems as the basis for kinship topology. Skinner proposes a hierarchy of markets in China, ranging from the smallest village market to the large market town and on up to regional market cities, forming an interlocking spatial system.

These markets are arranged in a regular spatial and economic hierarchy that also structures social and cultural systems (pp. 3–7). As one moves up the hierarchy, the number of households increases as the proportion of labor involved in agriculture decreases, with the central market town marked by worship of the ch'eng-huang city deity (p. 10). The periodic cycles of the markets concentrate demand and thereby allow for higher density of markets across landscape (pp. 10–11). Six market towns form a hexagonal grid as the environmental and human temporal cycles intertwine in the movement of people, goods, and services pulse through interconnecting transport flows (p. 11). While peasants attend markets as consumers, to make purchases, elicit services, borrow credit, and attend religious festivals, elite gentlemen come to find books, stationary supplies, and other luxuries, lend and invest money, and pass leisure time in tea and wine houses (p. 27). This total complex of nested marketing is secured through parallels of a downward flow of merchandise and upward flow of goods (p. 30).

Although these marketing centers may form administrative as well as economic levels, the administrative and the economic functions do not map one-to-one (p. 7). Government control decreases at the lower levels of the marketing hierarchy, especially in terms of (in) official activities, licenses, taxes, and regulations (p. 31). Moreover, Skinner makes some insightful contrasts in how marketing and administration order space. Administrative units are discrete and encompassing, while marketing systems are only discrete at the most basic (village) level (p. 31). By contrast, *every* marketing unit is oriented towards an ascending level of centers, therefore forming a networked and interlocking system with significant capacities for social integration (p. 31). This is how he arrives at the argument that the standard marketing community is also a culture-bearing unit, because the social field of the participating farmers is demarcated by their marketing area not by their village (p. 32).

Skinner emphasizes that when we think of marketing system as a community 'we are not dealing with a cosy primary group structured through bonds of great intimacy or intensity' (p. 33). However, as Fei also points out, this is a face-to-face world of known acquaintances. Skinner provides the example of his host, Mr. Lin, a 45year-old peasant in Sichuan, who in the course of his life would have attended his local market a 1,000 times with every (male!) household head (p. 35). Therefore, this social knowledge accumulates over a lifetime, as people develop a social map through their marketing area with structural consequences for economic, political, social, and cultural life (p. 35).

This social terrain of inclusion also serves to create marriage alliances, as marriage brokers are located in marketing centers, thereby creating a kind of marketing community endogamy, both in prescriptive and open alliance system (even between lineages) (p. 35). 'The affinal bonds of the peasant thus constitute another network which spreads through the standard marketing community and gives structure to the whole' (p. 36). In terms of lineage segmentation, Skinner even proposes a strongly economic (rather than ritual) basis focused on the market, such that a great lineage may also come to dominate a market economically (p. 37). In terms of ritual elaboration, Skinner points out how these marketing communities also focus on a shared major temple in the town for communal worship (p. 38).

Looking at the formation of lineages historically, however, raises questions to aspects of Freedman and Skinner's findings, particularly when we examine not only how lineages looked in the 20th century, but how and where they appeared over time. In the following sections we will examine how hierarchy was destabilized or bolstered through lineage formation, in particular when state or kin power holders consciously or unwittingly reformulated ideology in line with their interests. This can be seen as a culmination of long processes of historical change or as considered interventions by ideologues introducing new teachings.

Through the prism of first ancestor worship, we will see how families and lineages relate through hierarchy and equality. We will juxtapose a number of positions on when, how, and why first ancestor worship emerged, with a focus on the spread of these practices in the Song dynasty (960–1279AD), a time when agricultural intensification and urbanization occurred at the same time as neo-Confucian thinkers reformulated ritual prescriptions. However, how far changes were administered from the top down and how far they grew from the bottom up of the social hierarchy, and their varying causes and effects in economic, political, or ritual factors, are all up for debate.

3.3 Changes from above: The Role of Neo-Confucian Ideologues

In his historical analysis, anthropologist Chun shows that although the lineage-village complex was for a long time closely associated with Chinese kinship, he emphasizes how it was a geographically restricted and historically limited phenomenon (Chun, 1996). Chun focuses particular attention on two periods of history in which conscious intervention by ideologues influenced ritual practices and led to the rise of the lineage-village complex in certain areas. He identifies the neo-Confucian campaign focusing on family ritual orthodoxy in the 11th and 12th century and the rise of the concept of the "first ancestor" with its associated practice of tracing genealogies in the 17th century as key moments leading to the rise of the localized lineage in the southeast (pp. 432–439). Taking into account both its historical and geographical limitations, Chun questions whether "the lineage" should really be considered inherent to Chinese social structure and cultural patterns.

Chun takes Freedman's work as the starting point for his analysis, but differentiates his position quite clearly from this model, in large part because of its limited engagement with the historical trajectory that formed lineages and its alleged insufficient explanation of the geographic spread and organizational diversity of lineages across China. Chun points out that Freedman's model was in explicit dialogue with an Africanist lineage model, where kinship organization was supposed to compensate for decentralized state control, but in China lineage formation and evolution occurred very much in dialogue with the imperial state and therefore this historical trajectory should be subject to closer scrutiny (pp. 429–430). For Chun, Freedman's model 'failed to explain why lineage organization was strongest in those regions where centralized political control was weakest and vice versa' (p. 430). He even claims that the logical consistency Freedman projects onto the lineage model derive from his predominant attention to single-surname villages in south-eastern China to the detriment of the geographic and organizational diversity across the country. In point of fact, as we have seen, Freedman's exploration of the lineage was explicitly part of a model and he himself recognized that the reality on the ground was more complex than the organizational simplifications and generalizations necessary to construct the mode. Chun also argues that Freedman's use of village land surveys to examine agnatic organization meant that the corporate accumulation of land became the driving force in his cycle of lineage development with the Chinese lineage essentially being defined as a landed kin estate, a bottom–up 'agnatic organization and territorial settlement were products of the same rational, calculating activity' (p. 430).

Beyond Freedman's economic rationale for the lineage as a corporation, Chun follows other analysts in stressing alternate factors underlying agnatic solidarity for this Chinese kinship organization (p. 431). Chun characterizes the following factors: '(1) unambiguous descent-phrased rules pertaining to membership and succession, (2) clear-cut rules pertaining to the inheritance and transmission of a shared estate, especially in land, and (3) a set of identifiable rites, beliefs, and obligations pertaining to the worship of ancestors by members of the domestic group' (p. 431). To Chun, what is most important is not what a lineage does, but where it comes from, i.e. Chun seeks to go beyond explaining the operations of lineage as analytical constructs and trace its existence as a social institution historically (p. 431). Like Fei in the previous chapter, Chun remains skeptical of importing foreign analytical concepts, such as the lineage, into China, instead emphasizing the Chinese term of *tsu* as defying translation and distinct from the related term *tsung* (p. 432). Although Chun addresses both thought and practice in the historical evolution of lineages, his emphasis lies with the discursive imagination of neo-Confucian ideologues as the catalyst for kinship transformations, thereby strongly implying that this intellectual elite initiated changes occurring from the Song dynasty as part of a top–down process.

Although the 20th century lineage organization is only 200 to 300 years old, their composition relies on different elements, each of which was molded by its own historicity. Of particular note are the following three: first, ancestral beliefs and rites whose origins can be traced back to pre-imperial era elites in the Shang and Zhou period, which then became more widespread in the last millennium; second, patrilineal descent traced through the generational transmission of titles and surnames also emerged in the Zhou dynasty with the presence of ancestral shrines, but the practice of composing written genealogies only became fully institutionalized in the early Ming period (c.a. 1400); third, landed estates, those linked to large-scale localized lineages are the most recent feature emerging from c.a. 1700 and paving the way for single lineage-village complexes (p. 432). These three factors are linked through ideological revival of the Zhou dynasty *tsung-fa* system that amounted to a kingly succession through primogeniture, territorial sacrifice at ancestral shrines, and probably included loose agnatic communities tracing unilineal descent and equal inheritance of land (p. 433). However, according to Chun the neo-Confucian ideologues in the Song dynasty prompted widespread shifts in kinship organization through their debates. In essence, ritual fundamentalists wanted to oversee a revival of this ancient *tsung-fa* system while revisionists were keen to disseminate sacrifices made to founding ancestors more widely in the population, thereby conceptualizing ancestor worship through a focus on the first ancestor, and prompting the creation of local lineages as patterns of social organization (p. 433).

According to Chun, this ideological revolution in Confucian family ritual happened in two phases: the first occurred in the 11th and 12th century when elites panicked over the alleged state of moral decay due to the popularization of Buddhism resulting in changes in domestic rights in China (p. 435). In Chun's assessment, neo-Confucian discourse was a conscious and deliberate defense strategy against this foreign invasion (p. 435). Ideologues sought to revive Confucian ethics based on rites that everybody in Chinese society could practice (p. 435). However, the government set up obstacles to universalize these practices by restricting the privilege of ancestral shrines to officials (p. 435). Therefore, many practices advocated by the neo-Confucians remained upper class literati practices, especially the new orthodox canon of domestic rites and writing genealogies (p. 435).

Then the second phase of transformation occurred in 17th and 18th century, when the first ancestor became the focus for communal ancestor worship, creating the basis of communal ancestor worship of agnates in a village locality (p. 435). The effect was that both charitable estates and ancestral halls were established and genealogies took on the new function as documentary evidence for 'tracing the relations of all known agnates to that common first ancestor, including glorious personages in the imperial and mythic past' (p. 436). However, popular dissemination of ancestral rites was not standardized, with handbooks often including popular rites mixed with neo-Confucian philosophy. Despite criticism by ritual fundamentalists, kin groups throughout China increasingly worshipped ancestors beyond the prescribed four generations and began recognizing shared agnatic status rather than official rank, as destratified ancestral worship spread throughout the country (p. 436). The outcome was that the following practices became widespread from the 18th and 19th century: building public lineage halls devoted to first migrant ancestor and writing genealogies based on that principle (p. 436). This allowed for the formation of charitable estates and therefore the emergence of nucleated lineage-village complexes in Southeast China, while central China continued to have a looser agnatic organization, and northern China lineages mostly eschewed collective ritual activities and corporate estates (p. 436).

Like Bloch's thesis, Chun's analysis shows how kinship can be mobilized to accommodate the contradictory principles of hierarchy and equality through ritualization of ideology. Chun summarizes that 'while the localized Chinese represented the institutional culmination of an imagined agnatic (egalitarian) ideal, in practice it was highly dependent on the role of elites in regulating the affairs of the group in a way that made it an appropriate nexus of power' serving gentry interests (p. 437). In short, to Chun the change in ideological orientation among elite literati scholars created the basis for the resulting ritual changes that turned ancestral cults into vehicles for the formation of large-scale corporate kin estates (p. 436). While corporate kin estates may have solidified agnatic solidarity, this solidarity was a precondition for their establishment. While Chun sees this solidarity emerging from rituals that were consciously and willfully constructed by elite ideologues in a top–down fashion, the historian Ebrey (1986) views the rites and rituals as the primary driver of change that proceeded to alter ideological commitments of elites and commoners alike.

3.4 Bottom–up Rites as Drivers of Change

Bloch's theory of ritualized authority includes insights into how rituals may be usurped over time by changing power holders to create continuity and justify their hierarchical positions. This contrasts somewhat with Chun's analysis that ideologues consciously revive, or revise the ritual repertoire to serve ruling interests. Ebrey's argument forms an opposite movement to Chun's by viewing bottom–up changes to rituals as altering kinship ideology, rather than the other way around. Ebrey goes further than either Bloch or Chun in viewing rituals as drivers for change from a sweeping historical perspective, focusing in particular on the period of 1000–1400AD.

Ebrey points towards the beginning of the Han period (202BC–220AD) as the time when agnatic kinship was already focused on family and family line, particularly for male household members and their patrilineal descendants and ancestors (p. 18). In the T'ang (618BC–907AD) and Sung (960BC–1279AD) dynasties the ritual repertoire largely continued, with a number of subtle yet significant additions, that 'altered the relationships of the old constants' (p. 20). These included the Ch'ing-ming festival as the occasion for visiting graves in which agnates gathered to worship their shared ancestors (p. 21). At the time, only high officials had family altars so this occasion created a new basis for elite agnatic solidarity (p. 21). As neo-Confucian ideologues had mixed opinions about the practice of worshipping ancestors at the graves (p. 22), Ebrey argues (contra Chun) that sacrifices at graves developed from local customs as a bottom–up development, very explicitly stating that she sees 'no evidence at all that ideological motives led Confucian scholars to promote worship at graves' (p. 23).

The two ritual innovations that Ebrey argues fostered solidarity between local agnates were 'the inclusion of *early ancestors* in rites and the practice of everyone visiting graves on *the same day*' (p. 23). The spatial concentration of graves in a single area and the increasing number of generations being worshipped created a mutually reinforcing cycle as graves were neither abandoned, nor neglected. Through the temporal concentration of visits on a single day, clearer lines were drawn for inclusion of agnatic members of descent group around earliest ancestors, with later migrants being excluded from ritual participation (p. 24).

Keen not to neglect the ritual practices of the elite, Ebrey also discusses four Song men's relationship to graves and descent groups, one of whom is a disciple and son-in-law of the famous neo-Confucian Zhu Xi. Ebrey highlights five shared assumptions between them: the association between graves and descent groups; the value placed on burying people in proximity for ritual purposes; an emphasis on the arrangement of graves to reflect descent and seniority; the commitment to defend graveyards from incursion by outsiders; and the practice of collecting money to pay for descent group rites (p. 28). The primacy of the ritual basis over economic and political needs seems critical to all of their positions. Ebrey rather forcefully criticizes anthropologists for overemphasizing the role of economic property and political influence in the formation of descent groups and their group consciousness, instead advocating more attention paid to the role of rites (p. 29).

Ebrey also discusses a related phenomenon to the lineage in some detail that separates the lineage from the notion of the family, not by size, but due to its communal ethos based on a shared budget and the absence of an estate separable from the household. The "communal family" was a domestic unit of undivided 5, 6, even 10 generations who lived together with a common budget (p. 30). According to Ebrey, communal families could be considered precursors to lineages, because 'they were large localized groups that shared in a common estate and were organized on a basis of patrilineal descent' (p. 30). Their only hierarchical distinctions were age, generation, sex, as members attempted to keep inequality in wealth from affecting living standards (p. 32). Rules regarding management, budgeting, courtesy and etiquette attempted to solidify this ideology, as did the common budget that minimized differences in wealth and social status (pp. 32–33). The big change from the undivided family to the lineage emerged through the establishment of a separable estate (p. 34). So why did these lineage estates emerge?

Ebrey contradicts Chun's claims that the neo-Confucians wanted to modify kinship across China, arguing that Sung dynasty intellectuals aimed to reform kinship *within* their social class, despite their romanticized notions of commoners' family spirit as a motivation (p. 35). For these ideologues, the house and the state were analogically linked in need of management and conservation, such that the neo-Confucian Chang Tsai lamented the division of wealth that would happen in a family by writing that '[n]owadays those who accumulate wealth or honor can only plan for thirty or forty years. They may build a residence and occupy it but when they die their sons will divide and separate and soon be bankrupt, so that the house (*chia*) does not survive. If, in this way, they cannot preserve their houses, how can they preserve the state?' (quoted in Ebrey, p. 38)

Ebrey concurs with Chun that the neo-Confucian ideology in the 11th century solved a number of problems, but argues that these ideologues were actually sanctioning the already growing practice of rites to early ancestors (p. 39). Furthermore, while anthropologists focus on the presence or absence of estates in the making of lineages, i.e. defining them as descent groups with sizeable corporate property, the comparison between the lineage estate and the communal family leads to a more nuanced picture of joint property and budgeting (p. 40). A main difference in relation to the estates was that with the rise of the lineages, independent households were able to separate assets (p. 41). Simultaneously, by securing ritual and charitable expenses through an endowment, lineages pooled financial responsibility for their agnates, thereby dissolving the principles of mutual aid within the communal family (p. 41). Although the state encouraged the formation of descent groups with estates, estates for non-agnates also existed, especially charitable estates for community-based activities (p. 42). Nonetheless, ritual expenses were in all likelihood the material motivation for establishing the estates, rather than the charitable dimension, because they provided basis for lineage formation (p. 43).

In relation to genealogical formation, Ebrey again nuances the argument, pointing out that tracing the emergence of written genealogies does not provide sufficient insights into the motivation for creating them, while analyzing their content reveals much more about the men who penned them (p. 44). In fact, it is not always entirely clear if the descent group precedes or follows its written genealogy. On one hand, an active descent group may ask a scholar to compile a genealogy, particularly to establish status through the identity of the first apical ancestor, to settle the transfers of land, residences, and burial grounds, to locate graves, as well as name members and their relationships (pp. 44–45). On the other, a group of ambitious men may try to establish a pedigree and evidence of social status through this document (particularly for marriage purposes) (p. 45), or to create a means to link patrilineal related descent groups together and form higher-order descent groups (p. 48).

Ancestral halls were also a major addition to agnatic kinship practices, because previously only high officials had ancestral altars with domestic rites going back four generations (p. 52). These new halls allowed for joint worship and the focus of rites across agnatically related men within a descent group (p. 51). Like all the previous authors, Ebrey also points out that the rich and poor, powerful and weak were tied together in the lineages (p. 52), but also that the coexistence of variation in kinship organization, even within a single township, means that any normative generalizing explanation is unsound (p. 53).

In sum, in Ebrey's reformulation, rites preceded the subsequent sanctioning of these rites by ideologues. Her point of departure for this argument differs from both Freedman and Skinner's approaches of scaling up from the smallest household to larger institutional formations of the lineage and market town, respectively, as well as from Chun's focus on an elite perspective of ritual fundamentalist ideologues. Instead, Ebrey proceeds from a contrast between large communal families and lineages. Ebrey's reasoning has wide-reaching consequences for arguments about hierarchy and inequality in ideology, as it undermines a straightforward shift away from elite aristocratic privilege in ancestor worship towards communal agnatic rituals based around the first ancestor. Instead, shifts in ritual practices actually pave the way for material inequality through extended lineages that hail symbolic solidarity through their rites.

To Ebrey, lineages establish grand estates while simultaneously sanctioning internal differentiation and rising inequality. Lineages secure finance for agnatic solidarity rituals through ritual estates, while undermining financial claims of its weaker and poorer members, who are provided for through charitable estates, rather than the joint household budgets of the communal families. As these rituals take center stage, particularly through the establishment of grave visits and ancestral halls, their symbolic egalitarianism based around alleged common origins serves to mask the growing inequality between lineage members. Two changes in ritual practice form both consequence and driver of this transformation in a circular motion of cause and effect: first, everybody goes to the graves on the same day; second, the sphere of how many ancestors are traced through worship expands. Lineage worship at communal agnatic gravesites, thereby inculcate knowledge about the ancestors through their shared location and informative arrangement about lineage ancestors, such that lineage members learn about their own position in relation to each other's agnates. In short, in concurrence with Bloch's thesis these agnatic rituals serve power holders, even under changing political and economic conditions, and instill ideological knowledge of communal relations between kin that confounds and undermines experiences of growing inequality and differentiation.

3.5 The State, Laws, and Taxes in Kinship as Patricorporation

By contrast to all previous arguments focused primarily around hierarchy and inequality among the male lineage members, Hill Gates (1996) analyzes how lineages bolster privileges of their members while exploiting others through a Marxist–feminist perspective. Gates takes issue with kinship as a fundamental, irreducible, elementary structure, instead focusing on kinship as a mediator for a division of labor that naturalizes hierarchies of gender and generation, making the exploitation of women and juniors appear necessary, biological, and moral (p. 84). Although her model is broad and far-reaching, Gates points to the variation in lineages across time and place to question whether Chinese lineages really form a singular system at all. Furthermore, unlike most African lineage constellations, the Chinese state was unusual in generalizing the lineage formation beyond an elite (of aristocracy and chiefdoms) and mobilizing it in its own state interests. Gates asks two pointed questions that remind social scientists not to simply import Western concepts as models and cautions sinologists not to take Chinese conditions for granted: 'What is a *jia*, the "family" or household? Why do the Chinese organize themselves into lineages?' (p. 85).

Gates argues that the Song period reshaped kinship according to three changes of great impact: first, non-Han kinship variation grew on Han kinship as Han people settled and expanded into new geographic regions; second, state officials began to enforce state laws through making kin seniors responsible for junior members as "local subalterns"; third, the state secured stability in property relations and complemented this with the sanctioning of flexible labor use through lineages, thereby balancing two economic systems, a tributary and petty-capitalist mode of production (p. 85). Here, Gates is not employing the full Marxist elaboration of the concept of a mode of production (which would entail combining means, forces and relations of production). Her mode of production approximates to forms of accumulation, but forms of accumulation that occur through the extraction of value from women, male kin juniors, hired labor, and apprentices. Gates reveals how kinship masked this exploitation by making kin seniors appear as righteously managing family estates, while ancestral property that represented and reproduced inequality of household was protected by state law and kinship ideology (p. 100).

Gates makes a sweeping historical argument for the two interrelated modes of production in Imperial China from the Song dynasty onwards: the tributary mode of production based on agriculture, on one hand, and the petty capitalist mode of production based on marketization and commodification, on the other. In the tributary mode of production, the ruling classes of officials and the imperial court extracted money, taxes, and labor from a class of (predominantly) agricultural producers. This economy of tribute existed in many imperial states across the world and was the dominant mode of production in China for millennia. By contrast, the petty capitalist mode of production may have been unique to China and emerged with the rising population numbers in the Song dynasty. Unlike the Western model of capitalism where the individual laborer formed the basic economic unit of production, the Chinese petty capitalist mode of production relied on the patrilineal family corporation as its basic economic unit of production. Gates traces the emergence of the petty capitalist mode of production in the Song dynasty to agricultural advances, increased marketization, and on-going urbanization.

The glue holding together the two modes of production was the patri-corporation, which allowed producers to balance talent, labor, and capital through a shared economic unit. Men could achieve social mobility by either excelling in the official examination system (in the state-sanctioned tributary mode) or by balancing labor and capital in such a way that a surplus of capital meant that labor could be outsourced (within the petty capitalist mode). Shifts in the kinship ideology during the Song dynasty, with the rise of neo-Confucian family values, turned women into reproducers, labor, and capital at the disposal of their male household heads.

The state had an interest in keeping the household as a weak and convenient unit for the extraction of surplus and men in control of these stable households. The legal practice of equal inheritance amongst sons broke down estates every time they passed down a generation.

The equal division of property between brothers, an aspect of the state management of property rights, served the tributary ideal. In the extended households of the ruling classes, there was privileging of the primary wives' sons, and family headship continued by primogeniture (pp. 91–92). The state's sanctioning of having all sons inherit their share of household property was upheld while protecting other rights of the father to dispense of lineage members flexibly at his will. The obligation to inherit property between sons stands in stark contrast to other rights a father wielded over his son and other dependents, rights including the potential to expel, sell, or kill members (p. 92). Official kin norms could be imposed through courts, especially in relation to filial obligations, marriage transactions, and property transfers (p. 88). Nonetheless, government regulation was usually enforced through kin seniors of the patrilineage, such that these elders acted in the interest of officials, in line with gender and generational hierarchy and its resource distribution (pp. 88–89). Uxorilocal marriage occurred as an alternative, particularly for the poorest households without sons (p. 93). Legally, there was no consideration from the state if the lineage was too poor for property to be feasibly divided (p. 94). Women had less direct connection to the means of production (especially land) and were therefore more easily commoditized and also acquired and disposed of (p. 95). Women served as a kind of "ballast" in balancing petty commodity production goals of household expansion and property accumulation, thereby becoming central to the collusion between state and kin seniors through property law (p. 95).

The quasi interchangeability of men in the same kin generation, allowed for a pooling of talent for bureaucratic and official posts that could be greatly beneficial to a lineage as a whole (p. 105). This interchangeability was also useful for adoption if households lacked a suitable male heir in the patriline (p. 106). Upward mobility through a powerful lineage was available to a son born in a weak or impoverished family: 'the paternal generation made profits and paid for a son or nephew to earn a degree; the filial generation got appointed and received tribute. The protection state kinship ideology offered to productive resources labeled as ancestral — rather than individual or private — property was extremely important to successful social climbers. A rich man's wealth was easily confiscated: a lineage's sacrificial land (or brick kiln or pawnshop) was a sacred trust officials felt bound to honor' (p. 108).

The puzzle of why lineages emerged strongest where the state appeared weakest is that there households and village elders were enacting an indirect, involuntary, unpaid rule (p. 90). Far from kin and village elders operating in a vacuum, Gates frames lineage operations as part of political and legal power enacted through local agents of the state (p. 90). In Gates' reading, this collusion seems very conscious and deliberate (p. 102). Competition for tribute and capital was managed 'through amassing lineage estates that were ritually sanctioned, legally protected, collectively held, and inalienable' (p. 104). Gates makes clear that petty capitalism was not capitalism, because ancestral property formed the bulk of privately owned means of production (especially land) and the state regulated the transmission of land across generations of men, while delinking women from rights to land, thereby usurping any potential for free waged labor by subjecting labor to kinship relations (p. 99). In her iteration, labor only shifted from *jia* relations ordering labor as predominantly a duty to (kin) superiors towards a contractual market commodity with abstract monetary value in the late imperial era (p. 94).

According to Gates, in terms of inequality, there was no real class emergence as labor relations were largely managed by kin relations, not the market (pp. 112, 114). However, in other ways this was capitalism naturalized (p. 113). Even the poverty of poorer lineage members could be used as a way of moralizing over them, as they held unsavory occupations, engaged in improper marriage practices, and were shabby in their domestic rituals (p. 113). This may have reduced the moral burden on wealthy lineage members to alleviate their kin's consumption burden and provide lineage welfare (p. 113). In this point, Gates comes close to what Ebrey says when she contrasts the rise of the lineage with the responsibilities of extended families. Gates argues that smaller lineages often aimed to maintain stable economic positions rather than expand in a capitalist way, so in some ways stratified with small lineages closer to a tributary mode and large lineages closer to the petty commodity mode (p. 116). Gates' final analysis about gender hierarchy comes close to Bloch's conclusion that the reproduction of gender inequality was both the most universal and possibly one of the oldest core values of hierarchy (p. 120). As Gates concludes, '[l]ineage activities raised maleness to the status of the sacred [...] Agnatic ties were honored, celebrated, ritualized; other kinds of kinship, and female roles other than the relation of mothers of sons, were essentially ignored by the lineage' (p. 120).

Questions as to how and why lineage formations were reasserted with full force in the Market Era after their widespread suppression under Maoism, raises questions about how ideological knowledge and historical consciousness is learned, developed, and constructed among each generation, in ways that must bring together anthropological and psychological approaches. In addition to Bloch's general theoretical discussion, Stafford addresses these processes of intergenerational learning with the specificities of ethnography in rural mainland China and Taiwan in mind.

3.6 Development of Historical Consciousness

In his general book on separation and reunion in China, Stafford (2000) bridges anthropological and psychological approaches. Here we examine his chapter on how children learn to develop historical consciousness in rural villages in mainland China and Taiwan. This offers a contemporary perspective on some of the issues we have addressed so far, particularly how a sense of history is instilled at different scales, including the family, locality, and nation as temporal consciousness situates a person in terms of their relationship and agency to the wider pattern of events (p. 127). The chapter strongly echoes Bloch's position, that history is not simply inherited at birth or transmitted wholesale from previous generations, but is instead constructed, here *developed,* in an environment marked by not only changing contexts, but constant re-evaluation of what has been learned in light of new events and experiences (p. 128). Stafford traces patterns and processes by which space and time are learned, but also present and future becomes situated as children develop and grow (pp. 128–129). Periods such as "ancient" or "after liberation" become thinkable through a 'process of temporalisation [that] is facilitated by hearing of and reading about past events and eras (i.e. by being given ready-made historical narratives); but it is also shaped by children's own experience of the passage of time (e.g. their increasing grasp of the ageing processes and what time *means*)' (p. 129).

Stafford provides two very evocative mundane examples, both of which are mediated by persons, language, and the environment of the home. Northern farmhouses are insulated or, 'literally wall-papered with history' that surrounds the heated bed-stove platform, the *kang*, where families spend most of their time indoors in the freezing winter months (p. 129). Newspapers, manuals, textbooks, and magazines on the walls appear quite idiosyncratic, especially as the content of their written material is largely ignored, despite including propaganda from the Maoist period. By contrast, Stafford's second example arises from a father explicitly and meticulously teaching his daughter to recite classical poetry about filial duties. Within the home, these two kinds of historical references instantiate only a small sample of the many sources of historical knowledge a child draws on, illustrating differences in significance between what you are taught and what is ignored, or at least not explicated. These experiences instill differences in value and evaluation of history in children, as they learn history as a contextual and fragmentary form of knowledge that cannot be restricted to formal learning.

Stafford then proceeds to connect how folk models of child development meet with ritualization as an explicit formalization and transmission of knowledge within families. Folk models of child development stress fate and the temporal journey along a projected path against which children become measured and old ladies constitute the main moral authorities on this process. By celebrating children publicaly at various intervals, families not only surround them with supportive family networks, but also allow children to choose their destiny. For instance, sitting amid a range of objects on the bed-platform, children may choose a book indicating their future scholarship, a scale if they have the makings of a trader, a stone is chosen by hard workers, money selected by those with a bent for fortune, and a steamed bun for those who delight in food rather than work. The ritual not only indicates, but also brings about a child's future through safeguarding their righteous development and filial sentiments.

At other moments, family celebrations also connect public displays of childrearing and the management of this process of child development through improvisation. For instance, Stafford offers an example of when something goes wrong during the highly charged celebratory period of Chinese New Year, a time at which the home becomes a symbolically dense and fatefully charged environment, and bad omens for the coming year through the unfolding of misfortunate events or immoral acts must be avoided at all costs. One boy behaves rudely to his elders, makes a stroppy exit, before setting off firecrackers in the courtyard that explode in his hand. Family seniors scold him for this injury to a body that they deem not entirely his, but also as family property. However, the consequences of his disrespecting his elders and bodily safety are met with a subsequent meal that runs counter to what the child could have expected at any other time of the year, as he becomes absorbed into a circle of privileged shared consumption with the senior generation who ply him with food and drink in their midst. Thereby, '[h]is anti-social behaviour was met with the ultimate Chinese expression of sociability: eating and drinking around a table' with adults, where a child is normally not welcome (p. 138). 'The boy's dramatic personal experience — which surely must have seemed completely singular — was thus merged, or made to merge, with a flow of (momentarily "timeless") time, and with a pattern of ideas and events which is linked to the familial past' (138).

Stafford highlights an approach that focuses on the familiar and concrete rather than privileging generic and abstract learning in what is known and named (p. 140). Rather than simply looking at kin naming practices, for instance, in which kinship positions are made explicit, Stafford traces how children learn their social position in space and time through diffuse sensations and emotions in interaction with others. In this regard, Stafford's ethnographic exploration reveals significant parallels with Bloch's theoretical framework. Stafford also indicates some overlaps in power and knowledge that lead to common complaints of history being a burden in China. Complaints that history is too long and has too many people in it are commonplace in China (p. 142). This popular perception of the tyranny of history is shared by academics, who also relate this problem to a notion of quantitative thinking about history, especially as a fixed object of knowledge (p. 141). Thereby, Stafford reveals how certain forms of conservatism in generational knowledge are abstracted and translated into politics as ideology, and introduces mechanisms by which historical consciousness is acquired that brings together various forms of historical knowledge (p. 140).

3.7 Conclusion

This chapter has taken a long historical perspective on kinship in China. The chapter contrasted practical and experiential knowledge as individual, with historical and transmitted knowledge as ideological, and then connected them through critical engagement with Bloch's work on ritual. In this view, kinship itself comes from what a person learns in everyday interaction and becomes ideological through formalization in ritual. The chapter examined whether kinship could be said to be ideology in China. It looked at anthropologists and historians who argued that kinship was ideological in China, elaborating on kinship's long-standing relationship to the state, economy and patriarchy. However, contrasts were also traced in different approaches to explaining lineages as institutions that were political, economic, and broadly ideological. Furthermore, the realm of ideology as not just representing historical, but also confounding various forms of experiential knowledge emerged with full force in these discussions, as we traced the naturalization of hierarchy and the justification of inequality through lineages and their associated ritual practices and epistemological premises.

Freedman put forth a persuasive and encompassing lineage model for China, where they served as the institutions in the interest of the economic aims of agnates building up from the smallest domestic family to the political and jural functions of an extended lineage, and that this was implicated in the political governance of the state. William Skinner emphasized economic marketing structures and how these multinodal networks formed the basis for exchange relations ranging from trade in goods to the basis of affinal relations across marketing areas, as distinct from administrative hierarchies. By contrast to these more abstracted and synchronic models, Chun traced the formation of lineages through transformations in elite ideology, with particular focus on the promotion of first ancestor worship in the Song dynasty. Sharing in a historical approach that emphasizes the ritual basis for kinship changes, Ebrey compared the lineages with extended households to show how popular rites at gravesites served as catalysts and instantiations of ritual changes from below. By contrast, Gates provided extensive evidence from state legal codes to show how the state and kin seniors colluded to combine two forms of accumulation that encompassed both tributary and petty capitalist modes of production. Finally, we turned to a more contemporary exploration of these issues through Stafford's methodologically stimulating examination of how children develop a historical consciousness and form ideological knowledge from a medley of experiences in their family homes. In the following chapter, we build on the insights into kinship made in this chapter and yet move further away from formal abstracted models through focusing attention on the everyday processes and acts that constitute living relatedness.

Seminar Questions

How does Bloch's theory of ideology enhance understandings of the evolution and continuity of Chinese kinship?

How does Chinese history contribute to anthropological understandings of the relationship between kinship, power, and wealth?

Readings

Bloch, Maurice (1989). 'From cognition to ideology' and 'Hierarchy and equality in Merina kinship', in *Ritual History and Power: Selected Papers in Anthropology*. Athlone Press: London. pp. 106–151.

Chun, Allen (1996). 'The lineage-village complex in Southeastern China: a long footnote in the anthropology of kinship', *Current Anthropology*, 37, p. 3.

Ebrey, Patricia (1986). 'The early stages in the development of descent group organisation', in Ebrey, Patricia Buckley and James L.Watson (eds.) *Kinship Organization in Late Imperial China 1000-1940*. California University Press: Berkeley, pp. 16–61.

Freedman, Maurice (1979). 'The politics of an old state: a view from the Chinese lineage', in Skinner, G. William (ed.) *The Study of Chinese Society: Essays by Maurice Freedman*. Stanford University Press: Stanford, pp. 334–350.

Gates, Hill (1996). *China's Motor: A Thousand Years of Petty Capitalism*. Cornell University Press: Ithaca.

Skinner, G. William (1964). 'Marketing and social structure in rural China' Part I. *The Journal of Asian Studies*, 24 (01), pp. 3–43.

Stafford, Charles (2000). 'Developing a sense of history', in *Separation and Reunion in Modern China*. Cambridge University Press: Cambridge, pp. 127–143.

References

Freedman, Maurice (1966). *Chinese Lineage and Society: Fukien and Kwangtung*. Athlone Press: London.

Freedman, Maurice (1958). *Lineage Organization in Southeastern China*. Athlone Press: London.

Chapter 4

Relatedness and Gender

The last chapter engaged with kinship, particularly in its ritual, legal, and political dimensions. Taking a long historical view on the institution of the Chinese patrilineage allowed us to abstract and compare models over time and space. We not only traced changes and continuities to the institution with its characteristic attributes of patriliny, virilocality, and ancestral worship historically, but also considered its geographic variation across China's vast territory. In this chapter, we build on this classic perspective to kinship by examining more recent theoretical approaches to relatedness, which is the study of how people relate to one another.

Studies of relatedness tend to eschew abstraction, especially at the level of universal models, instead focusing on how people create, experience, and distinguish relationships locally or comparatively. Furthermore, relatedness takes a step back from the officially sanctioned models of both prescriptive and descriptive kinship studies that often prioritize those with the most power to represent their position in their field of relations to outsiders (such as anthropologists). Questioning the reach of formal kinship assertions has meant an increasing focus on women and children's ways of relating to others. By taking into account the varied positions that gender and generation often instill upon people and how different the resulting experiences of relatedness are, these studies question whether kinship systems may even be considered unitary *within* a given context.

By considering the experiential dimensions of forging, maintaining, and dissolving connections to others, studies of relatedness frequently highlights emotional dynamics involved in intimacy and closeness. These experiences not only incorporate belonging and connection to those nearest and dearest, but also reflect hostility, conflict, and rivalry with others on whom one depends in the fragile balancing act of life. As such, moral motivations and ethical decisions about how to not just constitute a relationship, but also how to acknowledge and honor its ideals, are never far away. Relationships are rarely simply given, but usually to a certain extent achieved, as one must rise to expectations of those to whom one is bound by responsibility and dependency. Therefore, relatedness resolves to venture beyond the confines of formal rules of kinship and explore the events and practices that unfold over a person's lifetime entwined with others.

In short, this chapter moves from more abstract and formal rules of kinship to everyday practices of relatedness. The chapter asks how social differentiation comes to be enacted through gender and the family in China. Beginning with Janet Carsten's pioneering work, the chapter traces the theoretical shift in anthropology from a focus on social cohesion to an engagement with social practices. In China, approaches to intergenerational cycles and broader inter-domestic cycles of reciprocity takes the discussions of family relations beyond the rules of patriliny we encountered in the previous chapter. We will also see how movement, especially through *virilocal* marriage practices and increasing migration, creates different gender roles for men and women, in relation to household and family in contemporary rural and urban China. Finally, this context of migration and rural–urban exchanges will be explored in terms of the changing value of work and space, and its intersections with the Chinese family planning policy. Chinese relatedness thereby offers anthropology an example of how intimate relations are infused with the effects of state policy and political economy.

4.1 From Kinship to Relatedness

As discussed in the previous chapter, the study of kinship went hand-in-hand with the establishment of anthropology as an academic discipline and has formed a mainstay of anthropological expertize ever since, changing, adapting, and evolving over time. One of the most profound changes in recent decades has been opening up this field of knowledge beyond bonds assumed to be "natural" through assertions about kinship drawn from "scientistic" Euro–American folk models to include an increasingly diverse field of relatedness in its purview. Emphases on the forging and unfolding of relationships through time as a *process*, as well as the ongoing exchanges of material *substances* and emotive *values* in forming persons, have emerged as particularly fruitful areas for enquiry cross-culturally. We will now turn to the highly influential volume Carsten edited on the topic in 2000 entitled *Cultures of Relatedness: New approaches to the study of kinship* that both initiated and substantiated transformation in the field. The volume revitalized the study of kinship beyond classificatory terminology and diagrammatic representations, and shifted attention from abstract formal models to living everyday relations.

Carsten takes relatedness as the starting point for her volume, thereby opening up an area of enquiry beyond any rigid definition of kinship and less loaded with theoretical baggage from her predecessors, opening up possibilities for anthropologists dissatisfied with the formalism in the literature on kinship through the less defined sphere of relatedness. Carsten (2000: p. 14) provides a quotation by Bronisław Malinowski that illustrates this frustration: 'The average anthropologist…has his doubts whether the effort needed to master the bastard algebra of kinship is really worthwhile. He feels that, after all, kinship is a matter of flesh and blood, the result of sexual passion, and maternal affection, of long intimate daily life, and of a host of personal interests.' (1930: p. 19).

Carsten views anthropological emphases on the body and gender as part of a shift away from kinship in anthropology, while the denaturalization of science and technology has broken down the idea of "nature" as a single universal base underlying kinship. Building on these developments Carsten seeks to move towards the crucial experiential dimensions of relatedness, including its emotional, creative, and dynamic potential. By focusing on "relatedness" she suspends a nexus of assumptions about what constitutes kinship to frame questions differently within a comparative domain. To investigate how people generate and sustain relatedness through everyday practices in both their own cultures and in cross-cultural comparison, Carsten focusses on processes of ongoing practices in everyday life, the role of substances in constituting bodies, and the gendered dynamics of creating different forms of relatedness.

To a certain extent, this shift from *what* kinship *is* (i.e. structural definitions and classificatory systems) to *how* people *relate* (as a fluid process across time, created by daily life, and including material substances in particular contexts) was preempted by critiques of the universality of kinship models generated by earlier anthropologists. Carsten explicitly outlines a shift in kinship studies that nearly dissolved the field of kinship in American anthropology: Schneider's critique of kinship as not having an exclusive domain, but being an aspect of other areas of enquiry, such as politics, economics, and religion. In addition, Carsten's relatedness approach challenges the Universalist claims of anthropological kinship models by taking its cue from Schneider's critique of the implicit role of biology-derived assumptions in its genealogical method. Carsten thereby pushes for a more nuanced understanding of Western folk models of biology underlying the allegedly objective anthropological approaches to kinship. Even in Euro–American contexts the question of where babies come from cannot be polarized between fairytale storks and scientific genetics, as children are thought to be partial products of shared bloodlines and bonds of love. Instead, relatedness studies frequently advocate examining how persons are constituted over time by considering the retrospective acknowledgment of contributions to reproduction. Tracing and retracing lines of connection between parents and children can occur throughout childhood, and even adulthood. Contributions to processes of making persons may be anything from material substances to affectionate exchanges, from disciplinary strategies to nurturing practices. Moreover, not just parents, but many care givers may forge relationships to children through their contributions, although the nature of the particular relationships may vary as widely as the distribution of care in raising children.

Carsten also cites precursors with a rising interest in the body and gender from the 1970s onwards. She signals that this is not strictly a shift away from studies of kinship, but a way of taking questions about what makes persons into new light. Through relatedness, Carsten brackets off the arbitrary distinction between biology and culture, which she calls a Western "folk discourse." Following Strathern's work the facts of nature are not so much discovered as constructed; particularly Strathern's later research shows how concepts of nature have been destabilized through matters of choice, with nature appearing clearly as part of knowledge, i.e. as something that can be manipulated through technology and legislation. New reproductive technologies are a particularly telling example of this, where nature and technology become mutually substitutable, breaking down the biological and social barriers. For instance, in third party reproduction the reproductive process can go beyond the traditional father–mother model through sperm or egg donation, or gestational carriers. Frequently, the third party's involvement is limited to the reproductive process and does not extend to the raising of the child. Thus, a child can have a genetic and social (non-genetic, non-biologic) father, and a genetic, gestational, and social (non-biologic) mother, and any combinations thereof. Theoretically, a child thus could have five parents, with all manner of legal, emotional, and social implications.

This emphasis on substance and process in constituting persons also comes to the fore in Carsten's (1997) ethnographic monograph exploring Malay relatedness on the island of Langkawi. She argues that people become complete persons by living and consuming together in houses where they share blood, milk, and rice as similar and convertible substances through activities that produce and reproduce bodies. As rice sustains bodies by creating blood, in women the blood becomes milk for babies when breastfed, so the cycles between rice, blood, and milk are mediated through women. Nonetheless, siblingship stands at the center of the house where the brother and sister form the gendered ideal of male and female, rather than the affinal stress on the conjugal couple as husband and wife, as the epitome of family unity. Children are strongly associated with house and complete a house through sibling sets. So, for instance, ideally a husband and wife eventually become close and affectionate similar to brother and sister, by a slow process of producing, eating, and reproducing together over their lifetimes. Here kinship is not given at birth or marriage, but slowly built up over time through ongoing practices anchored within everyday life.

Although this summary cannot do justice to the insights into daily life on Langkawi, a dual model of kinship emerges from Carsten's ethnography (see also Carsten, 1997). On the one hand, kinship comes to be associated with the house and hearth through the idiom of siblingship and shared origin, residence, property, and consumption. On the other hand, the community is related through reciprocal exchanges incorporating commercial transactions of the fishing economy and marital exchanges between houses. However, Carsten also shows how these two models cannot be represented as diametrically opposed, as they intertwine through living processes whereby differences are assimilated and unity is multiple.

More generally, Carsten posits relatedness as an ongoing process often mediated by conceptions of shared substances, but simultaneously cautions against naturalizing claims of inherited (e.g. genetic) material. Her criticism of claims made through appeals to "nature" rely on their assumption of universality grounded in biology compared to a culturally specific realm of the social, despite both being artefacts of knowledge subject to the interventions of technology. In addition, the notion of what becomes inherited between senior generations and their offspring generates an extremely variable terrain. Even Euro–Americans frequently impute scientific credibility to folk theories of common blood between kin, despite the symbolic basis for this idiom of shared substance. In China, folk theories of the contributions of substances in constituting kin often revolve around gendered oppositions between women and affine's associated with ephemeral flesh, sometimes symbolized by pork in food prestations, while men and agnates are instantiated through enduring bones mediated by semen and rice (see Thompson, 1988). The centrality of bones in death rituals and their role in ongoing ancestral rites at gravesites thereby constitute a nexus of symbol and substance that condenses understandings of the pure and lasting lines of male descent through the patriline.

Historical material from China similarly supports Carsten's skepticism with how the biological and the social are deployed as knowledge domains in the service of power. For instance, Bray's (2009) research with ritual instructions and medical manuals reveal that knowledge practices were used to sever childbearing from childrearing in late imperial China to constitute two distinct objects of knowledge, biological, and social motherhood. To a certain extent, this dual vision of motherhood was used as a technological tool to usurp the reproductive powers of those disenfranchised by gender and seniority in the kinship hierarchy. Particularly in wealthy extended households with first wives as the apex of cultivated female refinement were considered the most suitable for instilling these values and qualities in children through childrearing and therefore, children of other wives or concubines could be usurped under her maternal role as care giver. Motherhood's dual foundation in childbearing and childrearing could thereby be deployed as an instrument of kinship hierarchy within late imperial China through constituting the biological and social as distinct and privileging the latter form of reproduction.

Fei (whose work was discussed at length in Chapter 2) shares Carsten's skepticism with Western folk models elevated to the realm of general theory. Although Fei equally shies away from importing Universalist social science models, he nonetheless generates a distinct Chinese model of "differential mode of association" (*chaxu geju*) for comparison grounded in local concepts and processes. Far from the focus on normative social rules enabling the stable coherence of social organization posited during the heyday of kinship's elevation in structural functionalism, Fei's dynamic model of sociality could be seen as a proto-relatedness approach emphasizing how a person's creation of social networks and experiences of different forms of relationships transform across a lifetime. From a Western social science background in the "organizational mode of association", individuals are assumed to be the constitutive units for groups with delineated membership and making up stable and enduring organizations. From this perspective, lineages would appear as quasi-permanent and pre-given institutions in which the organization outlasts the individual through maintaining boundaries of inclusion and exclusion. By contrast, building onto his theory of the differential mode of organization, Fei views the lineage through the prism of ego-centered circles of social relatedness that spread out in concentric spheres, mediated by specific hierarchical relationships. Although Fei's theory resolutely forms a model or ideal type, the relationships he describes are never completely ascribed or given, but achieved and created through living up to the moral responsibilities that a given relationship entails.

The image that Fei deploys, of a pebble thrown into water, resonates with Astuti's (2000) evocation of an old Vezo man in Madagascar whose conception of kinship transformed across his lifetime. As a boy, he viewed himself as the outcome of a network of bilateral kin, while as a young man he saw himself as the center of concentric ripples extending outwards until they eventually disappeared, and by his old age he had moved towards the apex of a cone-shaped casting net, the tip of a pyramid of descent, where children and grandchildren stretched downwards from himself. The reflections of a Vezo elder therefore show that a person's experiential model of kinship can transform from a conception of cognatic to patrilineal descent via ego-centric ripples of relatedness within one lifetime.

An ethnographic example from China in Carsten's edited volume reveals an alternative perspective on Chinese kinship through the prism of relatedness that is less concerned with lines of descent and focuses much more on cycles of care. As will be discussed in detail below, Stafford (2000) breaks down the rigid patrilineal kinship image through a focus on *yang* as reciprocal intergenerational caring cycles between people and *laiwang* as a reciprocal process of coming and going of persons and things between families.

4.2 Nurturing Reciprocity

Similar to his chapter on developing a sense of history, Stafford's chapter on reciprocal relatedness in rural Taiwan and Northeastern China emphasizes how children learn to take for granted certain ways of thinking about the world. Stafford focuses on how children acquire knowledge of the obligations underlying nourishment and care within their immediate family and domestic environment, as well as how they learn to extend this expectation of reciprocal nurture to a larger field of social relations. In this regard Stafford lays down two interrelated cycles that he denotes with their Chinese terms: first, *yang* cycles encompass intergenerational "care" between children and those who raise them; second, *laiwang* cycles translate as the "coming-and-going" of exchanges and visits between neighbors, friends, colleagues, and other acquaintances through ongoing practices of give-and-take.

Through focusing on everyday reciprocal acts Stafford demonstrates the importance of domestic spaces in creating Chinese kinship beyond a rigid patriliny where women take on a central position of enactment. By expanding this field beyond parents and children, and connecting these cycles of nurture to reciprocally related partners exchanging visits, food, gifts, and labor, Stafford reveals relationships of mutual assistance in rural

China. Echoing Carsten's findings, Stafford's emphasis on the dynamics of processual relatedness opens up an incorporative tendency within Chinese kinship, and social relatedness more generally through taken-for-granted principles inculcated through the repetition of enacting practical relations.

The first cycle of *yang* translates as "to care for", or "to raise" (everything from children to pigs or flowers). Here it denotes an intergenerational relationship of nurture, whereby adults particularly mothers generate the notions of relatedness by raising children with the reasonable expectation that they will care for them as they grow old. But women more generally as wives and daughters are vital to creating and sustaining these relationships, which are generally placed within the domestic sphere. However, Stafford shows that this is neither restricted to parent–child interaction, nor synonymous with patrilineal descent ties mediated through mothers. The cycle of care initiated through childrearing should be reciprocated by those children as they grow into adulthood and take on responsibility for their aging care givers, regardless of whether they are elderly parents, kin or other relations. The *yang* relationship is also clearly not a one-to-one descent tie when enacted between parents and children, although it most commonly falls along that path: their children's failure to live up to the obligations of the caring cycle may even lead parents to sever ties with their descendants.

In some ways, this notion of *yang* overlaps with observations made by other analysts of Chinese kinship, including "intergenerational contracts" where a child's moral, material, and emotional "debt" to the parental generation is repaid later in life, or the notion of "filial piety" we discussed as a lifelong obligation to meet an ideal and unchanging hierarchical relationship of a child in relation to their parents that must be maintained and upheld by appropriate behavior throughout life. However, Stafford's notion departs from these predecessors by exploring this type of care beyond parent–child relationships, and also by examining how the failure to meet these caring expectations may even lead to the termination of descent relations.

Another historical comparison from rural Taiwan that comes close to Stafford's notion of *yang* is Margery Wolf's elaboration of the close and affectionate ties between mothers and their (particularly male) children through which young women seek to establish what she calls a "uterine family" (*niangjia*) at the heart of, and yet paradoxically also in defiant competition with, the patrilineal and patriarchal family. In brief, Wolf's (1968) early work on a Taiwanese family living under one roof contrasts the guest hall as the symbol of the extended ancestral family with the stove as the symbol of the living family. This form of inside–outside relations reveals the conundrum of women as outsiders of patrilineal kinship and yet crucial insiders in reproducing the domestic domain.

In her later work on the "uterine family," Wolf (1972) turns her attention even more explicitly to the processual and living dimensions of kinship from the perspective of Taiwanese women who are excluded from their husband's lineage. Due to patrilocal marriage women create a "uterine family" with their offspring, especially their sons, thereby binding their children to themselves through emotional and affective ties (rather than the territorial ties to ancestral homes and graves that male agnates are given). Wolf also shows how women gradually build up power and status within the home, beginning with very weak positions as young girls and ideally eventually becoming influential mothers-in-law within the extended family house. Wolf's "uterine family" essentially appears as a strategic practice, whereby married women gain status through sons and vie for power with patrilineal kin that see her as an outsider.

Like Wolf's "uterine family," Stafford's notion of *yang* moves away from a descent-centered perspective that excludes family life and "affairs of the hearth" to focus on the central organizing role of women's practices and everyday acts in constituting sociality. However, Stafford simultaneously critiques Wolf's model as positioning women in largely negative terms as outsiders marrying into families and developing their power as a threat to the unity of patrilines. Instead, Stafford seeks to overcome the implications of a uniquely "female consciousness" and distinctive "women's strategies" by showing the continuities between the two processual cycles of *yang* and *laiwang* as reciprocal movements creating the bonds of relatedness (p. 52). To do this, Stafford connects cycles of *yang* or "caring" as intergenerational bonds manifested through material exchanges within the domestic domain to *laiwang* as reciprocal movements of "coming-and-going" between friends, neighbors and acquaintances within their various domestic spaces. These reciprocal movements of people and things as part of mutual assistance build up and form relationships over time. In the next chapter, we will closely examine how cycles of give-and-take may initiate social relationships beyond familiar faces with relative strangers through the skillful management of the art of *guanxi*.

Returning to the notion of *laiwang*, in close-knit communities in rural Taiwan and Northeast China, Stafford shows that acts constituting this form of relatedness can range from small favors, over shared meals, to money transfers, and often culminate in shared responsibility for arranging and financing grand events, such as weddings. The wedding that Stafford elaborates in his chapter is one of the main procedures through which a woman ostensibly becomes separated from her natal home and installed in a new position in her groom's home, taking pride of place in the bridal chamber where her role in producing children for patrilineal continuity is emphasized through rituals and symbols. However, the expense and effort that the groom's family expends in bringing the bride to their home (through not only the wedding ceremony, but also through the preparation of betrothal gifts and negotiation of the bride price) reveals how crucial their daughter-in-law is for their ideal future.

Echoing similar points made in the previous chapter on kinship as ideology, Stafford points to a number of factors that have led to the lineage paradigm appearing as central to social organization in China, including the formal definitions of kinship, regional analysis emphasizing public roles of men and their descent groups over private parts played by local women, and the use of historical sources rather than participant observation fieldwork. The dynamics of gender and generation that reinforce the lineage paradigm are thereby, intertwined with the question of records and recording, genealogies and graves are easier to trace over time than ephemeral acts of care.

In short, Stafford attempts to bring together different experiences of kinship by highlighting the often underexplored positions of women and children through connecting two cycles of relatedness. Sangren similarly contrasts gendered and generational experiences within the Chinese kinship. However, Sangren moves in a whole new direction, by taking as his point of departure not exchanges of nurture, but frustrations of desire that are brought to light through the particular positions that people find themselves in with relation to a unified ideal type of kinship system.

4.3 Engendering Desire

Drawing on Stafford's work on separations and reunions, Steven Sangren (2003) distinguishes between male and female desires as they move through the Chinese family system from childhood to seniority. Sangren argues that desires for autonomy and recognition are differently distributed between male and female family members. Structured through patrilineal and *virilocal* practices, Chinese kinship leads to different emotional responses for daughters and sons. Sangren's approach brings together Marxian notions of production with Freudian insights on how people's activities are motivated by desires around a normative kinship ideal in China. Not only does this approach venture to take psychological insights outside of a Western nuclear family model, but it also makes methodological use of myths, in dialogue with Chinese kinship as an ideal type. The processual temporal dynamics come to the fore as Sangren thinks of kinship as a system that structures people's experiences in relation to assessing the past, positioning them in the present, and orienting their desires towards the future. The self simultaneously moves through time and the differing generational, but nonetheless gendered positions in the kinship system. Particularly past frustrations orient desire towards overcoming denials of the past through seeking fulfillment in alternative imaginary futures.

Although Sangren accommodates different positions for Chinese sons and daughters between individual desire and the social, he adamantly rejects the notion of a distinct female ideology in opposition to an official male ideology. Instead, Sangren brings to light how the Chinese family can be viewed as a single system that induces different positions for male and female, as well as senior and junior members. Like Bloch and Stafford, Sangren views child socialization as key to how social reproduction, the production of production, as he describes it, unfolds in its dialectical complexity (p. 57). He therefore explores how people as products, as well as their desires, are produced in interaction with an environment that includes collective institutions, particularly the family (p. 57). To Sangren, both daughters and sons have reasons to resist the Chinese family system's structuring premises of patriliny and virilocality. Here gender and generation converge through desire for autonomy despite the constraints of dependence that are forced upon sons and daughters.

In short, the Chinese family is viewed as a system of production and reproduction of cultural subjects who struggle with an ideal type of patrilineal descent marked by equal inheritance among sons, virilocal marriage practices, with sons remaining in their family home for life, while daughters must marry out (p. 54). The system leads to various obstructions and frustrations that create emotional responses, as well as desires to transcend and fulfill what they have been denied through practices that promise redemption (p. 55). The kinship ideal Sangren posits cannot so much be understood as an abstracted sociological model, but more as an experiential refraction of the alienation produced by inherited kin obligations. This psychological alienation leads family members to project agency onto gods, ancestors, and fate, only further compounding their feelings of frustrated autonomy and enforced dependence on circumstances beyond their control.

Sons experience a privileged, but unchosen role in upholding the patriline and patrilineal continuity which generally occurs in the same place as their parents, often even under the same roof, where they cannot escape from embodying patrilineal continuity. Sons also spend their life under the continuing authority of their fathers which they only partially escape with their fathers' death and his transformation into an ancestor. Male family members of all levels of seniority actually carry the weight of patri archal authority, both in their positions as filial sons and as responsible fathers and they are expected to carry out their roles to meet the obligations as filial descendants to fathers and ancestors. Thereby, male family members forcibly hold the power to maintain and uphold the lineage, but simultaneously dream of autonomy from these constraints and freedom from these obligations. In short, men desire autonomy from patriliny and escape from virilocality as filial descendants who are both subject to and bearers of patriarchal authority.

Daughters, by contrast, are usually obligated by the Chinese family system to marry out, so they are necessarily and often involuntarily separated from their natal family at marriage. They grow up with this potential expulsion from the family weighing upon their childhood and often suffer miserably at the distance that marriage wedges between them and the life and kin with whom they grew up. From the view of the patrilineal family system, daughters are like "spilled water", and daughters-in-law are forever "outsiders" to their husband's patriline. After marriage only motherhood to a patrilineal heir provides an avenue of partial integration to her husband's kin through her son. In their marital homes, women as outsiders strive for the inclusion and recognition that they were denied in their family of birth and hope to overcome through the children they bear. Therefore, daughters seek to fulfill in the families they create what they were denied in the families they were given (see also Judd 2009). After daughters suffer the rupture of marrying out as a kind of expulsion from the family into which they were born, as daughters-in-law in their families of procreation they seek to fulfill what was denied in their natal families. They fantasize about completion and desire recognition. Completion arises as a dream of holism, and manifests in women's hopes for close, intimate, life-long ties with their children who are often kept as near to their mothers as possible. Recognition takes the form of acknowledgement, a sense of worth and value emerging from their creative power and productive agency in giving birth to children, especially sons, as essential to the continuity of the family.

Sangren traces this oscillation between frustration and desire for Chinese sons and daughters as they manifest in various cultural domains, particularly myths, ancestral rituals, and wedding ceremonies. The mythic narrative of Nezha, a son who strives to establish independence from paternal authority, ends when Nezha must eventually recognize his father's position through taking on his role as a filial son. Miaoshan, a Princess who defies her father's intent to marry her off, must await his eventual acknowledgement of her autonomous subjectivity. Both stories end with rapprochement between the disobedient children and their fathers, although Nezha and Miaoshan also manifest the alternate positions for sons and daughters in relation to paternal authority. In ancestral worship, the son as the sacrificer must ritually recognize and thereby instantiate the authority of the ancestors, such that the son effectively creates the father. Similarly paradoxically and yet structurally necessary, the patriline relies on the mother, the in-marrying lineage outsider, to give birth to descendants, and must therefore deny her central role in patrilineal continuity. At marriage, female bridal lamentations provide brides-to-be with the opportunity to vent their anger and grief at their relatives in highly charged performances with lyrics that liken marriage to death, thereby calling for acknowledgement of the tragedy of their natal family expulsion.

According to Sangren, the creative agency and productive power of the whole Chinese family system relies on the agency of members whose autonomy and subjectivity are simultaneously denied. This finding resonates with the very form of ideology that Bloch described in the previous chapter, although here the oppositions of male/female, insider/outsider, social/biological, or formal/informal, have been complemented with a very particular and specific positionality within the Chinese family as a single, unified and ideal system. To Sangren, the denial of agency and the desire for autonomy along lines of gender and generation within family position, appear as so ideologically pervasive that they manifest not only in rituals of ancestral worship, but also in the narratives of myths and the lyrics of bridal laments. In contrast to Sangren's treatment of Chinese kinship as a unified ideal, others have separated the experiences of Chinese relatedness further along the lines of gendered mobility and spatialized practice, even dividing kinship into male and female domains in China.

4.4 Families Women Create

Judd (2009) goes even further in saying that kinship itself follows two different models for Chinese men and women through intersections of gendered mobility. Judd characterizes male kinship and particularly patrilineages as associated with close and localized kinship, where men are born and remain tied to their birth kin through lifelong links with this particular locality. By contrast, due to patrilocality Judd sees women's kinship as definitely structured around rupture and space, where women always have had to uphold networks of kin across physical, social, and conceptual distance. Judd (1989) wrote of women's ongoing connections to their natal family and dual residence patterns for young married women in North-east China. In this early work, Judd contrasted two levels of kinship: first, formalized kinship that followed the classic model and norms of patriliny and patrilocality; and second, practical strategies of female dual residence and connection to their natal family after marriage without explicit ideological sanction.

In parallel with the shifting terrain of kinship studies and the emerging field of relatedness that Carsten describes, Ellen Judd's research has also become less focused on the abstraction of models and more concerned with everyday strategies and practices. Judd (2009) nonetheless retains attention to the crucial observation that the experience of spatialized practices within Chinese kinship must be viewed within the gendered context that Chinese patrilineages are tied to specific geographical locations and land division that keep men anchored to a particular place, while women's kinship, especially due to patrilocal marriage practices, is structured by rupture and by space. Rather than critiquing the import of inappropriate kinship models from Western social theory, Judd thereby criticizes the tendency to see the lives of women through the prism of close and localized kinship translated from the male domain.

Judd points out that the idea of spatial fixity itself really was by far the most pronounced during temporary period of 1950s to 1980s, when Maoist policies kept people tied to their place of work through brigades and work units (*danwei*). Periods preceding and following the period of Maoist high socialism actually exhibit far more movement and migration than tunnel vision on the earthbound patriliny would allow. Furthermore, the loosening of the household registration system since the 1980s has created large-scale rural-to-urban migration, resulting in significant depopulation, feminization, and age polarization of rural communities, with elderly and children in need of state social services left behind in the countryside. These shifts have only served to compound the tendency for women to take on caring roles in the countryside, although women increasingly move beyond domestic and agricultural work to seize new opportunities in the diversifying economy. Nonetheless, women's hard work and dedication are crucial in sustaining their families, despite the state benefits of health care, education, and pensions that tie citizens to their native place and secure the long-term reproduction of labor in the Chinese countryside.

Another gendered dimension to labor and migration relates to the higher accessibility for occupational migration and mobility for men than women. Opportunities for employment and income in the city are more ample for men, while the caring needs of rural dependents often keep women tied to the countryside. This leads to many cases where men and patrilines are conceptually linked to local places, but it is 'their in-marrying wives who are more likely to spend their adult life building a family in these (to them) new places' (Judd, 2009: p. 43). This often leads to a spatial acrobatics in maintaining diverse relationships across a region, with women seeking to maintain relations with natal kin in their place of birth, husband's families where they have married, but also daughters who have married into other locations. In some ways, Judd's observations on how women move through life after marriage attempting to build up family ties through children and affines are akin to Wolf's notion of "uterine strategies". But in contrast to Wolf's findings in rural Taiwan, Judd finds that these networks are not fixed or localized but shifting and networked, such that they can be adapted to the changing political, economic, and administrative circumstances women face. Furthermore, the priority given to sons that Wolf observed is waning in Judd's examples where daughters, at least as much as sons, are valued for the material, practical, and emotional support they offer their mothers. The eloquent assessment of a woman who explains that the family is her own creation ('*ba jiali kan shi ziji chuangzao de*') (Judd, 2009: p. 32), synthesizes how much these multilocal inter-connected families provide a set of strategies that 'works unobtrusively in the interstices of patriliny and patrilocality, and does not persist past the generation of grandchildren, but it figures very large in the everyday lives of women (and men)' (p. 37).

Judd provides dramatic narratives of how people have to negotiate patriarchal and statist patterns of control over work, residence, and family planning. In these situations, women must be flexible in handling situations ranging from work to divorce, widowhood to birth registration, as well as making difficult decisions in weighing up various interests for children and other dependents. There are also situations where women also must choose arrangements that are considered less than ideal from a formal model perspective, such as marriages taking place uxorilocally or contravening rules of village exogamy. As women's kinship emerges based around families that must be maintained across multiple locations, flexible movement, and ambiguous boundaries, Judd traces how these rural women over time experience 'building these families out of their own bodies, their nurturing work in families and communities, and their hard work in fields, homes and other places of work' (p. 35).

4.5 Migration and Gendered Spaces

Insights into migration and gender in an urban context are offered by Zhang's (2000) research with migrant settlements in Beijing. Zhang explores the relationship of power and gender through the prism of migrant households where men and women's work is differently spatialized and unevenly valued. Countering representations of migrant women forming a monolithic underclass, Zhang explores the diversity of positions that women encounter within the urban tapestry of migrants. Women's success in navigating employment and even spearheading entrepreneurship in the city does not necessarily translate into improved domestic status, or emancipation from patriarchy. However, young women who arrive in Beijing without extensive support networks mediated through their native place links to Zhejiang often struggle particularly in commanding social status and leaving behind poverty.

In the chapter discussed here, Zhang examines different types of households engaged in family-based garment production and city-wide market networks. These urban homes are domestic areas of commercial production, places where residence, manufacture, and even trading intersect. As such, the household and workplace are thoroughly integrated, not just spatially, but socially and personally, as migrant families frequently house the wage-earning young women who work for them. These young women are considered part of the household in everyday rhetoric and government demographic surveys, although they are not necessarily kin to their employers. These young women often struggle to fulfill their desires for an urban and cosmopolitan experience of youth in the city due to their employers' demands for labor and harsh restrictions on their social interaction outside the household. Their membership in the household frequently serves to mask their social domination and economic exploitation behind the veneer of a household-based cottage industry.

Zhang's research reveals that female participation in economic activities does not automatically lead to their empowerment, as many young women are never able to leave their employers' household. Although this might appear to be a class-specific form of domination of workers through the medium of gender ideology, the experience of Zhejiang women from prosperous migrant households complicates this image of the intersection between gender, space, and class. Notably, many of the wealthiest migrant households seek to increase the spatial separation of production from other domestic activities over time. In some instances, even the women who built up these successful businesses through their own entrepreneurial activities are pushed out of the productive realm and restricted to other domestic pursuits considered to be more properly and suitably female. Over time, even men "talking business" in the living room may make this space inappropriate for wives, who are then confined to the dining room or kitchen of the homes. Furthermore, as new places of public consumption arise, successful men venture out into karaoke bars, restaurants, and hotels for business negotiations, eating, drinking, and even extramarital affairs, while their wives are restricted to domestic consumption sites of supermarkets, department stores, and the homes of close kin and female friends. In short, for middle- and upper-class Zhejiang migrants in Beijing, women's social spaces shrink with increasing wealth, while men's expand, leading women to become increasingly dependent on their husbands financially and socially. Nonetheless, some women openly struggle to retain control over their economic activities and independent power in their social lives, even competing with husbands for entrepreneurial income within Beijing migrant networks.

Whether these cottage industry households are best considered through the prism of kinship or relatedness, even if they draw on native place networks, is open to interpretation, as they also form corporations for labor exploitation and social control. However, what emerges from Zhang's research are situations where the value and recognition of household members and their labor are not uniformly distributed. Women as Zhang describes, experience devaluation of their role in economic processes at levels of the family and household, sites of production and marketing, but also in domestic reproduction and public spaces of consumption. Even the wider availability of venues for public sociality may reinforce gender dichotomies of unequal access to leisure and labor.

Zhang's article brings to light issues surrounding the potential for women's distributed networks of relatedness to expand and contract over time, but not always by the power of their own hands. This research cautions us not to simply equate the rising economic power of women with their potential emancipation and autonomy, but to bear in mind that denying or usurping labor value, or forcibly withdrawing women from the labor process, are processes that can occur in any social class.

Having examined the role of women as outsiders and insiders from the view of relatedness, we will now turn to children. From the perspective of kinship, children literally compose the future generation, and especially boys form the backbone of patrilineal descent. However, the family planning policy that the Chinese state has promulgated since the 1980s, has drawn new lines of insiders and outsiders across the population, beginning with children at birth.

4.6 Family Planning

The past two sections touched upon some of the administrative procedures involved in registering people with the state as they move through various life stages and their relationships change. This can occur when people share a household registration in a rural home community, or become the entrepreneurial household heads of urban cottage industries within high-rise apartments employing kin and other dependents. The state also demands bureaucratic registration for lifecycle events such as marriage or divorce, as well as death and birth. We now turn to state demands for birth registration and its role in governing the population through China's family planning policy.

As we noted in the previous chapter on kinship in the last millennium, the interpenetration of the family, the state, and the economy is certainly nothing new to China. However, the demographic discourse and governmentalization of life in the late 20th and early 21st century certainly reframed the state's role in reproductive processes, as new concerns emerged in how to balance labor and reproduction at the level of the nuclear family, rather than the patrilineage. However, to frame the state as simply appropriating control over reproduction from kinship would be an overly simplistic narrative of coercion, without doing justice to how dreams are forged and hopes propelled in dialogue with the Chinese population policy.

In addition to revealing how women create their own networks of relatedness across multiple locations despite their roles as outsiders of the formal male patriline, Judd describes how women may rely on these networks when attempting to hide pregnancies and even children outside the family planning policy. Greenhalgh (2003) examines how the family planning policy has pushed certain children, who then grow to adulthood, into the position of outsiders of the Chinese state. Not formally registered at birth, they are denied the usual rights of citizens, unless they are later regularized, thereby becoming part of a demographic and bureaucratic blind spot of unplanned persons.

Greenhalgh's research over the last three decades provides an overview over the broader political and economic development and implementation of the family planning policy since the 1980s. In her earlier work, Greenhalgh (1993, 1994) provided bottom–up perspectives on women's resistance to the policy of the control and the medicalization of childbirth as the state increasingly accommodated the needs, desires and demands of rural Chinese families for offspring in a process she labels the "peasantization" of the one-child-policy. Through the family planning policy the state forged a powerful impetus for modernization through improving the human "quality" of the population that used both force and promise to create compliance.

In the later article discussed here, Greenhalgh focuses her attention more on the scientific origins and discourse of the policy, as an apparatus of development that not just measures, but produces its object, population. As Greenhalgh summarizes: '[t]he emphasis on classificatory schemes for life directs our attention to the *social categories* embedded in governmental technologies for population surveillance, management, and restriction. Such technologies include the census, the survey, and the family planning program'(p. 197). This article is based on fieldwork and cooperation with Chinese population scientists and draws attention to how the policy is not simply an instrument of coercive repression but a force for the inspiration of dreams.

By taking the reader through the socialist underpinnings to the policy, Greenhalgh breaks down "images of China as totalitarian Other" conjured by Western critics of the policy, who place its origins within one of the following two narratives (p. 198): first, a powerful communist state obsessed with control and regulation; second, a demographic explosion that created an excess population in need of dramatic intervention for a slowing growth rate. Both of these approaches undermine an understanding of the political and scientific ideas that informed the policy as a mode of governance through the production of "population" as an object of knowledge (p. 198).

Greenhalgh comes up with alternate answer for the origins of the family planning policy. Beginning with the early Maoist period there was a concern with overcoming a Malthusian image of an excess population beyond sustainable levels arising from resource shortage in line with Marx's concern with population through specific modes of production. In order to put forward an alternative to capitalist paths for development, Mao and his population scientists promoted a comprehensive model for socialist state-led birth planning. The historical progression of the policy followed three key emphases over time: location, quantity, and quality of the population (for detailed description, see Greenhalgh and Winckler, 2005).

The concern with location began in the Maoist period when household registration became a crucial administrative instrument for curtailing mobility of the population from their native place and tying them to rural brigades and urban work units. The household registration system was also crucial to the post-Mao family planning program by limiting migration of women and children, as formal government registration of births, as well as state-supported obstetrics and schooling, were only available in the area of parental household registration. Nonetheless, the Market Era saw a significant relaxation of locational restrictions, where the dualism between rural and urban worlds was ameliorated through partial incorporation of rural migrants into cities and the investment of more state resources into developing rural areas economically and extending state welfare to the countryside.

In terms of quantity, the 1970s saw a growing state effort to slow population growth through propaganda campaigns and local government family planning programs. In the late 1970s and early 1980s, the communist party developed its ambitious plans to enforce a one-child-policy throughout the country. Although the exact implementation differed throughout the country, the family planning policy was usually strictest for urban household registration holders, for whom the policy effectively continued as a one-child-policy until relaxation in 2013 and 2015. In the countryside, the policy became more diverse and lenient over time, with many rural local governments permitting a second birth if the first child born was a daughter. In addition, citizens officially registered as ethnic minorities were exempt from the strict quota systems of their Han compatriots and subject to alternate guidelines on childbirth.

The family planning policy not only involved restricting childbirth for each married couple. In order to meet target birth numbers of planned children at various administrative levels, there were also interventions into managing the timing of births and affecting their numbers in aggregate. For instance, the bureaucratic process of registering the birth with the presentation of the parents' marriage license effectively set a minimum parental age requirement for childbirth. Beyond the first child, the spacing of children often became important to policy compliance, such that significant periods had to lapse before a second child could be conceived within the policy. There were also other bureaucratic controls, including complex mechanisms of fines and rewards developed at the local level, as well as very invasive and even forced medical interventions, including contraception, abortion, and sterilization.

In addition to the infamous restrictions on fertility through the Family Planning Policy since the 1980s, successive Chinese population policies in the last two decades increasingly encompass a developmental paradigm of improving "population quality" (*renkou suzhi*) in terms of physical, intellectual, and moral characteristics. These shifts make themselves particularly visible in policies and discourses aimed at providing children with "education for quality" (*suzhi jiaoyu*), where imperatives of improving health and education come together through new family-based responsibilities and market-oriented possibilities for child-rearing. The emphasis on "quality" (*suzhi*) also creates social inequity across generations in terms of rural and urban background, levels of educational attainment and states of bodily health. However, by heralding better conditions for the next generation of Chinese children the state also created a promise and forged an implicit contract with its citizens, who could hope for a brighter future for their singletons born in compliance with the state's regulations.

Through this prism of Chinese family planning program Greenhalgh examines "population" as a domain of power in modernity and evokes a nexus of categories that divide the population into planned and unplanned births. She thereby reveals how the positive image of the future of the nation rests with the planned child as healthy, educated, civilized, and high "quality." By contrast, the desired child's alter ego emerges in a murky mirror of unplanned parenthood, a sea of illicit children who grow up to become the uncharted "black population," condemned to remain undocumented, unregistered, and illegal. Without formal registration and identification by the state, they are unable to access the state provisions for improvement of the individual, and the population, that the state offers its fully legitimized citizens. In popular discourse, these unregistered people are marked as signs of national backwardness, dragging China behind in the international race towards global success.

Although these children escaped the sight of many demographers and other scientists studying China's population, resistance to the family planning policy abounded throughout the country, partially producing these unplanned persons. Mothers concealed unplanned pregnancies and unregistered children within their homes, fled from their household registration offices and moved elsewhere, often becoming part of a "floating population" or "excess-birth guerrillas." Parents who came of legal age for marriage after the birth of their children sometimes managed to retrospectively register their children, while others gave up their children for adoption. On occasion, unwanted children would meet with neglect and even infanticide. The burden on these unregistered children was not just the state denial of social support and basic rights, but also the weight and stigma they carried as low quality non-persons eking out an existence in the bureaucratic cracks of the formal state system.

The state's family planning policy has encountered a range of reactions from citizens over time, including everything from enthusiasm to defiance. Although compliance was often enforced through coercive or punitive means, many citizens also strongly support the policy's aim of improving the population quality or positively embrace its assumption of smaller, nuclear families as a positive, healthy, and modern ideal. Especially as families increasingly desire to have fewer offspring and value the benefits of channeling more of their financial resources and loving attention towards fewer children, the more bureaucratic dimensions of the policy appear increasingly outdated. Particularly with the new rights-centered discourse assumed by both state and its citizens, the government has loosened the policy considerably in response to both popular pressure and demographic demands.

The family planning policy may have averted the birth of 700 million people on a planet already burdened with an unprecedented demographic explosion, but by the late 2000s China was facing a new set of demographic challenges as a result of the policy. At a basic family level the 4-2-1 problem results from singletons supporting two parents and four grandparents as they age. Married couples might face a double burden of caring for elderly dependents and their own children. At a broader societal level this means a shrinking working population supporting an ageing population with increasing life spans. The accelerated pace of demographic ageing China experienced has been compounded by male preference leading to distorted sex ratios throughout the country. Young men, particularly those from rural backgrounds and with low levels of education, experience difficulties in finding wives in a context where hypergamy (the bride marrying up in social status) is commonly considered the norm.

A significant nation-wide loosening of the policy under Xi Jinping's government began with the announcement in November 2013 that couples where one partner was a single child could apply to have a second child, even in urban areas. In October 2015, an even more significant overhaul occurred with the announcement that families would now be allowed to have two children. In the wake of this major revamping of the family planning policy, state media have begun to discuss the possible regularization of the legal status of those born outside the policy who were never formally registered and thereby allow them access to social services, such as healthcare, schooling, housing, pensions, as well as opportunities to join the formal workforce. The recent changes to the family planning policy not only addresses the labor relations, but results in reproductive rights being returned to citizens as technocratic concerns meet the rights-centered discourse of self-fulfillment in line with the shifts in morality discussed in Chapter 2.

4.7 From Holism to Partial Processes

In this chapter, we followed recent approaches in the study of relatedness by shifting attention away from the formal rules of kinship, as models and turned towards living practices and experiences of social differentiation through time. The roles of women and children came to the fore in discussions of reproduction, as much social as biological. Not only were the formal rules of patriliny and patrilocality broken up by differing experiences of kinship for male and female, senior and junior, and inside and outside members of the household and family, but political and economic transformations were also having a dramatic impact on the most intimate spheres of domestic life. The question could be posed whether Chinese relatedness, or even kinship, should be considered a unitary system, given its multiple patrilineal, but matrifocal dimensions across multiple locations, and the radically different positions, experiences, and desires of family members over the course of intertwined lives.

Instead, relatedness provides us with an approach to examine social processes and differentiation through a critical engagement with the resulting categories, whether enshrined in formal kinship genealogies or bureaucratic state registers. The abstraction that occurs in agnatic constructions of ideologically sanctioned ancestral patriline, and in state projects of categorization and administration itself reveals a partial representation despite the assumption of holism. Although Stafford explores informal caring cycles in contrast to formal lines of descent and Sangren evokes gendered desires in kinship ideals, both reveal the importance of gender and generation in alternate views of relatedness as a temporal process. While Judd focuses on rural sending communities of migrants, Zhang examines rural entrepreneurs in the heart of China's capital, but both reveal how spatial mobility comes to be gendered through spheres of labor. Greenhalgh's final analysis of the population policy reveals how the production of both planned births and unplanned persons govern the aggregate population and exclude individuals from recognition by the state. What emerges from this research is a terrain of relatedness where social cohesion and stable reproduction are not given, but social differentiation is achieved through ongoing practices that retain certain aspects while transforming others.

Seminar Questions

Are women outsiders in Chinese kinship?

What is the role of gender in creating and dividing families in China?

Readings

Carsten, Janet (2000). 'Introduction', in Janet Carsten (ed.) *Cultures of Relatedness: New Approaches to the Study of Kinship*, Cambridge University Press: Cambridge, pp. 1–36.

Judd, Ellen (2009). '"Families we create": Women's kinship in rural China as spatialized practice' in Brandtstädter, Susanne and Santos, Gonçalo (eds.) *Chinese Kinship: Contemporary anthropological perspectives*. Routledge: London, pp. 29–47.

Greenhalgh, Susan (2003). 'Planned births, unplanned persons: "Population" in the making of Chinese modernity' *American Ethnologist*, 30(2), pp. 196–215.

Sangren, Steven (2003). 'Separations, autonomy and recognition in the production of gender difference', in Charles Stafford (ed.) *Living with Separation in China*, Routledge: London, pp. 53–84.

Stafford, Charles (2000). 'Chinese patriliny and the cycles of *yang* and *laiwang*', in J.Carsten (ed.) *Cultures of Relatedness: New Approaches to the Study of Kinship*, Cambridge University Press: Cambridge, pp. 37–54.

Zhang, Li (2000). 'The Interplay of Gender, Space, and Work in China's Floating Population', in Entwistle, Barbara and Henderson, Gail (eds.) *Re-Drawing Boundaries: Work, Households, and Gender in China*, University of California Press: Berkeley, pp. 171–196.

References

Astuti, Rita (2000). 'Kindreds and descent groups: New perspectives from Madagascar', in Carsten, Janet (ed.) *Cultures of Relatedness: New Approaches to the Study of Kinship*, pp. 90–103.

Bray, Francesca (2009). 'Becoming a mother in Late Imperial China: maternal doubles and the ambiguities of fertility', in Brandtstädter, Susanne and Santos, Gonçalo (eds.) *Chinese Kinship: Contemporary anthropological perspectives*, Routledge: London, pp. 181–203.

Carsten, Janet (1997). *The Heat of the Hearth: The Process of Kinship in a Malay Fishing Community*. Clarendon Press: Oxford.

Fei Xiaotong (1992). *From the Soil: The Foundations of Chinese Society* (translated by Gary Hamilton and Wang Zheng). University of California Press: Berkeley.

Greenhalgh (1993). 'The Peasantization of Population Policy in Shaanxi', in Davis, Deborah and Harrell, Stevan (eds.) *Chinese Families in the Post-Mao Era*. University of California Press: Berkeley, pp. 219–250.

Greenhalgh, Susan (1994). 'Controlling births and bodies in village China', *American Ethnologist*, 21(1), pp. 3–30.

Greenhalgh, Susan and Winckler, Edwin (2005). *Governing China's Population: From Leninist to Neoliberal Biopolitics*. Stanford University Press: Stanford.

Judd, Ellen (1989). '*Niangjia*: Chinese Women and their Natal Families', *Journal of East Asian Studies*, 48(3), pp. 525–544.

Thompson, Stuart (1988). 'Death, Food and Fertility', in Rawski, Evelyn and Watson, James (eds.) *Death Ritual in Late Imperial China*. University of California Press: Berkeley, pp. 71–108.

Wolf, Margery (1968). *The House of Lim: A Study of a Chinese Family Farm Family*. Appleton-Century-Crofts: New York.

Wolf, Margery (1972). *Women and the Family in Rural Taiwan*. Stanford University Press: Stanford.

Chapter 5

Love, Emotion, and Sentiment

This chapter analyzes changes and continuities in romantic love and intergenerational love in China to address the recent anthropological issue of the formation and performance of emotion. Anthropologists have examined where to draw the line between cultural particularities and human universals in the creation and expression of emotions. This is particularly important in tracing how emotions are related to notions of self and the shifting attachments people make to each other and wider society through the intimate field of emotion. This chapter examines the changes and continuities to love, both as a romantic and an intergenerational phenomenon in China, and addresses these issues through three interconnected areas: first, whether changing expressions of emotion in China are the result of increasing autonomy and privacy, second, whether there has been a shift in expressions of emotions from actions to words, and third, whether love affirms or transcends dependence.

The chapter will examine the study of emotion in China while asking whether and if so what is peculiar to China and what might be universal.

In the last three decades, the role that emotion plays in Chinese social life has been the subject of anthropological debate, particularly as it pertains to the notion of qing, meaning affection and sentiment. Anthropologists have analyzed this through two intertwined ways: first, through the wider field of ganqing or emotion; second, and more recently, through the rising prominence of the specific emotion of aiqing or love. Earlier discussions of ganqing connected personal affection and collective sentiment to social life more generally. Anthropologists discussed how notions of ganqing were culturally formed and enacted, through acts of generosity, kindness, and care, as well as the provision of work done for others. However, more recent debates have turned towards personal expressions of emotional attachment, specifically through the notion of aiqing or love, within the current Market Era. Love has emerged as the central pillar sustaining both romantic relationships and intergenerational relations in ways that shift intimate relations into an increasingly public sphere, while simultaneously offering new opportunities for privacy. Chinese ethnography thereby contributes to the anthropology of emotions by combining various performances of love and emotion with the different selves they imply in relation to others over time.

5.1 Love as Transcendence of the Self

Exploring love as a universal phenomenon, Lindholm (1995) posits love as an experience of transcendence. Rather than linking love to sexual reproduction, Lindholm traces the origins of love to the desire to escape isolation of the self. He thereby creates a subject-oriented, even existentialist approach to love that could run into problems cross-culturally, especially by flattening out issues of duty and desire as they pertain to practices of sexuality and institutions such as marriage. Pointing to a powerful and expansive sense of self-loss through merger with the beloved other, Lindholm claims a form of self-transcendence as the essence of romantic love. Debunking the prevalent view of a correlation between falling in love, sexual desire, and reproduction, he points out that if this was true, societies favoring cultural expression of love would have higher birth rates. However, in northern Europe, where there was a highly evolved tradition of romantic love, the opposite has been the case: a high value on romantic love historically went hand-in-hand with a low birth rate, late marriage, nuclear families, and individual autonomy. Therefore, romantic love cannot be causally linked to sexual lust as the basis for reproductive success. Lindholm explores romantic love as a cultural expression of a deep existential longing of escaping the self, akin to charismatic movement and large-scale religious celebrations, where elevation, idealization, and incorporation of leaders and lovers form self-loss. Lindholm quotes sociologist Francesco Alberoni, claiming that, 'the experience of falling in love is the simplest form of collective movement' (p. 68). To Lindholm, romance characterizes the expression of the human impulse towards self-loss in ecstatic states of union with an idealized other.

Lindholm compares the transcendence of the self in love to belonging to a collective movement or partaking in a shared religious experience. By scaling up the experience of love to a social experience, Lindholm's thesis eclipses how love creates an intimacy that is only shared between two people in relation to wider society. There is an exclusivity or secrecy to the nature of love as self-transcendence, through merger, union, and knowledge with an idealized other. The question therefore emerges how love is emplaced within social constellations that condone, monitor, or reject this form of personal intimacy in relation to a wider public.

In order to view love's place in a broader social context, Gell's (2011) discussion of love as knowledge of the self and other within a society's wider distribution of knowledge provides important insights. In particular, Gell devises a comparative scheme for thinking about varying degrees of love as part of social structures.

5.2 Love as Knowledge Revealed and Concealed

Gell (2011) links love to the social distribution of knowledge within differing informational universes in comparative perspective across cultures. Societies differ in the distribution of general information that everybody shares and specific information that fewer people are privy to. Gell argues that '[l]ove is constituted through the dual process of mutual exposure (between lovers) combined with concealment (from everybody else).' In a highly stratified and large-scale society (such as France, to use Gell's example), there is a wide gap between what everybody knows (general information) and what only a few people know (intimate information). By contrast, among the Umeda (a small community in the Sepik District of New Guinea where Gell conducted fieldwork), everybody knows everything about everyone else.

Among the Umeda, marriage is fundamental to the reproduction of society, but there is no intimacy in marriage as the institutional arrangements for marriage are made in public with full disclosure to the whole community. Children are raised with their future spouse and their marriage partners are decided for them in childhood. Therefore, romantic love based on choosing an intimate relationship with a relative stranger does not occur through marriage. Moreover, when this kind of romantic love occurs, this usually happens out of wedlock, or at least away from the village in secret trysts in the bushes. As such, love is seen to generate lethal knowledge, associated with risks of betrayal and sorcery, and the maintenance of romance necessitates the preservation of secrecy and discretion.

Gell contrasts love as an extrastructural force among the Umeda with Euro–American societies, where love is seen as structurally essential to marriage and reproduction. Importantly, in these societies, there is a high degree of contact with relative strangers, many of whom could potentially become romantic partners. However, like with the Umeda, the creation of love in Euro–American societies rests on the revelation of intimacies between people who generate secret and exclusive knowledge. Gell argues that this occurs through ongoing and reciprocal exchanges of indiscretions (that range from the verbal to the physical) as couples simultaneously share their secrets with each other and shelter them from wider society. As such, dating becomes a process of revealing oneself to another.

But how, Gell asks, does one validate the choice of a particular partner, of all possible partners, for life? In order to convert the arbitrariness of selecting another person as one's lover into an inevitable choice, Euro–Americans construct fictions of predestination, so that '[e]ach modern couple has to devise of itself a history which will justify its existence as a couple.' The bases for these fictions, or scripts, come from novels, films, and other publicly available cultural referents that serve to guide the construction of an apparently exclusive and intimate narrative of finding each other.

Even the phenomenon of love at first sight confirms rather than confounds this logic. In this extreme instance of fictional selection of a beloved, information based on a scripted fantasy fills the absence of actual knowledge about the other. Gell sees this process of scripting as a characteristic of modern romantic love. In his pensive conclusion, Gell asks whether future development will see love as becoming increasingly based on fiction, such that scripted prototypes will supplant actual lovers, or whether a complete disenchantment with the arbitrariness of choice will lead to new forms of genetic matching in societies.

Originally published in 1996, Gell could not have foreseen the potential for new relationships created by the explosion in telecommunications, such as online social networking, that have vastly expanded people's capacities for intimate exchanges and the potentially infinite extension of possible marriage partners. However, comparative parallels can be drawn between contemporary dating websites and long-standing matchmaking practices through marriage-by-introduction in China and elsewhere, where a third party connects important traits between potential partners. The possibilities for self-realization through love, romance, and sex, nonetheless often sit uneasily with family obligations to marry and reproduce. The following section provides a short overview into how different generations face each other reciprocally in relation to love, both in terms of romantic passion and family affection, in China throughout the last century. In order to see how dynamics of revelation and concealment have played out in the Chinese context, the chapter will then discuss different ethnographic examples throughout the Market Era.

5.3 How Structural is Love in China?

A brief history of love in China would be vast, so a few historical notes will have to suffice. The May Fourth movement in China already championed love-based marriages as part of promoting greater gender equality across society. Maoist policies also sought to foster marriages based on choice and affection, particularly through successive Marriage Laws that banned polygamy and child marriages, and set in place a legal framework against coercive arranged marriages by ensuring consent between both parties. Nonetheless, marriages by introduction remained common and parental approval strongly influenced spouse selection, as did the matching of partners by social standing and class background. Brigades in the countryside and work units in cities ensured strong community surveillance over romantic relationships and public practices of casual dating did not emerge during the period of high socialism.

In the 1980s, the loosening of the household registration system and the possibilities of pursuing new workplace opportunities across the country created unprecedented mobility for Chinese citizens. The proliferation of spaces beyond the watchful eyes of the community and family was matched by increasing contact with strangers as potential classmates, colleagues, friends, and partners. Simultaneously, the family planning policy made contraception and abortions widely available across the country, making non-marital sex less risky in terms of unwanted pregnancies. The resulting demographic changes of the longer life-spans and population policies curtailing fertility have meant the increasing prevalence of the 4-2-1 problem, where four grandparents and two parents often come to rely on a single child in their old age. In addition, this problem of intergenerational dependency can become compounded after marriage, when a couple may even face a situation of up to eight members of the grandparental generation and four parents and parents-in-law. Despite curtailing reproduction through the Family Planning Policy from the 1980s, the 1990s are the decade largely credited with China's sexual revolution based on love. Not only were young people remaining single well into their 20s, but they were also increasingly engaging in premarital sex and even sex beyond aims of institutional marriage. The population policy also shifted during this time to encompass not just the number of children, but to emphasize their quality in terms of education, morality, and health.

These changes accelerated in the 2000s as possibilities for romantic love and sexual intimacies proliferated with new communication technologies. Not only the privacy of these interactions but also the sheer volume of potential contacts skyrocketed with the use of mobile phones and the internet. Demographic changes also meant that the interdependence between generations became even more pointed as family planning policy decreased the number of children people could rely on in old age. The market reforms brought a new level of choice as well as a proliferation of material, emotional, and sexual desires to light. Nonetheless, the rising value of personal fulfillment and individual autonomy has emerged hand-in-hand with increasing risks and uncertainties as people face a competitive social environment, where moral institutions and ethical choices multiply at rapid speed. In order to track these changes in love, sentiment, and affection, this chapter now turns to earlier studies of emotion in the Chinese Market Era.

5.4 Expressing Emotion through Action and Words

Potter and Potter's (1990) work on the cultural construction of emotion in 1980s. Guangdong Province is often taken as an early point of reference for anthropological studies of sentiment in China. However, their account is also heavily criticized for emphasizing social continuity external to the self, and focusing on the importance of the perpetuation of social institutions over the expressions of inner emotional life. There are two main points within this chapter of their book: first, that people in Guangdong do not so much express their emotions through words, but through an 'idiom of work and mutual aid' (p. 192). They assert that the basic principle of "good feelings" underlying marriage formations is based on social responsibility, altruism, industriousness, work, and sacrifice (p. 192). All these qualities are underwritten through 'the significance [that] lies in the work done on another's behalf' (p. 192). Furthermore, this type of work not only brings marriage partners together but also forms the basis for parent–child relations as well as neighborly relations within the village. To the Potters, this means that when villagers speak of work, they are actually speaking of an affirmation of human relationships. Their second, more heavily criticized argument, is that the open expression of emotions, often negative emotions, in direct verbal confrontation are dismissed as idiosyncratic and therefore lack 'symbolic significance for the creation and maintenance of social relationships' (p. 187).

By contrast, Kipnis (1997) argues that relationships are not determined by social position, but have to be constantly produced and reproduced, such that relationships are 'the result of purposeful human efforts, of a type of practice' and simultaneously 'constitutive of oneself' (pp. 7–8). Kipnis directly challenges the Potters' argument that expressions of emotion are deemed irrelevant to social life in China. Instead, Kipnis argues that emotional expressions are about creating solidarity through generating collective ganqing. Particularly in situations of conflict, taking sides through expressing emotions through confrontation creates ethical and emotional ganqing. Kipnis also takes up the Potters argument that ganqing is founded on work rather than words, but reads this as part of the material obligations that are fundamental to generating ganqing. To Kipnis, the emotional and material obligations implied by ganqing form part of a larger web of social reciprocity.

Kipnis explores the notion of ganqing through 'nonrepresentational ethics' that are tied to material obligations and emotional expressions. He posits that Western thought has a Cartesian bias that translates into a tendency to value language and thought over the material world, on the one hand, and representations over pragmatic ethics and speech acts, on the other. As such, American society considers the importance of emotions as grounded in 'sincerity' that express the 'inner' feelings of one's heart. Within the Chinese context, he frames this as a problem of moving between representational and pragmatic ethics of feeling and speech, though he makes clear that this is a matter of degree, as there is no place where the value of representation is completely ignored, nor where the effect of pragmatic expressions is deemed wholly irrelevant. Nonetheless, Kipnis leans towards emphasizing the public outcome of emotional expressions over their internal authenticity.

Kipnis also traces this dynamic historically as oscillating between these two poles. In the early 20th century, the May Fourth movement rejected 'li' as propriety in favor of 'impulse, sincerity, sentimentality, and individual, subjective experience' (p. 108). However, in the Maoist period, labor became increasingly important in generating ganqing, both in households (e.g. through doing chores) and in public (e.g. by exchanging favors). However, in Dengist China of the 1980s an 'intense sentimentality' emerged in the public sphere through TV, films, novels, and short stories that made emotional expressions increasingly verbally explicit (p. 109). Kipnis also argues that socialist speech, in general, emphasizes the purpose (and not just the content) of the language one uses and the material effects this has through taking responsibility for others.

The fieldwork Kipnis did for this book was largely in 1989–1990 with some return visits between 1992 and 1995. This meant that during fieldwork, these villagers were still tied locally to people they knew through ongoing face-to-face interactions, so that any interaction was placed within long streams of exchanges, and their motivations and outcomes were more clear than they would have been among strangers in the city. The following discussion will trace this oscillation between emotional exchanges in constituting relationships in urban and rural contexts, as well as romantic endeavors and intergenerational attachments as they shift through time.

5.5 Love between Passion and Affection

Around same period as Kipnis conducted fieldwork in rural Shandong in the late 1980s and early 1990s, Jankowiak (1995) researched love and emotion among urban Chinese residents in Hohhot, Inner Mongolia. Jankowiak separates two domains of love through ecstatic desire in the short term and the incremental formation of attachment in the long term. Jankowiak argues that there are two orders of love: first, romantic passion as 'any intense attraction involving the idealization of the other within an erotic context', and second, the companionship phase of love 'sometimes referred to as attachment' (pp. 4–5). While the former is characterized by urgent, intense, and ecstatic emotions, the latter often leads to more peaceful, comfortable, and fulfilling emotional states. Despite definitions of love frequently emphasizing long-term attachment, it is the short and heightened period of attraction that captures the romantic imagination. Jankowiak draws these two temporal dimensions out of relationship narratives in China, with a focus on literature and film, on the one hand, and personal accounts based on interviews, on the other.

The short-term period of "falling in love" (*lian'ai*) can be contrasted with the formation of long-term attachment through "sentiment" (*ganqing*), as the basis for relationships between husband and wives. Jankowiak draws on historical examples of the distinction between marriage (based on duty) and concubinage (based on desire and choice, at least for the elite men involved). In addition, a wealth of stories about fox fairies draws on the dangerous elements of female sexuality and lust in destabilizing the socially sanctioned etiquette of family life.

However, Jankowiak's main material are interviews that trace urbanites' narrative representations of dating, in terms of what is revealed and concealed in romantic scripts. A contrast emerges between levels of formality in relation to the processes and outcomes of dating. Formal dating constitutes a more prescribed social form that usually constitutes courtship leading to marriage and is usually conducted in public, often even with parental encouragement. Informal dating is frequently concealed from family and friends and does not necessarily lead to marriage. Furthermore, the rules of the game are far less rigid and prescribed in this informal world of dating. This leads to both higher degrees of freedom and higher stakes of risk in informal dating.

The dating histories of Jankowiak's interviewees are punctuated by feelings of anxiety, excitement, idealization, uncertainty, fear of rejection, and abandonment, as well as sexual involvement and its manipulation. Despite these diverse emotional states, practical compatibility issues influence the dating field in Hohhot as romantic fantasies of an ideal mate also attempt to bring together (filial) duty to parents and (romantic) desire towards partners. If a relationship becomes formalized and moves towards a potential marital decision, parental approval enters strongly into consideration. Within marital relationships, childbirth may signal a second shift within the attachment phase, as lovers become parents themselves. Within Jankowiaks's framework there is a strong division between desire-driven romance and ethically informed duty, although the two may also converge in choosing a partner and bearing children in ways that link autonomy and dependence as well as family and fulfillment. The following engagement with the romantic revolution and increasing youth dominance in spouse selection makes this clear.

5.6 The Romantic Revolution

Yan (2003) traces what he calls a, 'romantic revolution in courtship' in rural China through three prisms: premarital sex, ideal mate selection, and expression of emotion. Yan takes up Potters' emphasis on how work generates attachment (though he ignores their argument about the irrelevance of emotion), and criticizes Kipnis for a focus on formal propriety (which Yan sees as too static and immutable). Yan argues that their approaches (especially Kipnis) are too utilitarian in dealing with emotion and this 'underestimates the great potential of rural Chinese to cope with the rapid social changes in the wider social context' (p. 83). Love (*ai*) has gained salience in the vocabulary of romance and intimacy in China, circulating not only through the media and popular culture but also through aspirations towards urban lifestyles and self-fulfillment. Yan's longitudinal study of Xiajia village in Heilongjiang is based on seven years of living in the village in the 1970s, and another seven periods of fieldwork between 1989 and 1999.

Yan traces the history of premarital sex within this village, linking its emergence to the rising importance of urban consumption and more opportunities and spaces for intimacy for couples. Young couples increasingly enjoy the possibility of private interactions in both cities away from their families and in the heart of family homes, particularly after their marital engagement. In the 1950s and 1960s, future spouses could visit future in-laws to provide assistance, but in the 1970s, engaged couples increasingly made a shopping trip in preparation for their wedding. Taking a trip to the provincial capital to buy betrothal gifts and take engagement photos would often lead to sexual activity as couples stayed in a hotel overnight. For the future married couple, these experiences of leisure and pleasure provided a romantic experience that helped solidify emotional ties. Parents increasingly condoned premarital sex as it helped secure that marriage intentions were followed through, particularly for women who had lost their virginity. In the 1980s and 1990s, prospective spouses would even stay overnight, sometimes for weeks, with their future in-laws. The separation of domestic spaces into personal bedrooms meant couples were often sleeping together with the privacy of their own rooms such that 'intimacy of all sorts developed behind closed doors' (p. 66).

In parallel with these spatial shifts in privacy and intimacy, Yan traces the increasing verbalization of love in Xiajia through the changing discourse of what constitutes a "good match" in the village. Under Maoism, a "good match" constituted both partners sharing similar family status, economic standing, and future goals. However, in the Reform Era, "matching dispositions" often involves an emphasis on individual personality traits and being able to express ones feelings to create intimacy, often through verbal means. An ideal spouse is no longer purely characterized by diligence, industriousness, and reliability, but explicit expressions of love and romance take center stage. Yan links this to the rise of romance in popular culture through love songs and soap operas, but also through a shifting materialist orientation that validates men and women differently in their marital roles. The turn away from agricultural labor has meant that men ideally have a good financial standing and the ability to make money through skilled labor, while women should be good-looking, gentle, and sweet.

These direct tokens of love contrast with older villagers' emphasis on actions as more important than words, where every minute act could be a gesture and instantiation of love. As Yan points out 'generational differences in expressing one's affections seem to suggest a shift from more symbolic, indirect, and work-related modes of expression (such as shared foods, mutual help, and body language) to more direct forms of expressing love and intimacy' (p. 76). Yan argues that '[w]ork can be used as an idiom of love, as can food, care, or just a few words of comfort. It does not much matter whether the expression is verbal or nonverbal; what counts is whether the two individuals have found a way to express their affection to each other' (p. 82). Yan goes on to show that 'without uttering the phrase "I love you", — villagers successfully conveyed their affections to their loved ones in obvious, easily understood ways. It is true that Xiajia villagers normally did not hug or kiss in public, yet public displays of intimacy between people were not unusual in everyday life contexts, albeit in ways that were often difficult to spot' (p. 82). These themes of marriage and sex, informal and formal dating, as well as verbalization and mobilization of romantic scripts in a rural context can be compared with recent research among urban youth in Shanghai, where romance has become increasingly delinked from marital outcomes.

5.7 Romantic Scripts, Sex, and the City

Farrer's (2014) study predominantly focuses on 'love relationships' among Shanghai residents and their different forms of dating and maintaining relationships, in particular through a focus on the 'scripts' people use to validate and justify their position in relation to their partners. Farrer's analysis is based on the transcripts of qualitative interviews of 33 men and 35 women, age between 20–28 who were Shanghai residents at the time of interview. Graduate students carried out the interviews with interviewees recruited from their personal networks between 2003 and 2007. A clear finding that emerges from these interviews is a delinking of romantic relationships and sexual intimacy from the institution of marriage, but 'not simply the weakening of institutional structures and their replacement by individual strategies but the production of new cultural scripts for intimacy' (p. 89). In particular, a 'fragmentation of romantic love' has been occurring in terms of commitment, passion, and intimacy, — which simultaneously leads to a proliferation of alternative scripts (p. 92).

The context of urban Shanghai in the mid-2000s is characterized by the high volume of contact with potential relationship partners, where people struggle to justify their choice of a particular partner over all the possible partners for a romantic liaison. Echoing Gell's proposition of the importance of fictions of predestination and devising a relationship history in these contexts, Shanghai youths also seek to attribute a form of inevitability to counteract the possibility of arbitrariness in their romantic entanglements through fate-based narratives. What is notable in the Chinese context is, of course, as Yan already noted, that there has been a rapid shift from a context on arranged marriages and marriages by introduction, to a world where a wide possibility of potential partners emerge. This brave new world of urban dating landscapes involves not only the possibility of online dating through the logics of algorithms in matching potential partners, but also the new possibilities for privacy and intimacy extended through technological innovations such, as mobile phones and online trysts.

Farrer describes the first meeting and choice of a partner as part of a struggle 'to explain why one would choose a particular individual as one's most important and only life partner' (p. 69). Evoking notions of destiny or fate (*yuanfen*) emerge as particularly meaningful scripts that describe meetings. A particularly evocative example involves a young man who met his partner on Skype, where he voices his incredulity at the destiny involved in meeting his partner in his first attempt at using the tool for an internet chat. Mythic predestination and prosaic compatibility thereby coexist and help young people explain the leap of faith needed to express attraction and affection to their potential partner.

These expressions of attraction and affection can be verbal, through face-to-face interaction or through texts or chat messages on electronic devices, and may also include sexual behavior and gestures. All of these expressions can signal loyalty and trust in the more long-term as 'acting responsibly' is crucial to an outcome-oriented concern for the present and future of a partner (p. 74). Protecting a partner's feelings and providing practical support are central to revealing care for a partner in ways that are simultaneously emotional and material. At times, the symbolic burden of these interactions can become overwhelming when there is a mismatch between a love script and a marriage goal between partners. In ongoing relationships, frequent contact and communication through digital media, including cell phones, emails, and chats are deemed essential for relationship maintenance.

Building on Jankowiak's and Yan's earlier research on the sequential unfolding of relationships, Farrer also traces how people are 'talking love' (*tan lian'ai*) through three successive stages: '(1) the initial stage of being attracted and expressing passion and (2) the second stage of getting to know each other (increasing intimacy), which may lead to breakup or to (3) the third stage of the relationship based on deeper emotional ties instead of mere feelings of infatuation' (p. 68). Farrer points out that a fundamental change in the relationship script is the potential for alternative endings, not just in marriage, but in potential breakups that are no longer seen as humiliations or moral failures, just possible outcomes of the circumstantial nature of life. However, breakups are occasionally viewed as problematic when sex involved the "sacrifice" of virginity to a partner, particularly for women (p. 82). Young people generally consider sex based on love as part of a responsible form of interaction that helps cushion the role of sex in breakup scripts. Breakup scripts focus on the lack of intimacy or decline of passion in ways that strongly emphasize emotional components in explanations. This emotional dynamic also makes up the central crux in breakup narratives with strong circumstantial changes, such as geographic distance, sexual promiscuity, income differentials, or diverging career prospects. All of these factors are seen to lead to a potential or actual loss of mutual feeling between partners.

A major stage marker indicating the potential for marriage is meeting a partner's parents. Especially if both partner's parents meet for dinner together the event may stand for an informal engagement party, where partners appease their parents' anxieties and expectations of marriage. Young women may also "borrow" their parents' voices to express concerns over a partner, implying that they prefer to outsource their reservations about the potential for long-term commitment (p. 76).

Farrer points out that young people in Shanghai are caught between two conflicting principles: exclusivity for a chosen partner and the potential choice of alternative sexual and romantic partners in the city. Resulting from the wider social, spatial, and technological changes, casual sex, sex with married people, and same-sex partners, are some of the emergent possibilities within the city. In addition to the "love relationship" scripts already described, there is a burgeoning field of alternative relationships, and associated scripts emerging. Short-term sexual relationships may include a variety of practices described by a diversity of terms. For instance, 'ambiguous relationships' (*aimei*) may not necessarily be heading towards a common future nor be based on romantic or sexual exclusivity. Internet memes abound with a multiplicity of terms for the partners that are not boyfriends or girlfriends, as Chinese relationships move further away from marriage as an institution.

Within such a context, the salient issue may be the resilience rather than demise of marriage as an institution. Farrer points out that a number of strong pressures favor marriage as an institution, including the state's emphasis on conservative public sexual politics, family values oriented towards childbearing, media concerns with sexual health, and educational curriculum championing sexual self-control and chastity. Despite these forces of sexual conservatism, the urban dating scene emerges as a realm, where emotional and material uncertainty abound, and young people navigating this risky terrain seek reassurances from their partners. As relationship goals and outcomes become destabilized by the separation of sex from marriage, the fluidity in types and partners and relationships, and the diversity of relationships scripts, potential partners seek new ways to make their romantic attachments explicit and implicit in novel ways.

5.8 Affection and Dependence between Parents and Children

Finally, we return to questions of love (*aiqing*) as a form of emotional attachment within family constellations by moving from partners to parent–child relations. As part of parent–child relations, emotional dynamics of affection also entail economic and ethical dimensions. Fong's (2004a) work brings to light how intergenerational love between parents and children in urban China cannot be separated from their structural interdependence as they move through life. This means that parent–child relationships, although affectionate, also carry pressures of risk and uncertainty through their intertwined lives. The provocative title of the chapter analyzed here makes this very explicit through the quotation of a child who threatens his parents: 'beat me now and I'll beat you when you're old.' Fong reveals shifting power dynamics between parents and children as they move through life: from childhood dependence on parents to elderly dependence on children. Love between generations can be expressed through different ways, through nurturance and care, but even through the use of violence, for example when parents try to get their children to study. Many of the experiences Fong describes show that mutual dependence between parents and their predominantly only children put a great burden and strain on their relationship.

Fong's fieldsite is in urban China, the city of Dalian in Northeast China, where almost all children are only children. With rising unemployment among older parents, and the simultaneous dismantling of pension and healthcare schemes, many older generations were left dependent on the success and care of their only children. Parents frequently saw it as their duty to make children study hard, get a good job, and thereby make it possible for their children to support them in old age. Sons and daughters were frequently invoked as having the same obligation to their parents based on their parent–child ties, although boys often had closer relationships to fathers, and girls with their mothers. Fong quotes a maternal grandmother who says that 'a good daughter-in-law is better than a good son, and a good daughter is best of all' thereby implying that care work up in the generational ladder is generally done by women rather than men (p. 133). Parents willingly sacrifice their comfort, even life, for their children. Fong argues that parents with less children focus all their love and attention on the only child. But those children, in turn, come under immense pressure to reciprocate parental love.

For instance, when expressing love in material terms teenagers often have detailed fantasies of expensive gifts they would someday buy their parents, like luxury cars or jewelry. Nonetheless, parents and children both experience anxiety, for instance over children's education, as a vehicle for mobility. What is at stake in these interactions is their shared future. In short, children are both subjugated and empowered by the expectation of parents' future dependence, and some parents even compete for a single child's favor. These dynamics of intergenerational solidarity and affection can even be scaled up further into the public sphere through the realm of what Fong calls, "filial nationalism."

5.9 Patriotism as Love Extended

By comparing feelings of filial attachment with feelings of nationalism among Chinese teenagers with global identities, Fong (2004b) reveals a contradiction between teenagers' sense of nationalism and their identification with global imagined community in which China is unfavorably compared to wealthier developed nations, especially in Europe and America. Fong argues that despite seeing China as backward or inferior in the material sense, teenagers have a strong sense of nationalism that runs parallel to their sense of filial duty to their parents. Parents are often less educated and less global than these urban teenagers, but they would always defend them to outsiders. Fong draws parallels between these emotional responses and the teenagers' relationship to the Chinese motherland.

Teenagers see themselves as vanguard of a new China, carrying the responsibility for modernization of both their families and their society. Tracing Chinese nationalism through the 20th century reveals how China self-consciously became part of an imagined community within the capitalist world system, particularly in the late imperial era and the republican government period up to 1949. However, in Fong's narrative, Maoism emerges as a period of exception, where the country became inward-looking and sought autarky and self-reliance in relation to other nations. Maoist movements turned young people against authority figures such as officials, teachers, and even their own parents through criticism, denunciation, and violence in the Cultural Revolution. However, in the post-Mao period filial devotion re-emerged as a powerful metaphor for nationalist feeling.

In Standard Mandarin Chinese, the very word for patriotism (*aiguo*) literally translates as a compound word meaning 'love-country' and has very positive connotations, such that people are shocked if one is not a patriot of one's own country. As a Chinese American woman, Fong experienced frequent complaints about China and unfavorable comparisons with the USA, which she would often try to redress with critiques of the United States. However, when Fong went the other way and also criticized China, people furiously objected to her criticisms. In short, the following pattern emerged: I can complain about my mother or motherland, but if somebody from another family or another country does this, I will defend her to the last. Fong's work thereby shows how discourses and domains of love from the intimate intergenerational love between parents and children can be extended into the public discourse of love and patriotism between young people and the nation.

5.10 Love and Emotion in China

Anthropologists frequently interrogate the crux between human universals and culturally formed particularities. In order to explore this tension, tracing historical shifts of certain concepts, practices, and experiences through time can be illuminating. The specific forms that love, emotion, and sentiment in rural and urban China take over time can be placed within more general theories in revealing ways. Tracing tensions between transcendence and dependence, romantic passion and long-term attachment, as well as how intimacy is articulated, sanctioned, or channeled allows shifting relationships between couples, parents, children, and even citizens and the nation to emerge.

Culturally formed avenues to express emotion (*ganqing*) are learned over time, allowing for comparisons with Charles Stafford's notions of processual ties through 'care' (*yang*) and 'coming-and-going' (*laiwang*), as well as Yan's and Yang's' work on social networking through exchanges of gifts, favors, and banquets (see the next chapter). If this form of affection is culturally formed, how are experiences and expressions of love and emotion changing within contemporary China? In order to answer this question, the chapter examined how notions of love, sex, and romance are shifting across different generations in China.

This chapter began with Lindholm's proposition that love expresses the human impulse towards self-loss in ecstatic union with an idealized other, while Jankowiak took romantic love to be a psychological emotion that was closely aligned with lust or sex, and temporally distinct from long-term attachment or dependency accrued over time. By contrast, Gell's exploration of love as secrecy and intimacy between lovers depends on a comparative analysis of the social distribution of knowledge, contrasting worlds with close contact with a finite number of people to experiences of potential infinite extensions through engagement with lives peopled with strangers.

Due to its comparative dimension between a closed and open social world, Gell's thesis could be juxtaposed with Chinese rural and urban, as well as Maoist and Reform Era experiences. In the Maoist period, brigades and work units constrained social interactions, while kin and colleagues kept a close eye over people's romantic and emotional conduct. Subsequently, the Reform Era entailed a romantic and sexual revolution, where love and emotion increasingly entered the public stage in explicit ways. Gell's work on the fictionalization of love, and the production of romantic narratives and scripts this entails, can be compared with Yan's work on the confluence between shifts in matching tempers turning towards increasing verbalization of love. Furthermore, Farrer's work on urban China reveals how a diversification of relationship potentials entails a proliferation of activities and scripts that go hand in hand with technological extensions of intimacy.

Broadening realms of consumption within the capitalist era have allowed a diverse range of films, pop songs, and online engagements to deeply alter the terrain of intimacy and attachment as people engage with emergent cultural forms. However, larger structural changes such as shifting marriage laws, youth dominance in spouse selection, and the anonymity attached to mobility and urbanization mean that new opportunities and possibilities for love and self-fulfillment also carry with them new risks and uncertainties in relationships. Not only romantic relationships between potential spouses reveal that love is uneasily juxtaposed between transcending and affirming interdependence. Vanessa Fong's work shows that intergenerational family love also carries new weight within a context, where larger numbers of grandparents and parents rely on fewer offspring for their old age. Demographic shifts mean that both urban singletons and their relatives face hardships that bring the close relationships between affection, ethics, and material obligation to light. Furthermore, scaling intergenerational emotions up to the level of the patriotic attachment to the nation, reveals how loving one's country mingles material obligation and ethical emotions. Chinese ethnography thereby reveals how love, affection, and sentiment are differently expressed over time, throwing light onto the different selves that emotional lives imply.

Seminar Questions

Is increasing autonomy changing expressions of emotion in China?

Is Chinese romance a product of capitalism?

Do "actions speak louder than words" in performances of love and emotion?

Readings

Farrer, James (2014). 'Love, Sex and Commitment: Delinking Premarital Intimacy from Marriage in Urban China', in Davis, Deborah and Sara Friedman (eds.) *Wives, Husbands, and Lovers: Marriage and Sexuality in Hong Kong, Taiwan, and Urban China.* Stanford University Press: Stanford. pp. 62–96.

Fong, Vanessa (2004a). '"Beat me now and I'll beat you when you're old": Love, Filial Duty, and Parental Investment in an Aging Population', in *Only Hope: Coming of Age under China's One-Child Policy*, pp. 127–153.

Fong, Vanessa (2004b). 'Filial nationalism among Chinese teenagers with global identities', in *American Ethnologist*, 31(4), pp. 631–648.

Gell, Alfred (2011). 'On Love', in *Anthropology of This Century*, 2. Available online at: http://aotcpress.com/articles/love/, last accessed 03/05/16.

Jankowiak, William (1995). 'Introduction' and 'Romantic passion in the People's Republic of China', in William Jankowiak (ed.) *Romantic Passion: A Universal Experience?* Columbia University Press: New York, pp. 1–19, 166–183.

Kipnis, Andrew (1997). *Producing Guanxi: Sentiment, Self, and Subculture in a North China Village.* Durham and London: Duke University.

Lindholm, Charles (1995). 'Love as an experience of transcendence', in William Jankowiak (ed.) *Romantic Passion: A Universal Experience?* Columbia University Press: New York, pp. 57–71.

Potter, Sulamith and Potter, Jack (1990). 'The cultural construction of emotion in rural Chinese social life', in Sulamith and Jack Potter *China's Peasants: The Anthropology of a Revolution.* Cambridge University Press: New York. pp. 180–195.

Yan, Yunxiang (2003). 'Sex, intimacy and the language of love', in *Private Life under Socialism; Love, Intimacy, and Family Change in a Chinese Village 1949–1999.* Stanford University Press: Stanford, pp. 64–85.

Chapter 6

The Exchange of Money, Gifts, and Favors

This chapter examines the exchange of gifts and money in China, and how they are not just a product of, but simultaneously produce, social relationships. The chapter begins with a classic assumption in social theory contrasting impersonal transactions of money and commodities through the market, on the one hand, and interpersonal exchanges of gifts that hold emotional and personal values, on the other. The chapter asks: How appropriate is this contrast in the Chinese case?

China not only has an extremely long history of a money economy, but also a strong legacy of ritual gift exchanges, in which even money itself circulates as a gift. This continues today at life cycle events when guests give hosts money wrapped in red envelopes at weddings and white envelopes at funerals. Paper money forms a spirit currency as an alternative to the money of the living, and is burned to the gods as an offering or to the ancestors for use in the underworld. Historically, there was also a large market in exchanging money for people who might be bought and sold as slaves, adoptees, wives, and concubines. These historical factors beg the question of where to draw the lines between impersonal and personal exchanges, as well as between alienable and inalienable property.

Of course, the history of state socialism was crucial in curtailing and transforming these processes. Maoist policies of socialist redistribution promoted an ideology of social and economic equality, but the revolutionary transition was also accompanied by a new political hierarchy and stratification of status at the level of work units and in collectives. This had particularly detrimental effects on those designated with negative class labels, but all citizens were subject to situations in which government cadres and party officials gained control over crucial decisions deeply affecting their comrades' lives. Gifts often flowed up the administrative chain as workers and farmers vied for favor from those responsible for their fate. In the Reform Era, establishing social connections has become even more important for success at the individual and family level within a competitive market economy, and renewed interest in the art of social networking (*guanxixue*) has emerged in rural and urban areas.

This chapter takes a closer look at the difference and commonalities between utilitarian and affective exchanges in both rural and urban China. Furthermore, it will address the intersection between displays of prestige, the production of selfhood, and the creation of relations that one can depend on for future reciprocity. Overall, the chapter analyzes how Chinese processes of exchange fit into more general anthropological theories on commercial, personal, and emotional transactions.

6.1 Money and the Morality of Exchange

In order to arrive at a broad anthropological theory of how money affects the moral evaluation of exchange, Bloch and Parry (1989) compare monetary, commercial, and gift exchanges cross-culturally. Parry and Bloch survey general social theory on the topic before engaging with the qualities of relationships involved in transactions, as well as the temporal dimensions shaping cycles of exchange. The varied ethnographic examples in their collection reveal the following: first, 'the enormous cultural variation in the way in which money is symbolized and in which this symbolism relates to culturally constructed notions of production, consumption, circulation, and exchange' (p. 1); second, by comparing this wide range of ethnographic examples, Bloch and Parry tease out a unifying pattern based on the 'totality of transactions' that can neither be explained by 'shared meanings attributed to money nor in the moral evaluation of particular types of exchange' (p. 1).

At this more general level, Bloch and Parry put forth a contrast between two types of transactional cycles that belong to distinct but overlapping moral worlds. The first focuses on short-term, instrumental relations that often connect individuals to each other through exchange that is codified and guaranteed by laws, contracts, and markets. While these transactions rarely extend beyond a person's life-span, Bloch and Parry also recognize a second moral world of exchange based on more long-term transactional cycles. Transcending the immediate and self-interested acquisitions of particular individuals, this second realm connects human relationships to broader social organization through lasting cycles of exchange that reproduce ideological systems. Here ongoing relationships over time are safeguarded by morality embedded in institutions such as religion or values such as status or trust. To a certain extent, capitalism, or at least analysts of capitalism, have tended to raise the short-term transactions arising within capitalist market exchanges to the level of the long-term, transcendent, and enduring social orders, thereby blurring the distinction between them.

Western discourse often assumes a set of revolutionary implications for money as unleashing individual profit-oriented exchange that may be demonized as aberrant or heralded as natural (pp. 2–7). At the celebratory end of the spectrum, intellectuals have faith in the benign influence of money and the pacifying effects of monetary exchange (p. 3). Whether Bernard Mandeville's vicious greed or Smith's virtuous self-servitude forms the catalyst, this school of thought places the basis for a prosperous society with the individual pursuit of monetary wealth (p. 3). Representing an intermediate perspective, Simmel attributes money with the potential for freedom through expanding individual capacities and extending circles of trust, while simultaneously cautioning against its threat to exceptional achievement by distorting incommensurate values through a quantifiable monetary order (p. 4). While Western social theorists identify money with an intrinsic power to revolutionize social interaction, the ethnographic record challenges this assumption, not least because actors themselves do not necessarily recognize this power through money symbolism.

Critically engaged with the mystification of monetary processes, Marx, as later Simmel did, described the growth of individualism at the expense of the solidarity of communities (p. 4). To Marx money allows productive and reproductive '[r]elations between people [to] masquerade as relations between things' (p. 7), and drives a wedge between producers and their products (p. 11). 'Anonymous and impersonal', money reduces quality to quantity (p. 6). However, these earlier social theorists rely on implicit dichotomies between monetary and non-monetary systems of exchange that ride on further sets of oppositions that anthropologists have shown to be problematically reductive (pp. 6–7). These include such social categories as traditional and modern, pre-capitalist and capitalist, use-value and exchange-value (p. 7). These ways of classifying exchange relations and scaling their economic differences up to levels of an allegedly universal social order may reduce and distort the diversity of exchange relations in the world. Furthermore, this type of economic analysis based on Western social theory may obfuscate common and enduring patterns beyond the diversity of the immediate transactional realm.

Arising from Mauss' influential essay on the gift in cross-cultural comparison, many anthropologists have focused on the contrast between gifts and commodities to disentangle the boundaries between persons and things in exchange relations. The power of money to segregate persons and objects arises from a different source for Mauss, than for Marx. To Marx, the separation between product and producer generated through money as a wage confers on the commodity the appearance of an existence severed from its relations of production (pp. 5–6, 11). To Mauss, it is 'the lack of separation between persons and things, which gives it the appearance of being animated by the personality of the donor (Taussig, 1980: pp. 36–37)' (p. 11). Bloch and Parry point out that this echoes a contrast 'between the 'fetishism' or 'objectification' characteristic of capitalism, where for the most part persons are spoken of as though they were things, and the 'personification' characteristic of pre-capitalist economies where things acquire the attributes of persons (cf. Gudeman, 1986: p. 44)' (p. 11). In a related anthropological analysis, they point to Gregory's (1982) characterization of gifts as based on 'an exchange of *inalienable* objects between *interdependent* transactors;' while commodities are part of 'an exchange of *alienable* objects between *independent* transactors' (p. 8, italics in original). In addition, Kopytoff (1986) and Appadurai (1986) have offered a process-oriented approach by tracing the biography of things to reveal how the gift- and commodity-state of an object may be temporally bounded (pp. 15–16).

Euro–Americans may resist giving money as gifts because this signifies an "economic" sphere that they bracket off as impersonal, amoral and calculating, and therefore the opposite of what their gifts are meant to convey. However, in China money, especially when wrapped in red envelopes, is often deemed a highly, often *the only*, appropriate gift at ritual events in line with a general moral economy. To Bloch and Parry, contrasting processes resulting in gifts and commodities or the line between persons and things appear overdrawn when confronted with the diversity indicated by ethnography. Instead of tracing symbolic pathways, they advocate a shift from focusing on the meanings of money toward the processes of whole transactional systems and their transformative processes. This is how they arrive at the analysis of money and the morality of exchange in relation to long-term and short-term transactional cycles. This chapter will now turn to the history of the monetary economy and its ritual and social consequences in China.

6.2 Money in Chinese History

Emily Martin's lectures from 1986 and published in 2014 compare the meaning of money in China and the United States. She traces the contrasting role that money plays in their respective moral systems and regimes of value by integrating historical processes, social theory, and fieldwork in both contexts, including participant observation in a village in rural Taiwan and a Christian Methodist sect in Maryland. Martin proposes a bold thesis: in China, money has historically tended towards social integration by complementing the growth in personal autonomy with an increasing density of social exchanges. Institutions and practices concretely safeguarded moral constraint on individual profit accumulation to bolster this social integration. By contrast in the USA, money delinks the mediating effects of social relationships from the circulation and accumulation of capital, thereby masking and legitimizing individual pursuits that cause social harm under the divine mandate.

Martin begins with money's paradoxical tendency to serve both socially integrating and disintegrating functions. Western social theorists have been particularly concerned with how money dissolves the qualitative differentiation in human relationships and emancipates individuals to deal with each other impersonally and interchangeably. To Simmel, this creates a modern spirit of rationality, calculability, and anonymity in social transactions that leads to a concomitant shift from community (*Gemeinshaft*) to society (*Gesellschaft*). To Marx, money helps to disguise inequalities of exploitation, particularly as capitalism commodifies all production through labor and its products. Furthermore, money instrumentalizes all relationships so that they can become contractual, for instance in employment. One can derive two patterns from this in relation to what money does (in Western capitalism): first, money increases social exchange and fosters personal autonomy; second, money confounds everyday perception of interactions that form the social basis of exchange, potentially legitimizing socially damaging activities.

Martin then goes on to explore the socially integrating effects of money in China. In her first lecture, she traces how money moves through Chinese communities within three contexts: labor, marriage, and rotating credit associations. In her second lecture, Martin goes on to explore how monetary exchanges between the world of the living and the spirit world of gods, ancestors, and ghosts serve to solidify bureaucratic restrictions on the convertibility and accumulation of money. She argues that the Chinese circulation and symbolism of money may superficially appear like nascent capitalism, and yet concentrates on the first tendency of increasing the density of exchanges while enhancing personal liberty. However, these transactions do not necessarily lead to the second process highlighted by Marx and Simmel in Western capitalism: the legitimization of the socially harmful pursuit of profit. Martin argues that the restraint on the second dynamic largely results from the limiting effect of various institutions, including the state, kinship, law, but also moral philosophy and ritual symbolism in China.

Martin sets out the historical context of money in China in the following way: money and exchange have a very long-standing history in China, with coins and bullion used in exchange by the 4th to 3rd century BC, and even taking on their characteristic circular shape with square middle hole by the Han dynasty (206BC–220AD). These coins were used until the end of Qing dynasty (1912) and continue to appear widely in ritual contexts laden with money symbolism. From the 11th century, large transactions of gold and silver were supplemented with the exchange of paper money in lieu of the weighty metals. The use of paper money as valid currency helped facilitate the market integration brought out in Skinner's research (discussed in Chapter 3), as markets at different scales functioned as nodes for financial transactions including borrowing and lending money and built up a network of commodities markets.

In Chinese philosophy and state policy, there was a status ranking of four professional categories with the scholar-officials at its apex, and in descending order the peasants, followed by the artisans, with the merchants at the bottom of the moral hierarchy. Merchants derived their negative association from trading in commodities produced by others for profit, in contrast to the state-sanctioned elite, their feudal agricultural peasant backbone, and the secondary producers of wealth engaged in manufacturing and services. Like Gates (discussed in Chapter 3), Martin points out that state restrictions on the accumulation of wealth by merchants dampened the possibility of growth of a bourgeoisie in the Western sense.

Money suffused ritual symbolism in various spheres, including shared substances, property, and income. Here, Martin turns to the divergence of money symbolism in regimes of labor and accumulation. Historically, the role of kin groups in tilling land and dispensing labor meant that labor was not freely traded in commodity markets. Kin had claims over each other and the disposal of each other's productive and reproductive capacities. There was also restraint on trading in land due to the desire to retain land and gravesites, although desirable kin ties to land could come under strain due to partible inheritance that fragmented land holdings. Martin points out that even wage labor relationships in rural Taiwan are characterized by recognition of employers and workers as whole persons: the amount and nature of workers' labor are not strictly delineated, employers usually provide food to those working, and workers' wages are not held individually, but pooled as a collective sum of common substance within their families to be consumed together.

Martin continues with the value of marriage (in the normative sense of patrilineality and patrilocality discussed and problematized in Chapters 3 and 4). At marriage, a bride is exchanged between two families alongside a variety of goods and payments of cash. However, these exchanges do not amount to buying or selling a person as a commodity. The bodily, emotional, and caring bonds that a woman's natal family creates by raising her cannot be severed with a material transaction. Nonetheless, at marriage material transactions do flow in both directions, and women's sexual, reproductive and labor capacities are transferred to wife-takers who are then forever in symbolic debt to her family. The transfer of money and goods allow both families to display their wealth, endow the newly formed conjugal couple and even the bride herself with the material basis for married life. In particular, the bridal trousseau of cash and gold could be read as convertible value distilled out of the various forms of exchange, but this usually remains part of the bride's personal fund, to dispense as she sees fit. The cash may be spent or invested, but the trousseau is ordinarily kept as a material reminder of her connection to her natal family. Especially the gold is treated as a family treasure that the woman only parts with in an emergency, often accompanying her until her final resting place in the grave. This money (both cash and gold) secures the married woman's autonomy through a reserve fund of private wealth, but simultaneously it materializes the indissoluble links made between the two families through martial exchange.

Martin then turns to rural Taiwanese rotating credit associations (*hui*), which she argues are similar to marital practices in that they are "building pure interaction and allowing personal liberty at the same time". Through these financial institutions, farmers share economic responsibility for each other in ways that can be contrasted to profit-generating money institutions characterized by usury. The rotating credit societies act as proto-banks, a form of community organization that pools money for borrowing and lending to members as between peers. In its simplest form, members regularly contribute to a shared fund of money that is then paid out to members in turn. A more complex version accommodates unforeseen expenses and varied needs, so that members may request the fund sooner, but then pay higher contributions than those who wait longer for their payout.

The rotating credit associations are not only about pooling money, but sharing financial risk as members commit to obligations to pay and receive as need arises between them. Sometimes the associations even set out explicit rules that their funds may only be used for purposes that do not undermine community solidarity. For instance, the funds may be used to finance funeral ceremonies, but not an investment to launch a business that would generate income inequality in the community. As Martin summarizes: 'In other words, using the accumulated profits to increase stratification within the community was not permitted.' In formal discourse, the activities of rotating credit associations are described through metaphors of organic and biological processes, a naturalizing discourse of growth and decay, flourishing and extinguishing in line with principles of heaven and earth. By contrast, in the case of usury, where profits are extracted from the debtor through excessively high rates of return, these natural metaphors are turned to processes that contravene nature as reprimands from heaven.

Summarizing her analysis of labor relations, marital transactions, and rotating credit associations, Martin argues that 'in all these contexts, two contrasting faces of money — its ability to make transactions denser, on the one hand, and its ability to act as a node of personal freedom, on the other, were held together within the same institutions.' In her second lecture, Martin focuses on the use of spirit money as a currency that parallels the monetary economy of the living and further bolsters social integration in China.

Different kinds of spirit money are burned as offerings to transfer it for use in the spirit realm of the underworld and in offerings to the gods of heaven, as well as to ancestors. In late imperial China, people were used to converting between currencies in the world of the living, with copper used for local purchases and retail transactions in everyday subsistence, silver for interregional trade and paying taxes to officials, and gold reserved for large payments and removing wealth from circulation. Spirit money as a form of currency is made entirely of paper, but indexes these into three different spheres of value and use: copper coins are offered to dead relatives and ghosts; silver money is used for less powerful gods, ancestors, unrelated spirits, or ghosts; and gold money is reserved for offerings to powerful deities.

Martin again draws on material from Gates who describes how the imperial state moderated markets, preventing them from expanding into full cycles of capitalist accumulation, while the religious domain offered a parallel representation of untrammeled capitalism in the world of the gods. Gates conducted research among petty-capitalist Taiwanese shopkeepers, where she sees this divine sphere as a counter-hegemonic alternative to the feudal-like bureaucracy of the state. By implying that capitalism forms the basis for transactions between people and the gods, these shopkeepers advocated that the same should hold for commoners and state authorities in a larger system of unfettered capitalism.

Martin puts forth another possibility based on her research among Taiwanese farmers. In her rendition, the divine bureaucracy runs analogically to the imperial state as tributary models where surplus is appropriated and held by the center. She argues that in issuing and burning money, commoners may have used ritual means to usurp a power normally reserved for the state. Therefore, these ritual practices form a kind of parody or mimicry of state authority. Especially in late imperial and republican era China, the risks and pitfalls of rampant capitalism were being felt as precarious encroachments on livelihoods throughout the country due to fiscal instability. As money was increasingly accumulated capriciously at the expense of others, the Gods of Wealth may have emerged like a commentary on the danger of money circulated as profit-generating capital.

A relevant contemporary transformation in Shanxi Province, North China, can be added from more recent fieldwork to complement Martin's argument. This was that farmers often hung a poster of Chairman Mao in the place of or on top of images of the God of Wealth above the spirit altar where villagers gave offerings to the gods. During fieldwork in the late 2000s villagers reasoned with me, Charlotte Bruckermann, that these two figures were transformations of each other, because the Chairman had provided land and houses so they could fend for their livelihoods, thereby making him a source of wealth. Some of the farmers even lived in grand courtyard complexes appropriated from wealthy merchants in the 1950s. As Chairman Mao and The God of Wealth shared the spirit altar during the Market Era, villagers frequently complained of rapidly growing social inequality and the erosion of utopian aspirations of socialism. Offerings to the God of Wealth and Chairman Mao provided a powerful way of expressing critique of the earthly state in its current capitalist form.

In late imperial China, Martin points out that although conversions could be made between different domains of money, both in the spiritual and the mundane world, and even between the two worlds, the forms of currencies nonetheless created bounded subsystems. Therefore, in contrast to Simmel and Marx's postulation of money as an abstraction of value from quality to quantity and its subsequent infinite convertibility, in China there was a more concrete value that was not only differently materialized but also socially embedded and institutionally contained within discrete spheres of circulation and transaction.

In the later two lectures, Martin turns to her fieldwork in Baltimore and the analysis of texts that proselytize "prosperity theory" or "prosperity thinking" to a Christian Methodist sect. Martin argues that in the absence of the morally moderating institutions encountered in China, this religious community not only traces evidence of God's plan in individual accumulation of wealth, but further expounds personal prosperity to be the result of capital circulation without the mediation of social relationships. In Martin's analysis, this is part of 'what happened in the development of Western civilization to set loose the side of money connected with evil and destructive forces at the expense of the side of money connected to sociability and the many roads of human exchange.' Notably, unlike the many analysts who have focused on China's "failure" in developing fully-fledged capitalism, Martin turns the "failure" argument on its head, focusing on the absence of moderating institutions that allowed capricious, self-interested, and socially harmful capitalism to develop in the United States.

Extrapolating from the concrete historical insights that Martin makes in her lecture series, we can also reread her argument from more contemporary Chinese critiques of extractive mercenary activities by individuals and businesses, and forms of corruption and nepotism by state agents, through critical appraisals of social connections (*guanxi*). In interpersonal relations, *guanxi* is often contrasted to the moral principles of affective and material reciprocity sustained by personal relationships of 'human feelings' (*renqing*). In the governmental domain, *guanxi* accusations against state officials are framed through the state's responsibility for maintaining order and stability, beyond which lies the threat of "chaos" (*luan*). In order to further trace how the socially integrating and disintegrating effects of monetary and other forms of exchange on relationships in China, the following sections will turn to the historical developments of personal exchange relations in the Maoist and Market Era in both rural and urban China.

6.3 Rural Relationships

In thinking about *guanxi* as personal networks of relationships, it is worth recalling once again Fei's notion of the ego-centered spheres of relations developed in Chapter 2. Like the ripples from stones thrown into water, these concentric spheres of relationships expand and overlap with the spheres of association made by others. Similarly, *guanxi* relations emanate outwards from persons as they build up expansive networks throughout life, through ongoing activities of hosting banquets, giving gifts, exchanging favors in work settings and family life.

Yan (1996) approach even explicitly echoes Fei's notion of relatedness, as Yan analyzes how flows of gifts, and especially receiving gifts, enhances social prestige in the village of Xiajia in Heilongjiang province in the northeast of China. Xiajia villagers maintained that a person with success in making and maintaining social relationships (*guanxi*) is judged to be a moral person. This is because they are meeting the standards of the local moral world through fulfilling their obligations of material and affective exchanges (*renqing*). Therefore, Yan follows villagers in differentiating the overlapping concepts of *guanxi* as personal networks and *renqing* as the moral norms and human feelings created in this context.

Yan develops a peculiarity of the Chinese gift that adds to general anthropological debates on the topic by highlighting a dimension that has rarely been addressed elsewhere. Other anthropological theories of gift exchange emphasize the spirit of the gift and how the obligation to reciprocate leaves the gift giver in a superior position to the gift receiver until the debt is repaid. In short, anthropological theories of gift exchange rely on a notion of reciprocity that ultimately equalizes relationships, or at least creates a seesaw motion between the status of the giver and receiver in relation to the obligation to reciprocate.

By contrast, the Chinese gift actually enhances the status of the receiver rather than the giver. Instead of explicitly calling for reciprocity (*bao*) or being inalienable in its attachment to the giver, the Chinese gift itself symbolizes prestige that attaches to the person who receives the gift and enhances their public esteem through the notion of "face" (*mian*). This means that gifts may flow up the chain of social status hierarchy, with recipients remaining immutably superior and retaining higher prestige than the givers. Competitions in prestige may occur when people attempt to expand the reach and scope of their personal networks through gift-giving, but ultimately the aim is to become a superior gift-receiver through this extended network. Instead of a dyad of balanced reciprocity oscillating between a giver and receiver, this flow of gifts forms an expansive and open-ended process centered on a particular person within their *guanxi* network.

The history of state socialism in Xiajia and China more generally interacted with this particularity of Chinese gifts in complex ways. The irony of state socialism was that its experiments aimed to foster social equality, and yet ultimately resulted in the creation of new forms of inequality and novel concentrations of power. For instance, as gifts could be given up the social hierarchy without being reciprocated in kind, most villagers in Xiajia were giving gifts to those in positions of authority, most notably village cadres, without definitive expectations of return. As already noted in Chapter 2, the socialist system of hierarchy put ordinary villagers into inferior relations of dependence with their brigade cadres. Villagers were giving gifts with the hope of return favors or social protection, but the gifts were not returned in kind, and sometimes not at all. Instead, cadres might use their position of power to help advance the gift-giver's aims further down the line. Such favors could include allocating them jobs, residences, and food, or pulling administrative strings to allow for movement, for instance in marriage.

During the initial period of decollectivization cadres were often instrumental in redistributing or privatizing collective resources to individuals, often again wielding their structural power in the interest of fostering their own networks. As valuable resources were rechanneled through personal connections, in many areas the divide between cadres and ordinary villagers was reinforced. However, in the Reform Era this inequality in power hierarchies underwent a renewed restructuring through the additional status and weight placed on wealth as a realm of prestige and the consumption of commodities as a marker of superior social networks. The following author engages with how urban dynamics of fostering networks played out with particular focus on the early phase of the Market Era.

6.4 Urban Connections

In contrast to Yan's view of *renqing* as a dimension of *guanxi*, Yang (1994) contrasts the male urban art of *guanxi* with the female rural practice of *renqing*. Her ethnography predominantly focuses on the production of *guanxi* connections and networks in the urban context of Beijing, although her comparison of the urban art of *guanxi* and a rural *renqing* gift economy is suggestive. Yang argues that her informants considered the 'aggressive tactics and instrumental aims' of making *guanxi* as masculine skills associated with the hardened, cynical and politicized sphere of the state (p. 288). The urban context of *guanxi* thereby instrumentalizes and politicizes a more traditional body of practices that are based on emotional and affective interpersonal relationships found within the rural gift economy, which her informants associated with a "feminine" art of *renqing* (p. 320). Yang suggests that in the 1980s and 1990s a rising sphere of *minjian* 'refers to a realm of people-to-people relationships which is non-governmental or separate from formal bureaucratic channels' (p. 288).

Yang's research focuses on the use-contexts of *guanxi* and its wide scope in affecting quality of life in the first two decades of the Reform Period. For instance, *guanxi* networks were often crucial in obtaining goods that were in short supply, or better quality, or at lower prices. This was especially an issue in the early 1980s when manufactured consumer goods were rare, and frequently allocated through work unit quotas. Engaging with work units and then private employers remained important in managing hiring practices, arranging job transfers, and gaining promotions. As the household registration system was loosened, people used their native-place networks and urban connections to enable geographic mobility. This was particularly crucial in the early phases of the reform when urban housing was often allocated through work units and employers rather than bought and sold on the market. Even for maintaining good health "red envelopes" of cash appeared in hospitals in return for preferential care. With far fewer cars on the road than today, *guanxi* could be used to facilitate transportation through arranging drivers or buying coveted train tickets. Corporate deals between supply and demand chains were frequently not simple business negotiations but involved enjoying recreational activities together.

In urban context, the gendered dimension in *guanxi* came into play as women often focused more on the domestic arena of utilizing networks by exchanging favors and gifts among neigbours, kin, family and friends in everyday life. In particular, women often took charge of marriage introductions and matchmaking, as well as making sure to secure their children's educational opportunities through gaining entrance to prestigious institutions and programs. In addition to this domestic domain of urban *guanxi*, there was also the more overtly political sphere, where urbanites elicited benefits from officials and administrators in offices and bureaucracies. They also engaged in *guanxi* exchanges within the commercial sphere of business relations, where services and contracts were made between partners with the aid of other parallel exchanges. Both women and men engaged in this second sphere of overtly instrumental public *guanxi* through political channels or economic advancement. Yang even notes that some informants considered women as more skilled in smoothly activating *guanxi* exchanges due to their charm in handling men in positions of power. This same attribution of skill could, if a woman became too successful, led to questions about her virtue and integrity, a point developed in detail below.

6.5 Status, Merit, and Self-Interest

A point worth noting in regard to *guanxi* is the difference in status achieved through gift exchange and status achieved by other means, such as educational attainment, political promotion, wealth accumulation, or popular fame. While both may create an asymmetrical relationship between lower and higher positions, status derived from gift exchanges explicitly depends on a person's relationships to others, even if they occupy an inferior social position. By contrast, the latter forms of status achieved by other means are more readily attributed to narratives of individual merit. This difference is especially relevant within a capitalist market economy with its increasingly open and expansive fields of social competition among strangers. This distinction is therefore also important for the contrast between short-term transactional cycles in which material gifts are more easily quantified and abstracted, but also traced, than in the other forms of status. Status achieved by other means may be credited to personal achievement, despite being the result of idiosyncratic or structural inequalities of access in which the role of gatekeepers is often paramount.

Both Yang and Yan analyze moral evaluations of *guanxi* transactions among the people they study. Yang's analysis of popular discourse shows how people view the instrumental and self-serving characteristics of *guanxi* practices as symptoms of moral decline. They do this despite engaging in the practices themselves, justifying its logic and efficacy with standpoints ranging from *guanxi* as a necessary evil to a positive set of skills for adapting to the competitive market economy. Yang contrasts this diversity of private opinion with the more tightly controlled field of state discourse that is unequivocal in its denunciation of *guanxi* practices, particularly when involving state agents and accusations of official corruption. In the rural context, Yan argues that meeting *renqing* obligations enjoys unreserved popular approval, while *guanxi* networks as attributes of persons are also generally positively evaluated. However, lamenting the position of those lacking *guanxi* networks as well as the inequalities arising from gifts given up, the social hierarchies and exacerbating imbalances of prestige and status are occasionally criticized.

It is also important not to lose sight of the temporal dimension highlighted by Bloch and Parry, but also discussed by Martin, of long- and short-term cycles of exchange in relation to how and when the debt of a gift is repaid, or not. The difference between value that is accumulated and value that is consumed is of extreme importance in this regard, as individual prosperity or joint shared consumption ties into assessments of the morality of the exchange. The consumption of food and drink at a banquet differs from the exchange of red envelopes of money, but both may form part of long-term relationships built up over time. Therefore, one cannot simply categorize instances of consumption or moments of exchange as examples of immediate or delayed reciprocity without taking into account the broader temporal and moral frames of the transactional cycles.

The question of how far the gift is really alienable in either rural, or urban context ties into the role of ideology, the mystification of the exchange through the attribution and loss of "face" (*mianzi*). Furthermore, by ameliorating the extractive processes of value for status accumulation through the idea of *renqing*, we might also ask how and why relationships are personalized through emotional and affective bonds. Finally, the pastoral role of the state differs in the urban and rural context due to how close and dependent ordinary citizens are to their local cadres and party officials. The Chinese communist party addresses this issue through its insistence on serving the people, so that its personal patron–client relationships are established through mutual dependence, at the same time as justice and autonomy are guaranteed through its actions of state-citizen relations. We will now turn to some more recent examples from both urban and rural China to further develop these issues of moral judgment and conditions for the creation of *guanxi*.

6.6 Elite Networks

Osburg (2013) examines how elite men in Chengdu, the capital of Sichuan Province in China's interior, forged social networks. Osburg predominantly conducted fieldwork in the mid-2000s with later return visits, where he accompanied entrepreneurs as they courted business contacts, fostered friendship ties, and pursued women, often simultaneously. These *guanxi* relationships were mostly face-to-face and frequently very intimate including friendship ties and sexual relations, with the latter often mediating the former. However, kin connections between the entrepreneurs were rare, despite the idiom of brotherhood that often prevailed in creating these homosocial male relationships. Osburg's elites generally appeared as isolated individuals rather than embedded kin, despite their far-flung economic cooperation and expansive practices of social networking.

In his analysis of the rise of elite networks, Osburg places gendered patron–client relationships center stage. Male business entrepreneurs entertained state enterprise managers and government officials in teahouses, karaoke rooms, massage parlors, and banquet halls. These elite men nonetheless held personal aspirations of autonomy and independence from social networks as an unattainable ideal, unattainable precisely because of the necessity to network. Sharing food, drink, song, and sex were ways of transforming instrumental relationships into sentimental bonds, something men sought to do with friends, business partners, and sexual liaisons.

Exchanges underwriting male patronage were even scaled up to spectacular but illicit networks, such as a grey zone beyond legality dominated by Brother Fatty and his gang, a criminal sworn brotherhood. The acquaintance who introduced Osburg to this "godfather" figure even claimed that 'You know, in China there is no law. Relationships are the law (*renqing jiushi falü*)' (p. 77). The statement appears noteworthy for its commentary on a gap felt in lieu of the state in guaranteeing the rule of law, but also highlighting the key role that social relations played in governing Chengdu's urban landscape in the mid-2000s.

Entrepreneurs navigated the tension between pursing membership in elite circles that relied on the legibility of recognized consumption and desiring self-cultivation through pursuits that separate them from their social circles. This resulted in contradictory aims of striving for independence while expanding networks of patronage. Everybody wanted to be his or her own boss but feels the social pressures of 'having to live for others' (p. 45). Despite elites voicing chains of critique that others were leading a vacuous existence compared to their own lives, Osburg sympathetically sketches the loneliness of an aging gangster sipping whisky in his private karaoke room or the self-righteousness of an allegedly socially independent female boss surrounding herself with subservient followers.

Among Chengdu business elites, male friendship was often facilitated through the medium of women, ranging from mistresses to hostesses, girlfriends to sex workers. Women often struggled to find alternate roles in the interstices of these powerful male-dominated networks. However, Osburg also ventures a look at the men's female counterparts. Osburg introduces three groups of women in this regard, who all struggled to justify their position within the polarized gender hierarchy. Successful female entrepreneurs had to defend themselves against accusations that they were masculinized "strong women" or feminized temptresses who used their sexuality to get ahead. Young "female beauties" (*meinü*) deployed their charm, wit, and skills to meet wealthy male patrons to support them financially as mistresses. The male entrepreneurs' wives and other "rich women" struggled to retain their dignity in the face of philandering husbands and accusations of their own voracious sexual appetites. Nonetheless, all of these women strived for validation and recognition as individuals who reached their position through their own merit, again leading us back to the question of how far positions gained by *guanxi* exchanges and status achieved (or denied) by other means are commensurable.

Another question that emerges in engagement with Osburg's ethnography of these powerful and extractive elite networks is whether Martin's historical argument that money fostered social integration in China still stands. Osburg unequivocally concludes that '*guanxi* has failed in the domains of public morality and social justice. By personalizing and privatizing bureaucratic institutions that are intended to serve abstract citizens and the public good, they exacerbate inequalities rather than keep them in check. Elite networks are the primary mechanism that allows public assets, such as land, to be diverted into private hands' (p. 186). Osburg makes a strong case that rampant market capitalism has had a disembedding effect on the economy along Polanyian lines and that more protection is needed for those excluded from the elite networks that only serve their own self-interests.

The elite networks Osburg describes may offer a glimpse of what the untrammeled extension of *guanxi* networks does without Martin's ameliorating institutions of the state, kinship, law, and ritual. In the final example, we turn to a rural community where aspects of these institutions continued and even reasserted themselves under conditions of marketization.

6.7 Kinship and Property

Contrary to theories of modernity and capitalism that posit the inevitable and unilineal disembedding of kinship from property and economy from society, Brandtstädter (2003) argues that the moral economy of kinship and property serve as a 'mode of integration' in the Chinese postsocialist countryside. Brandtstädter traces a renewed emphasis on the material and emotional links between kinship and property relations in three fieldsites in the coastal area of southern Fujian. Not only kinship rituals of conspicuous consumption, such as weddings and funerals, reveal this integration, but also the rebuilding of temples, ancestral halls, and even graves.

This new emphasis on property and kinship as a mode of integration has occurred despite many developments in line with conventional modernization and marketization theories. The region experienced rapid economic success through market development and received overseas investments and labor migrants. No longer reliant on local subsistence farming and fishing, or even commercial fabric manufacture, young people from the region increasingly earned wages abroad (p. 423). Nuclear families became the norm and the ideal in the region, with couples increasingly attached to their conjugal partner for material assistance and emotional support (p. 426). Through participating in wage labor locally and abroad, most families no longer depended on the land or their parents for income and residence. Instead, most families included members who worked abroad for several years, so there was an expectation that young people would leave, but also send remittances (p. 427). This meant that many families' living standard depended on a son or daughter working elsewhere (p. 427). Despite all of these changes, there has been a revival of lineage structures and lineage committees, as well as a burgeoning in the value of gifts and prestations exchanged at marriage. As Brandtstädter puts it, this escalation of ritual expenditure amounts to 'an outright potlatch of property consumption at weddings and funerals' (p. 429).

Brandtstädter argues that this form of prestige building is nothing unusual in stratified and competitive societies, and yet she argues that this new emphasis on kinship as a mode of integration led to the exchange, pooling, and consumption of property in kinship rituals (rather than the other way around) (p. 429). This is because kinship increased in value after the economic reforms as 'investment in kinship was triggered by an environment in which the existing rules of the game in interpersonal relations were increasingly up for grabs' (p. 430). As the post reform state retreated from the reproduction of moral communities, a break-up of state-society relations occurred in which state representatives were 'unwilling or unable to create new binding rules to "re-embed" social relations' (p. 436). To ameliorate the risks the volatile economic environment posed to collective welfare, local residents established new institutional forms to secure property and morality, allowing them to gain status, build prestige, and seize opportunities in the competitive new era (p. 436).

Kinship offered two parallel forms of integration in a competitive, mobile, and stratified society. On the one hand, in the mutable sphere of *renqing* and *guanxi* relations exchanges of gifts and favors produce relatedness through affective and material ties. This is an arena of everyday economic cooperation where affinal and matrilateral relatives are often preferred partners, although good friends may also be considered reliable allies in weathering economic storms. On the other hand, agnatic kin, lineage organizations, and temple associations provide avenues for political solidarity based on descent and territory through inherited shares of collective property. Although lineage affiliations influence the outcome of village elections and mobilize resources from overseas, they do not only benefit elites through increasing their control over resources. By taking over decolletivized property after the market reforms, lineages and temples effectively served as institutions that recollectivized community property.

Brandtstädter argues: 'the dividends of a restoration of kinship institutions (along with temple communities) in post-reform rural China are not simply money and power but also integration, order, and collectivity — that is, the creation of moral communities' (p. 433). Lineages and temples (re)accumulated property through buildings, land, and donations, thereby bracketing them off from markets as inalienable property through collective relations with the ancestors and community. With the retreat of the state from safeguarding collective morality, these institutions bolstered collective ideals of good governance through "recollectivisation" of property. Communities also benefited as lineages and temples took on roles left unfilled by the local state, including maintaining infrastructure and running educational institutions (p. 434). In short, with the retreat of the state from safeguarding public morality, the moral economy of kinship and property served as a mode of integration to protect communities from some of the negative corollaries of rampant capitalism and the vagaries of the market economy. Brandtstädter concludes that the dividends of these exchanges were not purely economic, but 'first and foremost relatedness itself' (p. 435).

6.8 Conclusion

In this chapter, anthropological approaches contrasting transactions of money and commodities through the market with interpersonal exchanges of gifts as holding emotional and personal value were contrasted with historical and contemporary ethnography of China. The long history of money in the Chinese economy includes ritual gift exchanges of money, of people being exchanged, through marriage or adoption, and the imperial state's role in delimiting capital accumulation paralleled by a divine bureaucracy of gods. These dynamics problematized contrasts between long- and short-term transactional cycles, immediate and delayed reciprocity, and alienable and inalienable property in different ways. The role of the state in safeguarding collective property relations through kinship institutions and legal structures began crumbling in the late imperial and republican era.

Crucially, the history of state socialism combined Maoist policies of socialist redistribution and ideals of economic equality with a political hierarchy and stratification at the level of work units and collectives. This led to new forms of inequality as gifts were given up the chain of social hierarchy and not reciprocated in kind, but through favors and protection that advanced the gift-givers' aims at the discretion of the gift-receiver who wielded power. This inequality was exacerbated under decollectivization as the state redistributed collective resources to individuals, often those with personal connections to power-holders. The market economy has made the establishing of social connections increasingly important for the success of individuals and families through the art of networking, another interleaving of gifts with monetary exchange. However, the interplay of state and kinship institutions in upholding public morality and protecting collective welfare was explored through the rise of powerful personal networks brought on by market capitalism.

Seminar Questions

How does the cultivation of personal networks through gift exchanges both reinforce hierarchy and foster mobility in China?

How do *guanxi* exchanges challenge the separation between the market economy and social reciprocity?

What do *guanxi* practices reveal about the role of morality and status in theories of exchange?

Readings

Brandtstädter, Susanne (2003). 'The moral economy of kinship and property in southern China', in Chris Hann (ed.) *The Postsocialist Agrarian Question*. Muenster: LIT Verlag: 419–440.

Martin, Emily (2014). *The Meaning of Money in China and the United States*. The HAU-Morgan Lectures Initiative, HAU Press: Chicago, haubooks.org/.

Osburg, John (2013). *Anxious Wealth: Money and Morality Among China's New Rich*. Stanford University Press: Stanford.

Parry, Jonathan and Bloch, Maurice (1989). 'Introduction' to Parry, Jonathan and Maurice Bloch (eds.) *Money and the Morality of Exchange*. Cambridge University Press: Cambridge, pp. 1–32.

Yan Yunxiang (1996). *The Flow of Gifts: Reciprocity and Social Networks in a Chinese Village*. Stanford University Press: Stanford.

Yang, Mayfair Meihui (1994). 'The scope and use-contexts of *guanxi*', in her *Gifts, Favors and Banquets: the Art of Social Relationships in China*. Cornell University Press: NY, pp. 75–108.

Chapter 7

The Localization and Globalization of Food

Everybody eats. Despite the universal necessity for food, food does not just bring people together, but can also divide and separate humans from each other. Food's status as a universal part of human experience and as vital to biological processes makes it such a powerful substance for communication between people as they eat and act. What, how, and when to consume particular foods varies radically across the world, bringing together issues of economics and religion, politics and intimacy, livelihood and taste, nationality and family. A diversity of ingredients, agricultural practices, processing techniques, distribution channels, cooking methods, food taboos, eating etiquette, and consumption habits differ radically between and across populations, although this diversity also forges global networks of food production, preparation, and consumption. Therefore, food not only eats away at bounded concepts of place and identity, but highlights questions of universalism and particularity within and between different regions, locales, and contexts.

Earlier anthropological studies of food were often restricted to food production, particularly with a focus on agriculture and tools, ranging from an interest in the evolution of humanity through technological innovation to the arrangements of plots, farming and exchange beyond the confines of the home. In addition, the religious and ritual dimensions of food, and its strength in fostering relationships through commensality (the practice of eating together) was important in understanding the relations between this world and other, immaterial or insubstantial, worlds inhabited by gods, spirits, and ancestors. Over time, food grew in centrality to debates on how to understand the universality of human experience, especially as anthropology moved from its interest in food production and religious significance to emphasize the mundane, everyday experience of food consumption. Food was, for instance, one arena in which the theoretical contest between structuralists and materialists played out, with structural analysis emphasizing cognitive categories and classifications of food (e.g. Douglas, 1966, 1972), while the materialists put more stock in the conditions governing the production, processing, and consumption of food (e.g. Harris, 1985). However, this polarized debate was largely synthesized by contributors such as Goody and Bourdieu, who brought concerns of nationality, taste, class, and distinction to the table.

Today even anthropological studies of food focused on very distinct settings are usually conceptually couched in a wider political economy, bringing together different scales that range from the global to the local, while viewing food as both nourishment and medium in delineating boundaries and hierarchies of inclusion. This chapter focuses on consumption and change, globalization and migration, in the anthropology of food and the anthropology of China. The chapter thereby moves beyond narratives of the persistence of the local in a homogenizing world impacted by mass migration and global food ways, and critically engages with how food is localized under pressures of globalization in relation to Chinese food and beyond.

Broadly, the chapter asks: How do the universal and globalizing processes of food production, preparation, and consumption nonetheless delineate specific social groups? More specifically, it will address the question: How can we understand processes by which Chinese food has become simultaneously localized and globalized in comparison to other foods and cuisines?

7.1 Chinese Cooking and Cuisines in Comparison

In recent decades, anthropologists studying many different dynamics of cultural creativity have come to the conclusion that we must move beyond narratives simply marveling at the persistence of the local under the pressures of globalizing and potentially homogenizing forces. Instead, we must analyze how, exactly, local cultural forms not only persevere but also change in negotiation with globalization. In relation to food, anthropologists have found that foods and cuisines are, in fact, often localized in self-reflexive and self-conscious ways in dialogue with globalization.

The following section will compare two very different perspectives on this process: first, the emergence of a national cuisine in the small Central American state of Belize; second, the proliferation of cookbooks for a national cuisine in the largest and most populous state on the South Asian continent, India. Both of these examples reveal how national cuisines as localized phenomena are being articulated through both regional comparison and globalizing forces. Therefore, spatial dynamics of scale emerge as important vectors cutting across both perspectives, but the historical dimension of how a cuisine, as opposed to cooking, develops over time also emerges as a central theme.

As Mintz pointed out (2002: p. 8), we all share in the definition of the human as 'the animal that cooks,' while a cuisine can be defined as a more elaborated set of techniques, skills, and ingredients that form a recognizable system of knowledge. Both the Belizean and Indian examples differ significantly from Chinese cuisine(s), where a formalized and classifiable group of Culinary Schools can be contrasted to wider ranging combinations of tastes and preferences ordering local ingredients, cooking methods and culinary prescriptions outside of this traditional canon. The chapter will later trace examples from both the formalized grand traditions of haute cuisine and compare these with other local, ethnic, and religious identifications surrounding cooking and eating. Furthermore, the argument will be explored whether these diverse culinary practices have played off each other and thereby co-constituted one another through absorbing, borrowing, and differentiating each other's characteristics.

While these Culinary Schools are broadly regionalized (e.g. Sichuan cuisine) or centered on particular municipalities (e.g. Guangzhou cuisine), they are being increasingly globalized as regionalized exports in Chinese restaurants around the world. However, there are also diverse local foods outside of this canon that are not classified as cuisine, but understated through identification as simple domestic cooking, such that a proliferation of Chinese restaurants within the country serve 'home-style dishes' (*jiachangcai*). The selection of home-style dishes may vary across the country, but include a more or less stable repertoire of favorites from around the country such that they could be claimed as local dishes in many locales. Nonetheless, certain aspects of dietary knowledge are widespread in China, such as an underlying notion of balance, based around Chinese medical knowledge stipulating a combination of heating and cooling foods and Confucian ethics advocating frugality and modesty as part of food etiquette.

7.2 National Cuisines on a Global Stage

Wilks (1999) writing on Belize and Appadurai (1988) analyzing India both avoid propagating a bounded or stable culture concept and nonetheless challenge narratives of global homogenization. Both Wilks and Appadurai trace the construction of national cuisines historically through complex self-other relations at different spatial scales ranging from the local to the global. Following this approach, one cannot separate the local or national, on the one hand, from the global, on the other, as the latter actually produces and strengthens the former in a reciprocal process (Wilks, 1999: p. 244). They treat this dialogue between "self" and "other" at different spatial scales and through historical transformation. In their understanding, there is not only an aggregating continuity from the local to the national to the global, but a continuous and mutually reinforcing process in which the local comes into view through refraction in the global mirror.

However, there are also significant differences between their models of self and other, largely due the specificities of the contexts they analyze. In India, Appadurai works with a unity-in-diversity approach in which different local cuisines are contending for prominent positions in an overarching cuisine associated with Indian national identity. Wilks' depiction of Belize differs significantly from the large nation of India (or China, for that matter) and offers insights into a national "self" that has always taken a transnational and global referent as its "other". This is largely due to Belize's historical position in complex commodity chains, where imperial hierarchies and class divisions have deeply affected local understandings of food, some of which have been transformed into assertive and celebratory self-affirmation in comparison to other national cuisines since independence. The following section will deal with each of these two approaches in turn.

Appadurai eloquently points out how cookbooks form a written genre that 'combine[s] the sturdy pragmatic virtues of all manuals with the vicarious pleasures of the literature of the senses' (p. 3). Appadurai follows Goody's observations that the development of cuisine is intimately linked to hierarchy and class, as distinctions between high and low, aristocracy and peasantry, urban center and rural periphery, frequently become amplified and reproduced through the evolution of a high cuisine (p. 4). However, unlike many other literate and agrarian civilizations where a textualization of canonical cuisines has a long-standing history, in India, the written codification of cuisine is a relatively recent phenomenon that has emerged as part of a postindustrial and postcolonial process (p. 4). Appadurai seeks to investigate not only how regional inflection and national standardization are occurring in Indian cuisine, but also why the flourishing of a cookbook market only occurred from the 1970s onwards.

According to Appadurai, the reason the Indian culinary realm was not very textualized up to this point was because historical forces 'militated against the formation of a civilizational culinary standard in India' (p. 10). Prior to the proliferation of Indian cookbooks at this time, textual sources pertaining to Indian food had been restricted to moral and medical prescriptions, despite the establishment of national print media, thereby confining food to moral and medical modes of thought (pp. 4–5, 11). In the realm of eating and cooking '[f]ood taboos and prescriptions divide men from women, gods from humans, upper and lower castes, one sect from another' (p. 10). In particular, the caste system hindered the local variations across the country from forming spatially regionalized blocks, only further reinforcing the even wider religious divergence between Hindus and Muslims (p. 12).

Appadurai argues that only with the rise of aspirational middle classes across the country did an actual demand for Indian cookbooks emerge (p. 5). The middle class segment of the population, rather than its super-elite, has driven this proliferation of largely Anglophone material. Appadurai sees the middle class interest in Indian cookbooks and cuisine as part of a seesaw of culinary desire between familiarity and exploration (pp. 5–8). Appadurai writes of the '*seductiveness of variety*' that has driven people to test the boundaries under conditions of social mobility, internal migration, and urban anonymity (p. 10). However, unlike highly policed marital and sexual boundaries, food transgressions can be increasingly enjoyed in public settings with the proliferation of diverse restaurants (pp. 9–10). Moreover, through the use of cookbooks the exotic can be brought into the very heart of the family home by the adventurous wife-as-chef. Regional inflection has gone hand in hand with national standardization as middle class housewives sought advice and guidance on delicate matters ranging from interethnic and intercaste dining to how to handle leftovers and budget constraints (pp. 6, 8).

In a sense, cookbooks belong 'to the literature of exile, nostalgia and loss' as the once familiar become systematically salvaged for the future or the novel and exotic becomes domesticated to appease discomfort or diffuse excitement (p. 18). New cookbooks always have to make editing choices that compromise local diversity, such that a balance needs to be struck about eliminating anything deemed disgusting and elements included that are considered most popular, resulting in 'the exchange of culinary images [as] the elimination of the most exotic, peculiar, distinctive, or domestic nuances in a particular specialized cuisine' (p. 17). Inequalities of representation must also be overcome to gain 'appreciation and mutual recognition' especially from the dominant metropolitan view (p. 18). For instance, cookbooks may be complimentary about ethnic or caste traits that would be criticized orally and subject to complaints. Cookbooks thereby form part of a strategy to forge a new unified India as part of nationalist and integrationist ideology (p. 20).

Appadurai addresses the apparent paradox that the proliferation of specialized cuisines indicates the emergence of unified national cuisine in the following way: regional and ethnic cookbooks are about systematizing knowledge of and about the other through their culinary traditions (p. 15). Although these 'gastro-ethnic images' may be stereotypical, they nonetheless aggregate, map, and scale national diversity on a single plane (p. 16). As Appadurai puts it, 'all cuisines, however local, reflect the aggregation upward of more humble and idiosyncratic cuisines from as far down as individual household culinary styles. Such telescoping and recategorization is also doubtlessly a slow and constant feature of history in complex societies' (p. 17).

By contrast to India's vast territory, Wilks looks at the small nation of Belize that only gained full sovereignty in 1981 to examine how Belizean food has become established as an identifiable cuisine (p. 244). He begins with a general overview on food as substance and symbol, nourishment and communication, with the potential to instantiate personal and group identity and asks: How is food able to provide a stable pillar of identity despite changing tastes? (p. 244). Wilks compares two meals to which he was invited in Belize to trace some of the major shifts in the construction of a national cuisine. At the first meal in 1973, the hosts serve prestigious imported foods to their foreign guest. At the second meal in 1990, the hosts emphasize how they are providing Wilks with an authentic taste of Belize (pp. 245–248). By serving a Belizean meal comparable to other world cuisines offered on the global stage, this new generation of Belizeans asserts their categorical equality in power and knowledge to global norms of modernity and sophistication (p. 248). Wilks even proposes approaching these performances through the prism of drama, rather than culture, in which both national "self" and transnational or global "other" are staged (p. 248).

How, exactly, did the transnational become the "other" in Belize? To answer this question, Wilks turns to the history of Belize's position enmeshed in global commodity markets (p. 248). As a logging colony exporting local mahogany in the 19th century, Belize did not establish a substantial agricultural base (p. 249). Although rural subsistence farmers existed throughout the country, the wood cutters and middle-class urbanites shunned local and wild foods in favor of a colonial taste for imports, particularly flour and meat. Only with the increasing self-government from the 1960s onwards did Belize begin to establish food self-sufficiency, and with it pride in local cuisine gradually grew (p. 250). High profile events, such as the British media representation of Queen Elizabeth eating a "royal rat," while actually enjoying a gibnut, a prized specimen of local game, ignited indignation and resistance among Belizeans.

In addition to the wider availability of local foods, Wilks argues that colonial gatekeepers of taste were slowly undermined by flows of people, goods, and information that gradually broke up their monopoly of knowledge about the transnational other (pp. 252–253). Wilks explicitly frames his findings in contrast to Appadurai, pointing to the differences between the schemes of self and other they found in their respective research. In Belize, the externalized other is the transnational context, not the national unity-in-diversity that Appadurai describes for India where contrasts between regionalized others constitute the key ingredients to 'the superordinate national mélange' (p. 246). Of course, another major difference is how they approach the topic of a national cuisine, with Wilks drawing on more conventional ethnographic and historical approaches to the constitution of a discernable cuisine, while Appadurai turns towards the written construction of regional and national cuisines that explicitly contribute to creating an established culinary canon.

In order to determine how far Appadurai's and Wilk's approaches to the construction of national cuisines illuminate the terrain of Chinese food, the following section turns to the question of how one can actually define a "cuisine" and whether the term can be applied to Chinese contexts at local, national, or global scales.

7.3 Chinese Food as World Cuisine

Mintz's (1986) monumental contribution both to the anthropology of food and to global history took the form of an in-depth study of a single commodity, sugar, in a book entitled *Sweetness and Power*. In this work, Mintz portrayed a detailed and yet far-reaching picture of how sugar production and consumption deeply altered global labor relations by fuelling triangular processes occurring between the African slave trade, colonial plantations, and industrial factories. In the article examined here, Mintz (2009) explores Asia's contribution to what he calls "world cuisine" and traces a number of fascinating commodity chains across the globe. Mintz succinctly defines "world cuisine" not as a static object or stable system, but as a process that is 'now nearly continuous and ongoing, but it is also surprisingly ancient. World food history has involved the gradual but uneven spread of plants and animals, foods and food ingredients, cooking methods and traditions, over larger and larger areas, often penetrating and sometimes blending with local food systems, which vary in their openness — and the effects of that spread' (p. 1).

Mintz admits that this rendering of "world cuisine" may be uncomfortably close to outdated diffusionist paradigms for many anthropologists, but maintains that this approach captures how cultural materials, such as food ingredients, cooking methods, and their resulting palatable dishes have been circulated and spread across the globe through various flows of people and things. Mintz cites the most famous example of the Columbian exchange between the Old and New World, named after Christopher Columbus' unexpected arrival in the Americas on his voyage from Europe in search of a sea route to Asia. Bringing together culinary and botanical history with the twists of trade, not only did the European craving for Asian spices fan the sails of those early armadas, but later colonials like Benjamin Franklin also marveled at Asian techniques of food processing, such as the art of making tofu.

Following his signature approach of tracing commodities driving world history, Mintz takes up interesting examples of foods that have fanned out from Asia across the globe, such as soy, ginger, monosodium glutamate, rice, and tea. In the opposite direction, maize, capsicums, and peanuts were all relatively recently introduced to Asia with the Columbian exchange, although they now make up standard fare in many parts of the continent. However, there has also been a shift in the drivers of these translocal processes from earlier adventurous farmers towards contemporary enthusiastic chefs, aggressive restauranteurs and expansionist corporations. There are also long-term trends that dominate on a global scale, such as the shift from complex to simple carbohydrates, as cereal becomes increasingly refined and tubers lose their central role in diets. Middle class lust for animal protein is currently being met in ecologically devastating ways as soy becomes a key animal feed and pastures expand across the globe. Mintz also provides examples of how cultural appropriation, from the Sushi California Roll to Beef Chow Mein and Cajun Chicken all entail simultaneous indigenization and transformation, such that '[w]hen this happens, the borrowed element is no longer what it once was — even if it is or seems to be identical. More commonly, modification, simplification and reintegration typify food history, as they do in so much cultural borrowing, and tell us about culture's absorptive power' (p. 5). Mintz also points out that war and famine, as much as raising productivity and improving standards of living, may entail 'a heavy toll upon cultural locality and distinctiveness' (p. 5). On a lighter note, he also reminds us that 'imitation is supposed to be the sincerest form of flattery' (p. 6).

Notably, Mintz engages with global standardization argument from the perspective of gradual processual change, on the one hand, and radical historical rupture, on the other, that lead him towards two opposite but tentative conclusions:

1. 'That there is a continuous, creative culinary process by which the new or unusual is embedded effectively in the everyday, usually by the replacement or intensification of a customary or familiar item with a new and different one, seems absolutely true. I do not think that this kind of change has abetted standardization, at least not yet' (p. 5).
2. There are undeniably radical social and economic changes occurring that affect world cuisine, such as 'large-scale economic changes that move masses of people around, shift the rural–urban balance, or create big migrant labor forces. These changes may not have to do with food itself, but with the conditions for its production, the circumstances under which people eat, and the place of domestic groups in reproducing the eating habits of the previous generation. It should be clear that what I am enumerating does describe much of what has been happening in China, for example, in the last two decades. If by "cuisine" one means the haute cuisine (or grande cuisine) of the ruling stratum, that will probably survive nearly all of these large changes. But if one means the way that most people eat (or "most ordinary" people eat, in the American paraphrase), then the possibility of radical change and eventual standardization of some food habits on a global basis certainly exists' (p. 5).

In his preface to Wu and Cheung's collected volume on *The Globalization of Chinese Food*, Mintz (2002: p. 7) also emphasizes that the history of eating is 'tied to environment, ecology, technical achievement and evolving cultural forms.' Specifically in relation to Chinese food, he nonetheless succinctly pulls together some common themes, such as polarities of 'yin/yang, fan/ts'ai, hot/cold, wet/dry and clean/poisonous polarities' (p. 16). However, two major changes affecting Chinese, and Asian food more generally, are the 'cumulative consequence of growing affluence, a rising interest in novelty, and more sophistication and daring among consumers. They cook less, they eat out more; and they are willing to try more new things' as well as a parallel 'growth of healthy eating outlooks' (p. 18).

In their introduction, Wu and Cheung (2002) go even further than Mintz's analysis of cultural appropriation to argue that Chinese food ways have long been forged along intrinsically multicultural paths, both within and outside of China. On the fringes of Chinese territories, the global implications of its food flows have ancient precedents, such as the Indonesian spice trade in the 5th century (pp. 2–3). Historically, as much as today, Chinese food could never be discerned as a single or unified national entity (p. 4). Instead, Chinese food is composed of many regional and local cuisines that are not just subject to geographical differentiation but also to social stratification (p. 4). Foreign and exotic food items were often particularly high status elements of cultivated refinement in local cuisines, a phenomenon that is particularly well developed in Cantonese cuisine (p. 9). Moreover, the globalization of food pathways and the migration of the Chinese population across the world cannot be separated. Following Wu and Cheung, the reach of Chinese food necessitates attention to the interplay between the familiar and the exotic, the domestic and the commercial, both at home and abroad, to trace interactions with local and global forces.

7.4 The Generation Gap at the Table

Without attempting to conjure up a static image of 'traditional knowledge' about food and eating, Guo (2000) chapter provides insights into the effects of historical experience on generational knowledge formation among three cohorts of Chinese citizens. Her article thereby offers a succinct social history of eating in the PRC and how food relates to social, economic and family changes and knowledge construction. Through food knowledge conceptualizing self, group, and nation are literally ingested by three generations along dominant paradigms that shaped national history (p. 94).

Guo terms both the knowledge base and food outlook that various generations have acquired as their 'dietetic knowledge', specifically defining this as 'basic ideas that shape people's dietary desires and their explanations for their eating habits' (p. 95). Guo points out that age is a major variable factor in determining the Chinese citizens' dietetic knowledge and joins other common sociological factors such as gender, status, education, etc. Her sample also notably includes both urban Beijingers and rural villagers from Jiangsu province, thereby straddling the rural-urban divide in experiences and knowledge. Guo ascribes the three generations in her study with three basic knowledge outlooks, labeled "traditional," "scientific," and "commercial." Each generation has acquired their particular form of dietetic knowledge from its wider social field, and surprisingly the particular personal and social experiences are not always passed on along generational lines as one might expect.

The eldest, grandparental generation, was born before 1949 and their notion of "traditional" dietetic knowledge relies on popular ideas loosely derived from Traditional Chinese Medicine, such as the guiding role of "balance" in choosing what, when, and how to eat. Grandparents consider the twin potencies of yin and yang and their associated forces of "cold and heat, night and day, female and male, negative and positive, preserver and stimulator" in regulating the natural order in making food decisions (p. 98). Parents born during Maoism derive their nutritional concepts form modern science and biomedicine in line with a "scientific" dietetic knowledge. A modernist stance characterizes their emphasis on vitamins and nutritional supplements as akin to medicine. Furthermore, concerns about food safety and hygiene are paramount as the food pathways they must rely upon are often beyond personal surveillance and monitoring. Guo characterizes young, school-age children as engulfed in a lust for consumption, drawing on a growing repertoire of "commercial" dietetic knowledge. Children's relationship to food is highly market-oriented and consumerist as they develop a keen awareness and responsive opinion on available food products, their associated values, and changing trends from advertisements and peers.

Guo's findings challenge common assumptions about the intergenerational transmission of experiential knowledge, in general, and dietetic knowledge, in particular. Overall, the discontinuity in the dietetic knowledge each generation possesses shows how radical disjuncture in experience and orientation can occur at a rapid pace. However, more specifically, dietetic knowledge is not necessarily cumulative down a generational chain of transmission, as dietetic knowledge is not always passed on to younger generations. In a related point, knowledge acquired by younger generations may or may not be passed to more senior family members. Guo provides a number of examples that illustrate these points.

First, family celebrations reveal deep schisms of value between generations and their connections to food. For instance, in relation to traditional festival foods there is a generational stratification of religious significance and efficacy (p. 105). Not only do grandparents value the consumption of the appropriate foods at festivals above all other family members, but they are also more knowledgeable about the meaning and effect of eating particular foods at particular moments in the annual cycle (p. 105). This contrasts rather starkly to the inverse distribution of knowledge related to children's birthday parties. A relatively new phenomenon across most of China, these festivities form increasingly important events in children's emotional lives with their families and peers. Children experience conspicuous consumption lavished upon them as a demonstration of parental love, meaning that they have high stakes in securing family provision of the newest and most desirable food products at their birthday parties (p. 104).

Second, the intergenerational transmission of experience may also be disrupted by the vast shift in values underlying the various forms of dietetic knowledge. Stories relating to the catastrophic famine that occurred between 1958 and 1961 are often not shared with children for various reasons (p. 107). Some of the experiences are simply too horrifying to relay to children, while others are told and yet fail to be factually credible or emotionally comprehensible to those born and raised in the Reform Era. Children do not so much fear famine, or the quantity of food that their family has access to, but loss of face at the quality and types of food that their family consumes. Children's sizeable knowledge about food products and practices, especially 'names, tastes, appearances, or prices of new foods and drinks' allow them to assume 'the role of culinary instructors by offering specific information to influence their elders' purchasing and dining decisions' (p. 103).

Guo points out that the role of food in moral education appears to be diminishing, and at times Guo herself seems tempted to admonish and discipline the children she describes (p. 106). However, these changes in dietetic knowledge also reveal schisms of value that have been forged by the experiential circumstances of each generation. Habits formed around visions of the good life cannot be divorced from the historical ruptures that occurred as the eldest generation came of age in a time of food insecurity punctuated by actual hunger and starvation, while the middle generation would have acute memories of food rationing and an ingrained disposition towards frugality and health as key values guiding good eating (pp. 111–112). By contrast, children of the Market Era experience indulgence in complex material and emotional ways that make consumption part of self-fulfillment in relation to others (p. 112). While this could be purely related to political, economic, and social upheavals, these children may change values as they come of age and take more responsibilities for their health and families.

The main contribution Guo's article in relation to our general exploration is to raise a challenge to the assumption that "insiders" of any unit of scale in relation to Chinese food share a homogeneous system of knowledge or values regarding food. Not only regional or historical variations appear pertinent to the differing understandings of Chinese food, but even within individual families we may find significant stratification of food values, for instance across generational cleavages. Continuing this exploration of the boundaries between "inside" and "outside" in relation to Chinese food, we now turn from the intimate setting of the family meal to the public presentation of restaurant cuisine.

7.5 Inside and Outside Culinary Principles

Can we take cuisine, in Mintz's sense of a systematized set of techniques, skills, and ingredients forming a coherent set of food knowledge, and apply this to a regionalized perspective in one of China's great Culinary Schools, Cantonese cuisine? Regionalized thinking about Chinese food is so common that one saying even spatializes the country into flavors according to cardinal directions, such that 'the east is sweet, the south is salty, the west is sour, and the north is spicy' (*dong tian, nan xian, xi suan, bei la*). A common piece of archaeological history that persists in contemporary common knowledge is that the Yangze River is the great divider for the country's cultivation and consumption of staples, with the north relying on grain and the south on rice. Of course, this division is no longer (if ever) a strict delineation of Chinese diets. With such a long history of mixing and melting, but also separating and defining, what exactly is a Chinese cuisine? Following Mintz, it is most conducive to take a processual approach rather than a static system as the point of departure to explore this question.

Turning to a historical account of restaurants and eating out, Klein (2007) offers insights into how transformations in the 20th century have affected Cantonese cuisine, as restaurant chefs and managers seek to negotiate subtle balancing acts between offering the familiar and the exotic in the commercial realm of public dining. Historically, diverse cuisines have frequently centered on particular cities, such that Cantonese cuisine, from Canton, is centered on Guangzhou, but the term has expanded to encompass the cuisine of the whole province of Guandong and even sometimes includes the entire Pearl River Delta and Hong Kong. This leads to some dispute about the center of gravity and scope of encompassment of the designation of Cantonese cuisine (p. 527). The contemporary analysis of culinary systems (*caixi*) builds on these historical spatial differentiations, often defining four or eight schools of cuisine by region. The long-term integration of outside foods have frequently become inside cornerstones over time, but the exotic also often holds the potency and potential to be particularly efficacious and desirable, a process particularly apparent in Cantonese culinary principles. To investigate the adventurous search for new flavors and the expansions of tastes and preferences Klein offers insights into a gastronomical institution specializing in Cantonese cuisine.

Klein argues that one of the great culinary traditions, Guangzhou cuisine, partially defines itself at the core by integrating "outside" tastes, ingredients, and methods. Subsuming the outside on the basis of longstanding culinary principles, Cantonese cuisine manages to both incorporate the exotic and stress continuity. Chefs nonetheless deny this transformation at the core, instead positing tropes of unchanging essence and timeless principles that are conveniently vague, such as freshness and seasonality. Interestingly, Maoist massification campaigns sought to bring the elite pleasures of Cantonese cuisine to the masses and provide ordinary workers with culinary delights they had previously been denied, rare ingredients had to be substituted with common ones to make foods more affordable. In the Reform Era, struggling restaurants such as Glorious China where Klein conducted fieldwork employ the same methods to keep prices low and offer familiar flavors.

Today, chefs also study Hong Kong cook books, menus, and culinary shows to bring the most recent innovations to their diners. By expanding facilities and introducing new dishes, diners can be wooed into local restaurants despite the competition form more spacious establishments outside the city. However, considerations of social hierarchy and cultural identity are at play in what elements become appropriated and represented in local cuisine, such that the spiciness of northern Guangdong Chaozhou cooking is more attractive than similar tastes emanating from Sichuan Province in China's interior due to its association with regional "backwardness". By contrast, Hong Kong style Cantonese cuisine enjoys great popularity due to its association with a global cosmopolitan sense of taste and style. Thereby, regional hierarchies and social distinctions are blended with the ingredients, flavors, and textures of culinary consumption of the other.

7.6 Localism from Cooking to Cuisine

Far from the glitz and glam of the coastal region, Goodman (2006) examines the deliberate political construction of provincial identity on the Loess Plateau of China. Shanxi Province is generally associated with its revolutionary Maoist legacy and state-supported coal industry in popular perception. The provincial government has therefore sought to transform its image through promoting a new Shanxi identity as part of a self-reflexive translocal political and cultural imaginary. Part of this strategy to encourage development was to awaken local feelings and strengthen local commitments among Shanxi entrepreneurs and managers, thereby motivating them to bolster economic activity in their home province (p. 57). As Goodman points out, this strategy constitutes a complete turn-around from the Maoist skepticism towards localism, when these regional attachments were deemed harmful to the national project by fracturing the unified path towards flourishing socialism.

Goodman's main example for this top–down construction of localism is the fostering of a provincial cuisine in Shanxi, where a humble combination of noodles and vinegar gained prominence throughout the 1990s as the backbone of a culinary unity. Shanxi food had previously not been part of a recognized cuisine. Instead, these vernacular foods, such as Shanxi noodles and breads, were associated with particular prefectures, counties, and even townships. The provincial government therefore self-consciously scaled up the identification with these foods to create a unity within a new state-fostered unit of provincial localism. Goodman also alludes to similar processes occurring in relation to theater, music, literature, and other folk traditions (p. 63).

Much of Goodman's material is drawn from his wider social and demographic data focused on the middle class and its perception on place and culture, particularly the multivalent understanding of home. For Shanxi residents the notion of home forms a complex set of interrelations cross-cutting location and kin, including birthplace, native or ancestral home, parental home, and family residence (pp. 58–59). When asked to nominate three typical local foods, respondents overwhelmingly focused on noodles (76%), noodle dishes (47%), and steamed breads (37%) (p. 66). Interestingly, highly localized food items, such as Pingyao Beef, Taigu Cakes, and Qingxu grapes, were not nominated as typical foods of Shanxi as a whole (p. 67). When prompted to differentiate Shanxi food from food typical elsewhere in China, the closest comparable other, residents often noted seafood (72%) as one of the most exotic elements for those residing in one of China's driest inland provinces, and rice (69%), the staple commonly associated with China by outsiders and yet historically more prevalent South of the Yangzi River (pp. 65–66). Goodman traces how the conception of "the local" has changed from Maoism to the Reform Era, as the party state deemed this discourse increasingly acceptable, even commendable, as a form of identification (p. 69). However, by scaling up from villages, townships, and municipalities, the provincial government has created a translocal imaginary in Shanxi that does not rely on migration or movement (p. 69).

The implication of this process for regional and provincial cuisine is that a cuisine need not necessarily develop spontaneously or organically over time. In the case of Shanxi noodles and breads the government's top–down political intervention into a process of scaling up from the local was successful in consciously and deliberately constructing a provincial cuisine. This differs significantly from the bottom–up aggregation and encompassment in ever larger units of inclusion suggested by both Wilks' and Appadurai's analyses. Goodman's material also challenges theories positing that migration is necessary for a conception of translocality. By contrast, in Shanxi 'strong local identities are being shaped by networks linked to other places' (p. 71), such that perception of place does arise through a contrast with other places, but this understanding is determined by what is imagined rather than experienced elsewhere. Goodman thereby makes a strong case that there is not a center-periphery notion of locality operating here, but very much a multimodal translocal network spread across the Province. While the Shanxi case reveals a conscious construction of cuisine through political authority from above, the following example of fast food chains in Hong Kong shows that economic drivers, particularly global corporations, can equally initiate massive transformations on conceptions of food in a locale marked by translocalism.

7.7 Consumer Culture and Corporate Food

With *Golden Arches East*, Watson (1997) conducted an exciting experiment in the anthropology of food that very explicitly engages with globalization and homogenization debates. The edited collection focuses on how a single global corporation, McDonald's, introduced its cuisine to East Asia through a series of ethnographic encounters. McDonald's acts as a commercial vehicle for novel ingredients, tastes, cooking methods, and food pathways, but simultaneously imports corporate spaces that conform to its overarching corporate logic, which are in turn subject to appropriation and localization in different ways across the region.

Analyzing McDonald's therefore throws light on both the dynamics Sidney Mintz discussed in relation to the global standardization: first, how do outside, exotic, or foreign culinary processes become embedded in the mundane food processes of locally lived experiences? Note that this is where Mintz argued that cultural creativity seems to be winning out against global sameness. Second, and most explicitly addressed in Watson's collection than any other here is the far-reaching transformation to world cuisine propelled by social and economic changes at a global scale. In this regard, Mintz highlighted unprecedented global processes like mass migration and urbanization affecting labor forces and their livelihoods. These changes do not just affect how and what food is produced, but circumstances and choices for consumption. Mintz (2009: p. 5) also drew attention to how such processes may leave the haute cuisine untouched, but in terms of 'the way that most people eat [...] the possibility of radical change and eventual standardization of some food habits on a global basis certainly exists.'

In his introduction to *Golden Arches East*, Watson offers a general overview to McDonald's in Asia. His substantive article focuses specifically on Hong Kong and how McDonald's imported a new corporate set of foods and associated practices that have become appropriated and modified in a local context. McDonald's commercial strategies are not just restricted to the production and sale of new commodities, but a whole corporate process that leads from lofty headquarters down to the humble dining tray. Not just managers and servers, but diners enter implicit contracts regarding efficient behavior and skilled conduct. Standardized menus, sanitation facilities, food hygiene, as well as surveillance and safety of the premises raise a high bar on the fast food scene. Thereby, McDonald's promotes a uniform corporate product all over the world that consumers can rely upon to provide approximately the same services and comforts that they are familiar with from back home, whether that be in Hong Kong, São Paolo or Detroit.

Beyond selling a globally standardized experience, Watson argues that the rise of McDonald's in Hong Kong occurred in parallel with the rise, or even creation, of a new consumer. Generational change again appears as a dominant force in this narrative of social change. However, here the argument relates to the shift from an earlier cohort of first generation refugees to Hong Kong who lived for the moment, and how their central role has now given way to the economic dominance of their children. Now adult, this second generation is making a life and a home in Hong Kong. Watson sketches how this generational change parallels shifts in domestic power balance as this generation came of age with their own income and spending power, and further increased youth spending through the provision of pocket money to children. School-age children even use McDonald's as an alternative to overcrowded homes and disciplinary schools. McDonald's provides these youngest consumers with additional spaces to socialize and study. However, intergenerational distress often arises in relation to where and what to eat, both snacks and meals, as grandparents view McDonald's as a children's restaurant. Children do, in fact, view McDonald's as the prime venue for hosting birthday parties, and the franchise is partially credited with popularizing the birthday party in Hong Kong.

Watson also engages with the question of how this transition from a place associated with the distinctive, exotic, and foreign valued by 'self-conscious status seekers' has been transformed to a locale where 'busy, pre-occupied consumers' come to enjoy competitively priced meals in a familiar and everyday setting (p. 87). Despite building on local practices of snacking and drinking in teahouses, McDonald's very consciously provided an alternative rather than competitor to Chinese-style cuisine (p. 82). The managing director of McDonald's in Hong Kong strongly felt that serving uncompromisingly authentic American food would win a new consumer base, and even let this policy flow into McDonald's naming decisions when the first restaurant opened there in 1975. Initially, McDonald's in Hong Kong did not translate its name at all but only displayed it in English along with the golden arches, only later transliterating the sounds for McDonald's into Chinese characters, while retaining a distinctive foreign flair (pp. 82–83).

The generational differences in how residents relate to McDonald's has to do with the political and economic history of Hong Kong and its position *vis-à-vis* the People's Republic overall. Refugees who came to Hong Kong saw the area as a site of struggle and temporary making-do, whereas the next generation viewed themselves with a stability and self-confidence as residents Hong Kong. These new "natives" held stakes in the local community as a familiar place, and their aspirations built on visions of the good life in a cosmopolitan city. Furthermore, McDonald's formed part of a web of corporations, banks, and investors that secured Hong Kong's position in global capitalism. Contrary to the critical stance towards McDonald's environmental, health and ethical track record abroad, in Hong Kong McDonald's forms part of a positive image of capitalist forces securing political viability and local livelihood.

McDonald's corporate strategies reveal a particularly acute manifestation of more general shifts in the world economy. For instance, the spatial and temporal division of labor that happens in order to bring a Happy Meal to the table is part of a breakdown of any clear division between production and consumption in the commodity chain. Not only does McDonald's deskill or fracture the production process, but it also blurs the lines between manufacturing and service economy labor within its outlets, not least as skilled consumers pick up the labor cost through self-discipline that includes consuming meals quickly and cleaning their dining spaces. Moreover, consumers are vital to marketing through their creative engagement with the brand, and their experience and presence in a given restaurant means that consumers are the producers of the ambience, a big part of what McDonald's is selling.

There are also aspects of McDonald's that have been transformed for and by Hong Kong, for instance with the cultural expectations of service molded to admirable local etiquette. Rather than serving food "with a smile" as this would be considered 'an excess of congeniality, solicitude, or familiarity' employees in Hong Kong exhibit qualities of 'competence, directness, and unflappability.' (pp. 90–91). Furthermore, despite attempts to discipline customers in the ways of the fast food chain, customers continue to "hover" in anticipating tables and insist on amassing large provisions of napkins (pp. 94–95). After initial friction, it seems the franchise now accommodates these local particularities.

Both of Mintz's claims about globalization seem to be vindicated by Watson's astute research on McDonald's in Hong Kong where global standardization and context-specific localization go hand-in-hand. One could even argue that Hong Kong's ambiguous role as a Chinese beacon of capitalism created a betwixt-and-between position enabling it to switch insider and outsider status in relation to both the People's Republic and global capitalism, making McDonald's a particularly attractive franchise from both the local and global perspective. In contrast to this form of inside and outside in terms of political and economic systems, the following example turns to the ambiguous status of a Hui Muslim community as an ethnic and religious "internal other" within a dominant Han ethnicity city.

7.8 Faith, Food, and Identity

The Muslim district in Xi'an, the capital of Shaanxi Province, is the residential and commercial center for a community of about 30,000 predominantly Hui ethnic minority citizens (Gillette, 2000: pp. 74–75). None of the four Stalinist criteria for a nationality, defined by a common territory, language, economy, and psychology, actually applies to the large number of people officially classified as Hui who live scattered across China. Arguably, the Hui ethnic designation provides an almost residual category for people across China who share a Muslim heritage and observe Islam, but are often integrated with Han and other ethnic Chinese communities (pp. 74–75). For the Muslim community in Xi'an a core element of their collective identity is eating *qingzhen* food. Maris Boyd Gillette's (2000) research on food choices in the 1990s among Xi'an Hui community reveals how food can create, mark or reinforce ethnic and religious boundaries, but also transcend, bridge, and overturn notions of otherness.

This category of *qingzhen* literally translates to 'pure and true.' Like the term *halal* in Arabic, *qingzhen* can refer to any object or action considered permissible under Islamic law for a Muslim. In relation to food, the term *qingzhen* classifies food that meets the Islamic standards for dietary purity (p. 72). The most important criteria for *qingzhen* dietary purity is the abstinence from consuming pork, but Xi'an Muslims also include other important practices in food preparation (pp. 75–77). For instance, they avoid pollution of food through contact with pork products, including from utensils that may have previously touched pork; the segregation of different types of food in preparation and cooking; and performing a major cleansing ablution before cooking. Effectively, these *qingzhen* criteria amount to an avoidance of any food cooked by non-Muslims. Therefore, Gillette was taken aback when she observed a devout Muslim woman buying her granddaughter snacks that were not labeled *qingzhen*.

Gillette traces the variables that make certain snacks acceptable for Hui consumption despite no explicit *qingzhen* seal of approval. Factory-produced, hermetically-sealed, Western-style snacks are locally reconciled with a *qingzhen* lifestyle. These snacks fall into their own third category, beyond the dualism of *qingzhen* and forbidden, an ambiguous realm unmarked by explicit rules and sanctions. Foods made by Hui Muslims are effectively treated as *qingzhen* by definition, while those made by Han ethnic majority citizens are considered suspect (p. 80). However, industrial processed foods occupy an exceptional and permissible position if three criteria are fulfilled (pp. 80–87). First, the product must be perceived to be Western, i.e. originally developed in Europe and USA, even if the actual manufacturer is in Asia; second, the product must contain absolutely no pork, to the point that recognizably Chinese factory food, such as packaged mung bean cakes are excluded due to the potential use of lard; third, they must be produced with industrial techniques, rather than relying on extensive hand use, like local noodles, buns, dumplings, and flatbread.

In sum, foods produced in factories by machines, which are subsequently sealed, packed, and globally distributed are viewed as sanitized, scientific, and progressive. The unseen production techniques, exotic ingredients, foreign flavors and varied textures, represent and reinforce a local conception of the West, strongly associated with wealth, technology, modernity (p. 88). The Hui sense of self seems to play off two counterparts considered "other." The primary category of differentiation occurs with their Han Chinese neighbors, who live alongside the Hui and therefore mirror their dualistic classification into *qingzhen* and taboo forms of everyday life. This contrasts with the third category of foreign, exotic, and Western life beyond the PRC. By creating a permissible third realm, a space opens up for Hui people to fulfill ambitions to be good Muslims and good (global and national) citizens.

How do adult aspirations for their children to be good Muslims and good citizens come together through the consumption of foreign snacks? There seem to be a number ways that the snacks condense values of religion, technology, cosmopolitanism, and aspiration. Although this runs contrary to the Western secularization thesis that posits the advance of modernity is associated with the demise of religion in the name of science, Xi'an Muslims describe the Qur'an as 'extremely scientific' (pp. 88–89). Therefore, a scientific outlook and practice closely resonates with a Muslim worldview. Furthermore, adults want to offer their children with the experiences needed 'to live in an industrialized, technologically advanced, cosmopolitan world' (p. 89). Adults often find these Western foods quite unappetizing, but they provide them to children in the hope that the next generation will acquire a taste for them (p. 82). Gillette's findings therefore offer a wider application of Bourdieu's theory about the inculcation of social distinction through food, as Hui adults are not just passing on their own preferences, but actively awakening and inculcating aspirational tastes in their children (p. 89).

Social differentiation between self and other among the Hui is predictably asserted against their most proximate other, their Han neighbors, in a slippage that almost equates *qingzhen* with non-Han. Hui citizens may consider eating pure and clean food more "civilized" than the official state discourse of civilization imposed upon them. Civilizational centers can pull in more directions than Beijing and the Hajj pilgrimage to Mecca also forges a path towards globalization.

Food and faith often intermingle to create exclusion in the form of taboos, but they can also reinforce shared belonging through commensality. Although boundaries between the Hui self and the Han other are usually maintained in conventional *qingzhen* practices, by eating the foods of distant foreign "others" with neighboring Han as local "others" new possibilities for a shared sense of identity emerge. The foreign-style factory foods may provide a common basis for eating between Han and Hui children, another hope that adults may hold for their future. When turning from local to global others, these neutral foods provide a shared aspirational framework of technology, science, and modernity across the world. Thereby, global modernity can be consumed together in one's own home.

7.9 Eating Modernity and Consuming Exoticism

Throughout Chinese history, food consumption has been understood in a variety of ways that were not necessarily always focused on culinary appreciation or haute cuisine, although the joys of eating certainly came to the fore in the past as much as the present. In China, there is also a canon of literature on food and eating that focused on moral and medical principles, with analogies between the proper functioning of the body and sound systems of governance never far behind. Complementing bodily forces of *yin* and *yang* meant ingesting appropriate foods at the right time and in suitable quantities with the associated etiquette. Even following the most basic structural principles of combining staples with vegetables was part of maintaining proper balance and bodily integrity and went hand-in-hand with displays of frugality and skills of resourcefulness. However, the question of where to draw boundaries around a distinctly Chinese notion of food, sketching divisions internally through various cuisines, delineating Chinese foods from "outside" foods and tracing their co-constitution with globalizing forces emerge as a complex, possibly impossible, task.

In this chapter, we explored the examples of India and Belize to investigate the creation of cuisines through a dialogue between self and other. Neither the unity-in-diversity approach to Indian cookbooks, nor the local self and global other drama played out in Belize, provides an overarching framework for Chinese food and eating. Nonetheless, the interplay between self and other both texts employ translates into the Chinese realm where we cannot just speak of a survival of the local, but its production in dialogue with globalizing forces. Here Sidney Mintz's separation between cooking and eating as a set of practices, and its more systematic formalization as a recognizable cuisine becomes key. One might ask whether the self-consciousness needed to reflect on techniques, skills, ingredients associated with food as a system of knowledge only emerges through comparison at various scales, whether this be the family, the region, or the nation.

If scale becomes a central yardstick in measuring the limits of culinary principles, the intergenerational transmission of dietetic knowledge shows that even the family may shore up massive fissures across different age cohorts. The importance of a constitutive outside in defining the inner characteristics of a cuisine emerged in Cantonese restaurants where the integration of exotic elements as particularly desirable and potent actually formed a hallmark of its evolving culinary canon. In contrast to this established culinary system, the rising coherence of a Shanxi culinary unity consisting of a medley of noodles and breads reveals that top–down political integration can also foster a cuisine. This multinodal form of a translocal imaginary also resonates with Hong Kong, where openness towards global capitalism forms part of a local identity. The success of McDonald's in changing from an exotic corporate import to a familiar and everyday meal option reveals how far globalization is a local phenomenon. Furthermore, for Hui Muslims in Xi'an religious and ethnic identities may crystallize in both opposition and aspiration with culinary others at the local and global level. Overall, tracing Chinese food consumption links global and local processes in intricate and unpredictable ways. Chinese examples thereby join those offered in Sidney Mintz's classical anthropological work on food, showing that there is two-way traffic between eating modernity, consuming the exotic, and sharing the familiar both at home and abroad.

Seminar Questions

How does the consumption of Chinese food contribute to the formation of localized and globalized identities?

How has modernity reconfigured intergenerational knowledge, values, and practices at the table?

Can we speak of 'communities of consumption' in relation to Chinese cuisine?

Readings

Appadurai, Arjun (1988). 'How to make a national cuisine: cookbooks in contemporary India', *Comparative studies in society and history*, 30(01), pp. 3–24.

Gillette, Maris Boyd (2000). 'Children's Food and Islamic Dietary Restrictions in Xi'an', in Jing, Jun (ed.) *Feeding China's Little Emperors: Food, Children, and Social Change.* Stanford University Press: Stanford, pp. 71–93.

Goodman, David (2006). 'Shanxi as Translocal Imaginary: Reforming the Local', in Oakes, Tim and Schein, Louisa (eds.) *Translocal China: Linkages, Identities and the Reimagining of Space.* Routledge: London, pp. 56–73.

Guo Yuhua (2000). 'Food and Family Relations: The Generation Gap at the Table', in Jing, Jun (ed.) *Feeding China's Little Emperors: Food, Children, and Social Change.* Stanford University Press: Stanford, pp. 94–103.

Klein, Jakob (2007). 'Redefining Cantonese Cuisine in post-Mao Guangzhou', in *Bulletin of SOAS*, pp. 511–537.

Mintz, Sidney (2009). 'Asia's Contributions to World Cuisine', *The Asia-Pacific Journal*, 18, pp. 1–6.

Mintz (2002). 'Foreword: Food for Thought', in Wu, David and Cheung, Sidney (eds.) *The Globalization of Chinese Food and Cuisine.* Curzon Press: Richmond, pp. 12–20.

Watson, James (1997). 'McDonald's in Hong Kong: Consumerism, Dietary Change, and the Rise of a Children's Culture', in Watson, James (ed.) *Golden Arches East: McDonald's in East Asia*. Stanford University Press: Stanford, pp. 77–109.

Wilk, Richard (1999). '"Real Belizean Food": Building Local Identity in the Transnational Caribbean', *American Anthropologist*, 101(2), pp. 244–255.

Wu, David and Cheung, Sidney (2002). 'Introduction: The Globalization of Chinese Food and Cuisine: Makers and Breakers of Cultural Barriers', in Wu, David and Cheung, Sidney (eds.) *The Globalization of Chinese Food and Cuisine*. Curzon Press: Richmond, pp. 1–18.

References

Douglas, Mary (1972). 'Deciphering a Meal', in *Daedalus*, 101(1), pp. 61–81.

Douglas, Mary (1966). *Purity and Danger: An analysis of the conceptions of pollution and taboo*, Routledge: London.

Harris, Marvin (1998). *Good to Eat: Riddles of Food and Culture* Illinois: Waveland Press; originally published (1985). *The Sacred Cow and the Abominable Pig*, Simon & Schuster: New York.

Mintz, Sidney (1986). *Sweetness and Power: The place of sugar in modern history*. Penguin Books: New York.

Chapter 8

Nature, Environment, and Activism

Comparing the diversity of engagement between humans and their environments around the world challenges assumptions about a universal dualism between nature and culture. This echoes some of the anthropological debates we encountered in previous chapters, including critiques of classical anthropological assumptions of a universal biology and a stabilizing nature underlying a diversity of socially differentiated kinship systems. It similarly mirrors theoretical debates in the anthropology of food that polarized materialist approaches and structuralist or symbolic analyses of how particular culinary practices emerged that cannot readily be reduced to strategies of survival, on the one hand, nor abstract systems of cognition or meaning, on the other. In this chapter, we will examine related discussions emerging within the terrain of anthropology of the environment, analyzing a foundational text in this debate, as well as how Chinese conceptions of the environment have become intertwined with notions of social justice and political activism in recent years.

Particularly, as the human impact on the earth's ecosystems becomes increasingly apparent and unsettling, anthropologists have turned to examining links between economic activity and ecological degradation around the world, including everything from greenhouse gas emissions to rising sea levels, and from soil erosion to river pollution. As global climate change brings humans to the boundary parameters of survival as a species, scientists, politicians and citizens around the world have also been raising questions of historic responsibility and the limits of economic expansion and globalization (Chakrabarty, 2009).

Routine and acute experiences of environmental degradation form common experiences for humans, wildlife, and the wider global ecology, but these events do not necessarily translate into scientific evidence or political mobilization. Outright obstruction to demands for ecological protection occur, but there are also more subtle hurdles to halting ecological destruction, including the difficulties in tracing and linking the diffuse effects of economic processes to human and non-human harm with scientifically valid chains of causality. Furthermore, even when and if such causality can be established, there are other challenges in mobilizing these findings in creating political action in the interest of the common good. Even what form the "common good" takes is up for debate, and cannot be reduced to the greatest benefit and least damage to the greatest number, especially when we begin to account for non-human detriment. Even for humans, it is not always clear whether to prioritize economic development or ecological preservation or human longevity in addressing ecological degradation.

Geographically, the People's Republic of China covers a vast territory that includes a diversity of landscapes, a range of climates, a myriad of flora and fauna, and a large citizenship sustaining their livelihoods in very different ways. In China, as elsewhere, it is contentious to put a date on when humans became the drivers of ecological processes, something scientists are proposing through denoting the current geological era as the Anthropocene rather than the longer Holocene since the last Ice Age. China's ancient history of settled agriculture sustained a large population but also put long-term strain on the environment over its agrarian history and its urban centers. Industrialization gained pace from the 1950s onwards. A further acceleration of economic processes has emerged with the burgeoning of industrial and mechanized manufacturing in the market era, adversely affecting air and lungs, soil and growth, rivers and crops around the country.

The Chinese state increasingly acknowledges and combats its acute pollution problems and simultaneously seeks to contain the social unrest arising from ecological demands citizens are making in terms of their health and livelihoods. How are ideals of order related to the current authority of institutions and legitimacy of frameworks for environmental action by interested parties, such as international agencies, the Chinese state, its citizens, and civil society? This chapter examines how historical processes and moral economies resonate with contemporary environmental understanding in China to establish how far it conforms to a new globalizing economic and environmental agenda.

8.1 The Dualism of Nature and Culture

Early anthropology approached environmental concerns by analyzing them in terms of localized folk sciences, or through particular myths and rituals linked to livelihood and subsistence techniques. In order to reinvigorate the field, Descola and Pálsson (1996) engage in a classic anthropological approach of iconoclasm on Eurocentric concepts underlying the field, taking to task the dualism of nature and society underpinning the foundation of scientific modernity. From human ecology to social theory, they see nature–culture as 'the philosophical touchstone of a whole series of typically western binary oppositions which anthropologists have otherwise successfully criticized: mind-body, subject-object, individual-society etc' (p. 4). Descola and Pálsson argue that questioning this dualism is more than a post-modernist turn or constructivist affectation, as their resistance to the dichotomy rests on a range of disciplinary approaches and variety of ethnographic examples that make the abandoning of this dualist understanding towards a monist perspective pressing.

They show that neither materialists, nor structuralists do justice to the multiplicity of possibilities for social relations beyond the human. To materialists, nature shapes culture through survival strategies that amount to adaptive responses to physical conditions. Cultural institutions, common behavior, and whole societies are thereby reduced to the outcomes of environmental constraints or the unfolding evolution of genetic programming. They include a range of disciplinary and theoretical approaches in this broad materialist category including cultural ecology, sociobiology, and some Marxists. At the other extreme, culture imposes meaning on nature. These structuralist or symbolic approaches pay close attention to the 'conceptual discrimination between sensible qualities, tangible properties and defining attributes' (pp. 2–3). By making sense of how others understand "nature" through classificatory, symbolic, and representative systems, as well as the diverse instantiations of these conceptualizations in rituals, myths, and everyday behavior, this approach nonetheless leaves a shared realm of nature beneath cultural diversity unexamined.

Despite moving in opposite directions, with nature directing culture, on the one hand, and culture giving meaning to nature, on the other, both forms rely on the same dualism, the same underlying content, and the same ontological assumption of a world divided into a realm of nature and a sphere of culture. Furthermore, both assume that a single, unified, and universal nature underlies the diverse, eclectic, and specific assortment of cultures. One can also reread this problem through tracing commonalities and differences from an etic perspective, where the objective outsider grasps reality governed by natural laws and measurable by scientific methods, in contrast to champions of the emic perspective, where the exotic, bizarre, and idiosyncratic specificities of particular cultures are celebrated. The challenge to the dualism of nature and culture replicates the critiques voiced in relation to social diversity grounded in the biological confidence of Western folk models that crept into anthropological understandings of kinship in Chapter 3. Descola and Pálsson show how overcoming this duality necessitates audacious steps onto shaky middle ground, where discontinuous cosmologies and overlapping ontologies emerge to provide new possibilities of rethinking the world beyond this dualism.

Descola and Pálsson explore three examples that unsettle the dualism of nature and culture: first, how a person comes into being makes the specificity and isolation of "the human" from its environment difficult to sustain. In evolutionary terms, the emergence of humanity uniquely separated from other animals cannot be determined through a particular moment of phylogenetic branching or of capacity development. In human development a person builds up skills, techniques and capacities through interactive negotiation with their environment. Second, ethnography from around the world reveals how indigenous groups, particularly in Amazonia, do not necessarily divide the world along a differentiation of human from non-human, such as plants, animals, or spirits, but often attribute a wide range of beings with intention, consciousness, and kinship. Third, at the other end of the spectrum there is not the critique of the human as the uniquely cultural, but the breakup of the stability of nature, where modern scientists encountering hybrids must censor, separate and disguise anything that falls between the two realms through epistemological processes of purification. For instance, scientists generate knowledge through mathematical models in which the world never fully lives up to the ideals of nature, or they use technical extensions and interventions that destabilize the very notion of nature as separable from culture (e.g. in biotechnology, see Chapter 4). The division of labor between the natural and social sciences further replicates the nature–culture dualism and undermines attempts to cross-fertilize.

Descola and Pálsson avoid proposing a definitive way out of the nature–culture dualism, but instead suggest a very pragmatic approach for generating theoretical innovation when they argue that 'some constructs are less adequate than others for understanding the world, and when they fail to illuminate and are shown to be contrary to experience they should be revised or abandoned' (p. 9). By challenging a 'key foundation of modernist epistemology' they claim to be transforming states and substances into processes and relations, opening up a new area of enquiry where 'the main question is not any more how to objectify closed systems, but how to account for the very diversity of the processes of objectification' (p. 12).

There are urgent political dimensions to theorizing human-environment interactions and nature–culture assumptions, as public agendas are continuously forged through ethical concerns over ecological degradation at various spatial scales. The nation-state cannot contain the resolution for citizens and their governments as technological advances and economic expansions affecting the environment are global. Furthermore, not just growing economies, but the penetration of economic practices and market thinking into the very rendering of natural resources as "goods", with the privatization and commodification of the environment this entails, cannot be left unexamined. Therefore, epistemology emerges as key to understanding the world beyond humans, as social relations with non-humans, are critical to the survival of anthropos. Although their approach does not put forward a novel unified framework, their critiques provide a basis for meaningful comparison beyond the universal model of human exploitation of the environment as the domination of culture over nature.

8.2 Globalizing Nature in China and Taiwan

Globalization of nature' cannot be reduced to a unilinear import of forces from outside China into the country as part of a process of creating a homogenized world. In examining the nature of "nature" in China and Taiwan Weller (2006) advances a radically comparative view, tracing ideas of "nature" in very different milieus and comparing, juxtaposing, and intertwining them as they have been put into action. Weller's stance on current globalization theories of environmental consciousness is critical, due to their frequent assumption that environmental movements are middle class phenomena based on post-materialist values enabled through wealth and education. By contrast, the diversity of indigenous and local conceptions of the environment across the globe tell a radically different story, particularly amongst those who draw their livelihood from their immediate ecological surroundings or have become the victims of some of the worst excesses of environmental degradation. Although market thinking and cultural imperialism in global environmental approaches abound, reducing these to homogenization treats a diversity of forces as uniform and negates the very interactive, creative, and diverse practices that the mixing of environmental ideas has made.

In short, Weller seeks to see how local categories of knowledge shape globalizing culture, here through the realm of "nature". Notably, Weller's local understandings of nature are not placed against a foil of universal knowledge centered somewhere in Europe or America. Instead, he traces the entangled epistemological histories of conceptions of nature across Taiwan and China, in dialogue with understandings of nature emerging in Europe, North America, and Japan, as well as broader institutional structures, scientific ideas and governmental forces shaping the world's ecological epistemologies.

Weller shows that a strong vision of nature as separable from humanity, a variant of the nature–culture dualism, has gained global influence, whether in thinking about nature in exploitative or protectionist ways. Narratives of humans conquering or preserving nature proliferate globally, partly because they have been built into state projects that are both socialist and capitalist. States may celebrate control over nature, championing their scientific research, technological advances or engineering projects as evidence of their victory of humanity over nature. States may also tap into utopian visions of untrammeled wilderness as escape from the artificiality of industrial modernity, advocating appreciation of nature for its own sake, or glorifying the bucolic world of the peasantry and their way of life. However, both of these visions have the nature–culture dualism at their core, although with the major difference where to place positive value. Weller traces the origins and effects of these ideas in both socialist China and capitalist Taiwan, as well as exploring similarities between their understandings of "nature" that diverge from global norms, thereby highlighting some of the shared specificities in relation to the concept.

The word for "nature" in the Chinese translation of *ziran* is now commonly established and accepted, with the two characters forming the word meaning "self-evidently" and "spontaneously" (pp. 20–21). However, the most common term before the 20th century and still sometimes used today to denote nature is the concept of *tian* that translates as "heaven." *Tian* refers to the divine order of heaven as part of an ethical order and natural world. This world includes heaven, earth, and humanity, and is made up of cosmic energy that flows through everything, human and non-human, the animating force of *qi*. In this worldview, humanity is differentiated from rest of the world only as a realm of adjustment in the vital substance and essential material of *qi*. Yet, pre-modern China entailed a diverse elaboration of environmental ideas. Daoism advocated following the path and embracing the patterns created by the unfolding of natural processes, the Dao or way of the world. Confucians emphasized the distribution of political power and proper social order. Buddhism taught compassion towards all living things. Furthermore, the centralization of forces of power, especially imperial power, led to the attribution of alternate liminal powers at the margins.

Despite this diversity in pre-modern China, Weller points to a shared understanding of the working of the cosmos and flows of *qi* that subsumes the human and physical world within its order, rather than following the Western sense of "nature" as a sphere beyond human culture. Here Weller follows the philosopher Tu Weiming's argument that traditional Chinese conceptions of the environment are embedded within an 'anthropocosmic worldview' that entails human use of the natural world and its energies by establishing 'a mutual relationship between humanity and the cosmic order of heaven, in which each of the parts resonates sympathetically with all the others' (Weller, 2006: p. 23). Weller states that '[e]arly views of heaven-and-earth as a system of energetic resonances, or of an anthropocosmic system that placed human benefit as the goal of environmental manipulation, allowed massive reshaping of the land and water. They did not, however, subjugate a de-animated nature to a ruling humanity' (p. 48). Nonetheless, the establishment of *ziran* as a more standardized notion of nature was commonplace by the 1920s. Even so, Weller not only tracks the multiple paths leading to this development, but how diverse understandings of "nature" remain in both contemporary China and Taiwan.

Weller's entangled history of epistemology between East and West begins with early Jesuits in China. From the Ming dynasty onwards and then later as astronomers at Manchu courts these Jesuits were exploring nature as way of understanding God's divine work on earth. This conception of nature intertwined with neo-Confucian views of the cosmos from the previous 500 years, and the Jesuits' activities became part of valorizing Chinese forms of knowledge at the imperial courts. However, with the Scientific Revolution in the early modern period, God became increasingly removed from nature in the West, particularly through theories advancing technological progress and ecological exploitation. The Enlightenment furthered this process as humanity was recast as a conscious subject with agency in contrast to nature as an increasingly objectified mechanism. In China, technological dreams of scientific progress increasingly linked material progress to the exploitation of environment, including the 20th century May Fourth movement, but also engineering projects like the Grand Canal. Furthermore, both the Guomindang Nationalists and the Chinese Communists were committed modernists, who sought to use science to engineer the environment. The Maoist slogan of 'Man Must Conquer Nature' (*ren ding sheng tian*) (p. 48) captures this sentiment, although Weller points out that the political implication of the slogan would be better captured by translating *tian* as Heaven, an idea unthinkable a century before (p. 50).

The Western counter-movement was encapsulated by romantics who valorized nature for its own sake, as a wilderness devoid of human culture that held its own strength and power beyond rationalism or as a bucolic ideal of rural life. Although romantic movements are frequently associated with arts and literature, these ideas were influential beyond aesthetics and became part and parcel of political projects as well. In the United States, Jeffersonian hopes for an American democracy was based on small farmers, whereas in China Sun-Yatsen initiated his Land-to-the-Tiller program and the People's Republic sent youth down to the countryside. By imbuing rural ideals with utopian impulses, these movements form a critique of modern urban life. Moreover, Weller points out that through the desirability of nature in Western nature–culture split it is possible to find 'echoes of exactly this split today when anthropocentric pro-development arguments meet anti-growth biocentrism. Both sides presume a fundamental difference between nature and culture (quite unlike Chinese anthropocosmic views)' (p. 55).

Having traced these diverse understandings of nature, Weller examines how they come to be expressed in practices ranging from national parks to ecological policies in China and Taiwan. Weller shows how understandings of nature are turned into social resources for environmental action. They not only evoke particular relationships between humanity and nature, but also resonate with political orders at different scales including local, national, global. Furthermore, Weller extends this analysis to the moral economy and spheres of responsibility through a variety of examples, ranging from industrial pollution of crab farming operations in the PRC to temple divinities intervening in industrial construction plans in Taiwan, thereby teasing out a number of parallels and differences.

A major commonality between China and Taiwan is the patterning of effective environmental activism into three main phases (p. 115). First, activists begin with petitions, particularly through appeals to officials close to the centered of political state authority. Second, they move on to blockades. Despite being a legally dubious practice, blockading is commonplace and granted legitimacy through its weight in negotiating with local economic and political interlocutors. Blockading thereby forms part of the wider moral economy regardless of its official legal status. In the third and final phase, environmental activists usually reach an agreement based around compensation. Although this outcome is usually focused on financial redress, it may also include support for community projects or the establishment of environmental bureaus, pollution monitoring, or health checks.

Another notable commonality between China and Taiwan is that the state does not form a monolithic entity as different levels of government act and negotiate in different ways with relative specificity to the particular case at hand. Furthermore, parallel to the different scales of state, various parts of society become mobilized in environmental activism with different goals and visions of nature. These conceptions may even come into conflict in differences among interlocutors seeking environmental action. As a tendency, grassroots activist struggles focus on localist and human-centered issues, often involving temples, lineages, neighborhoods, even gangsters in defending their causes. Here a major difference emerges in ecological activism between China and Taiwan, as the Republic of China accommodates a more established realm of non-governmental organizations than the People's Republic. However, in both countries NGOs tend to defend a global, universalist, and dehumanized notion of nature, often out of touch with localized understandings of "nature".

8.3 Social Justice in Environmental Protest

Jing's (2000) research concurs with Weller's proposition in revealing the human-centered orientation of rural environmental protests that aim to protect human welfare and preserve human livelihood rather than a non-human realm of nature (p. 143). Rather than examining urban activism, Jing focuses on rural protests among villagers forming the front-line for political action against ecological degradation. Through historically sanctioned avenues for popular protest they attempt to influence government policies, court decisions, and the behavior of enterprises (p. 144). After providing the background of environmental protection laws, agencies, and campaigns in China (p. 145), Jing turns to two case studies in the Market Era, where the form of protests reveal local value systems by enacting symbolism couched in death rituals, cosmological beliefs, and morality narratives (p. 151).

The first campaign focuses on securing access to clean water in Dachuan village in Gansu Province northwest China. Most Dachuan residents rely on an agricultural livelihood that has become endangered by a fertilizer factory that predominantly employs outside migrants, leading to a struggle that has lasted for decades (p. 146). A series of dramatic public protest actions in the mid-1990s included the destruction of a bridge, demanding factory officials prove their faith in water quality by drinking contaminated stream water, and bombarding the factory with polluted water (pp. 146–147). Jing differentiates several phases of protest from the 1970s to mid-1990s as part of a 'cognitive revolution' in understanding of water pollution and the risks this posed. However, the factory's corrective measures always fell short of residents' demands for compensation for the detriment to their health and livelihoods. In addition to exploring legal avenues, which were frustrated and eventually barred, villagers therefore turned to social protest that included the actions described above.

Dachuan protests mobilized symbolism that revolved around descent group and worship of fertility goddesses. Early phases of protest for compensation for damages to livestock and humans were resolved through the compensation of hiring local people as temporary workers, providing villagers with below-market price fertilizer, and supplying a water tap to the village. However, when the birth control policy in the mid-1980s came together with miscarriages and birth defects, the fertilizer factory was seen as a threat to having healthy babies. With the health of women and children at stake, residents set about reconstructing local temples for a water-control god and various goddesses believed to protect childbirth, young children, and cure diseases, thereby creating spaces for leaving offerings to deities in return for their help in enhancing human health. The fertility goddesses emerged as religious manifestations of popular protest through a focus on the health of families. Furthermore, they made the demand mentioned above that not only factory leaders, but their wives, children, and grandchildren drink bottles of water from the contaminated river. This request proved particularly powerful in persuading factory officials to take action to remedy the situation, as drinking the polluted river water endangered their own family members, who normally drank potable water. Through both the divine temples and the mundane demands about drinking water mothers and children became symbols of moral mobilization to protect descendants.

Jing then turns to contentions around compensation and land reclamation in Gaoyang Township in return for resettlement to build the Three Gorges Dam. Residents turn to petitions made to the central government in Beijing, informing them of local corruption, accusing county officials of not distributing financial compensation, embezzling resettlement funds, and falsifying and exaggerating the land reclamation provided to residents (pp. 149–151). Gaoyang residents mobilized funeral symbolism and moral tales in their political protest, thereby articulating their grievances to Beijing officials in ways that forged allegiance between local petitioners and the central government in support of the project of constructing this major dam as a source of electricity. They cast their alliance around the modern engineering project with the benevolent national state in danger of being thwarted by corrupt local officials. The petitioners even planned to make white gowns with their slogans to wear on a trip to Beijing, but enraged county officials spoiled the plan and intimidated the residents into staying home. Jing points out that funeral symbolism has an important history in political protest in China, not only to express grievances but reveal preparedness for martyrdom. This motivation to the point of sacrifice was further reinforced through the petitioners' reference to the tale of Song Jiang, whose rebellions sought justice in the name of heaven. This morality tale therefore evoked how unpredictable the consequences of their petition were and appealed to the central government for help.

In addition to the petitions to government agencies and staging of demonstrations Jing focuses on, there is also a third form of environmental protest of filing lawsuits that will be examined in more detail below. In Jing's cases, he highlights the display of four characteristics contributing to their effective social activism and popular protest for environmental justice: first, mobilizing recognizable cultural characteristics to foster participation; second, voicing a sense of moral entitlement as citizens before economic, health, and legal issues; third, an awareness of environmental law; fourth and finally, forging an alliance with the central government. In short, Jing's research supports Weller's argument that the endangered environment incites political action through conceptions of social justice through a clear relevance to human existence, rather than protecting an abstract realm of nature beyond human intervention (p. 159). Jing's account also reveals how citizens may draw on different levels of the state to maintain social order and uphold their claims to ecological justice.

8.4 Compensation for Industrial Pollution

Lora-Wainwright (2013) builds on Weller's challenge to a 'post-materialist thesis' that environmental consciousness is a luxury of the global elite that lives above subsistence levels (see Weller, pp. 6–7). Empirical research shows that this is clearly not the case, especially for farmers whose livelihood depends on environment, but also for the industrial workers that Lora-Wainwright focuses on, for whom knowledge of complex environmental risk is coupled with a lack of a sense of entitlement to a clean environment, weakening popular resistance.

Lora-Wainwright points out that pollution resulting in potential illness forms a major concern for Chinese citizens, but links between the experience of exposure to environmental pollution and scientific evidence of the impact of that experience on human health are difficult to trace and prove. A jumble of factors come together in any human life, including risk factors ranging from genetic predisposition over stressful events to harmful habits, as well as long-term interaction with the environment. Therefore, it can be hard to point to a single cause in an illness pathway, especially as modern medicine traces many illnesses to a multicausal framework. Furthermore, there is the constant contestation that occurs due to high stakes in economic development and industrial production, for citizens as well as the government.

To investigate these processes Lora-Wainwright and a small team of researchers conducted interviews in a large administrative village on residents' relationship to pollution and health in Yunnan Province, in China's southwest. 10,000 migrants working in local industries and mines supplemented the registered population of 2,000 people. The main local employer was a fertilizer plant that was formerly a state-owned enterprise before becoming a joint-stock company partially owned by the provincial government as part of a multinational corporation in 2005. In this context Lora-Wainwright finds a strong "lay epidemiology" and a weak "popular epidemiology." The "lay epidemiology" refers to the perception and diffusion of illness causation based on personal experience. Residents are very knowledgeable about multiple risk factors and multicausal illness pathways, and identify pollution as a key factor in many illnesses. However, what is missing is a "popular epidemiology" that would transform these dispersed illness experiences linked to environmental health risks into collective strategies of resistance and activist demands to decrease pollution. Why is this the case?

Lora-Wainwright argues that people question the validity of their diffuse and experiential bodily ways of knowing about illness causation when compared with the positive and quantifiable improvements in life through economic development. Furthermore, local power relations reinforce this downplaying of contamination, as dependency on industry for employment fosters acquiescence to polluting industries. Moreover, environmental risks pose only one of many concerns that people face in going about their lives, alongside their children's education, elderly care and maintaining homes. In addition to the routinization and normalization of pollution, there is also a disciplining of demands and requests that may be met (like financial compensation) rather than those that fall on deaf ears (like regular health checks and treatment).

Local industries provide the residents with local infrastructure such as roads, a school, and a hospital, as well as renting land from locals. In addition, the community is stratified with unequal claims to compensation resulting in uneven distribution of returns for environmental risks. Most notably, the community includes five times as many migrants as locals, with only registered villagers receiving rent for land. Furthermore, even this relatively privileged part of the community is becoming increasingly differentiated through growing disparities of education, skills, and income. The fracturing of the community subjected to environmental risk means that where compensation is addressed, it usually remains an individual or family matter, rather than a community issue. The voicing of results-driven complaints also suggests that residents rethink risks through possible redress, thereby reinforcing the notion that more compensation rather than less pollution forms their most viable path forward.

8.5 Reason and Law in Rural Resource Management

Taking issue with the official discourse of a gaping moral "vacuum" in China (addressed in Chapter 2), Pia (forthcoming, 2016) argues that a moral and legal "plenum" is produced in Yancong Township, in another part of Yunnan Province in China's southwest. Common citizens and low level officials produce this moral plenum by engaging with legal pluralism in everyday management of resources, particularly water and land, to forge acceptable solutions based on "reason" (*li*). The state discourse of a moral vacuum generates the governmental imperative of sending the law to the countryside to enforce its legal framework. However, Pia contends that the state's intervention actually creates a divisive moral field, as common citizens and local officials already have at their disposal mediation sessions and a moral repertoire of "reason". Contrary to the state's vision of the law as guaranteeing moral authority, local residents see the law as an opposing and disempowering instrument to extract local resource management from them in unjust ways.

National media headlines frequently portray corruption with party members embezzling public money or commoners cheating each other, thereby reinforcing the impression of a general lack of normative principles. To a certain extent this vision becomes replicated on an everyday level by local government members who complain that villagers willfully destroy infrastructure (especially water meters) or divert resources (for example by channeling irrigation for private purposes), while villagers complain that the local government misappropriates funds. However, behind this discourse the everyday management of common resources appeals to a collective good, through persuasion and consensus, occurring through mediation in accordance with reason (*heli*) that contrast to the state's insistence on following the law (*hefa*). The state seeks to transform grassroots mediation though state laws, but thereby does not so much integrate local custom as produce a discursive schism between local standards of reason and central state laws.

Pia provides a number of cases to support the contrast between the two normative orders "law" (*hefa*) and "reason" (*heli*) that rural citizens navigate in their legal life. In the case of a land use dispute, the village party secretary effectively resolves the disagreement through balancing the interests and expectations of the opposing parties. In the case of water resource disputes, the preservation of infrastructure and accountable management take center stage in negotiating reasonable solutions. Both the land use and water resources disputes are resolved by drawing on various beliefs, values, and technical knowledge, as well as in-depth understanding of the context and persons involved. Lastly, in the case of land requisitioning where family farmland is appropriated for construction of government official homes, the law emerges as a mechanism of disenfranchisement, where legal instruments actively produce a moral vacuum and reveal the pro-development bias in the formal legal framework.

In short, mediation creates a space where public participation and the common good are both discursively and practically negotiated; it is embedded within an everyday plurality of legal frameworks as a counter-public to state law.

8.6 Global Environmentalism and *fengshui*

Bruun (2003) has studied rural fengshui practitioners in Sichuan Province in western China and Jiangsu Province in the east of the country. Bruun traces the fengshui revival after decades of official state denunciation as feudal superstition under Maoism, as it reemerged in the market era as a practice linking human fate to the broader environment. Fengshui also provides an explanatory framework and paths of intervention into a world marked by rising inequality, where fortune and misfortune often appear contingent. It provides an avenue for taking fate into one's own hands. Bruun also refers to Feuchtwang's (1974) research on fengshui as part of an ego-centered universe focused on a person or kin group that builds on the past and projects into the future, through burials, ancestral worship, and family homes. Furthermore, Feuchtwang has emphasized how a centralization of power (in contrast to a hierarchy of authority) accords with fengshui practices in dialogue with a moralizing political center. According to this view, fengshui acts as a cosmological model for both the physical environment and social fortune, as the natural and social come together through an ideal explanatory framework (Bruun, 2003: p. 16).

Fengshui literally translates as "wind-water" and focuses on tracing and manipulating the flows of *qi* as a "cosmic current" through the shape, flows, and forms of a given environment (Bruun, 2003: p. 3). Through fengshui practices, *qi* energies and substances become subject to modulation and management with the aim of bringing advantages to humans. The outcome of fengshui practices often include increasing wealth, bolstering happiness, fostering longevity, and encouraging fertility, as well as bringing an end to misfortune or illness. The practitioners are called fengshui masters or yin-yang practitioners and usually use a combination of techniques to assess a site and advocate a course of action. Techniques include viewing the general landscape and forces through "seeing fengshui" (*kan fengshui*), examining a geomantic compass (*luopan*), referring to the traditional calendar (*nongli*) and making calculations about correspondences between birth data and the elements by means of the Eight Triagrams (*bagua*) (3–4). Fengshui masters are frequently called upon to select auspicious sites for dwellings (*zhai*), both *yang* dwellings for the living in houses and *yin* dwellings for the deceased in tombs. Fengshui practitioners may also recommend interventions into the landscape especially through building or tearing down architectural constructions (such as houses or bridges) and altering or adding natural bodies (such as waterways or hills) to reflect, channel, and amass *qi*.

Despite these key ways in which fengshui practices bring the social and the environmental together within a single framework, Bruun takes issue with simply championing fengshui as a means to harmony between humans and nature. He argues that regulating human impact on the natural environment or moderating ecological intervention or degradation are absolutely not central tenets of fengshui cosmology as traditionally understood. In his chapter on fengshui as environmental ethics Bruun traces a movement back and forth that allowed such a discursive application of fengshui to emerge, initially through the import of fengshui elements into the West and now the reinsertion of these ideas into Chinese urban and intellectual spheres.

In Bruun's eyes, this Western tradition simplifies fengshui to the point of distortion by reducing it to a traditional philosophy for moralizing harmony between humans and environment. In the 1960s and 1970s, intellectuals initiated the Western study of fengshui as a form of natural philosophy of science that struck resonance with a growing market for alternative life philosophies at the time. This interest became compounded with the rising visibility of ecological degradation in China and abroad in 1970s and 1980s, which fed a growing fascination with fengshui as a point of intersection between nature and culture as an ecological ethics. From the 1990s onwards, fengshui was then reclaimed by a Chinese intellectual movement advocating a nativization of culture, which provided fertile ground for fengshui as an alternative and homegrown foundation of knowledge to Western science. In addition, the rising environmental awareness fueled a market for fengshui as a Chinese cosmology for understanding the relationship between humanity and nature.

Traces of fengshui may have inspired this two-way exchange for environmental debate between East and West, but the rise in discourse surrounding nature (*ziran*) in Chinese often mixes popular fengshui discourse with concepts from environmental sciences and Western ideas about natural balance, leading to a hybrid fengshui conception revolving around harmonious relationships between a human and natural world. Bruun emphasizes that fengshui practices are about improving human fortune through intervention into the environment, so certainly not about making the world more suitable for non-human life. If anything, they open up human-centered and ego-oriented strategies for exploiting the ecological environment towards one's own ends. In short, the form of fengshui being advocated as a simple compass for Chinese environmental ethics is more aptly described as a cosmopolitan intellectual pursuit than as a practice resonating with rural Chinese citizens on the ground.

Bruun points out that '[i]t is perfectly sound to explore the fengshui tradition's role in resource management and its capacity for environmental protection' (p. 232), but then cautions against hastily adopting fengshui as a native cosmology and practical cure-all for environmental destruction humans have sown around the globe.

8.7 Social Harmony Beyond Nature–Culture Dualism

This chapter began with the argument that a dualism of nature and society underpins Western science and takes for granted an identical, universalistic conception of nature. It then introduced anthropological approaches to sharing knowledge about the environment and responses made to changing environments within China, and compared this to a Western dualism of nature and society. It engaged with the possibility that an 'anthropocosmic worldview' is evident in Chinese grass-roots activism against pollution where a desire for human benefit within a larger system of political and cultural order does not revolve around human conflict with or opposition to nature.

In response to experiences of environmental degradation in China, various ethnographic examples reveal how some people mobilize moral imperatives to seek social justice, for instance, through local institutions of moral reason and mediation, while others settle for economic compensation for the environmental cost to human health. Lastly, the chapter examined whether Western "nature" is a globalizing concept by turning to a critical appraisal of *fengshui* as a form of environmental ethics amongst global consumers and urban Chinese elites, arguing that *fengshui* discourse revolving around its harmonizing function between man and environment is not an ancient tradition but constructed in dialogue with Western visions of nature, far from *fengshui* practices in rural China.

Seminar Questions

What can the Chinese anthropocosmic worldview contribute to anthropological theories about the relationship between nature and culture?

Is a global, universalist, and dehumanized notion of nature taking hold in Chinese engagements with the environment?

Readings

Bruun, Ole (2003). 'The Construction of a Discourse: Fengshui as Environmental Ethics', in *Fengshui in China: Geomantic Divination between State Orthodoxy and Popular Religion.* Nordic Institute of Asian Studies: Copenhagen, pp. 231–254.

Descola, Philippe and Pálsson, Gísli (1996). 'Introduction' in Descola, Philippe and Pálsson, Gísli (eds.) *Nature and Society: Anthropological Perspectives.* Routledge, pp. 1–21.

Feuchtwang, Stephan (1974). *An Anthropological Analysis of Chinese Geomancy.* Vientiane: Vitagna and 2002, Bangkok: White Lotus.

Jing, Jun (2000). 'Environmental Protests in Rural China', in Perry, Elizabeth and Selden, Mark (eds.) *Chinese Society: Change, Conflict and Resistance,*Routledge: London, pp. 143–160.

Lora-Wainwright, Anna (2013). 'The Inadequate Life: Rural Industrial Pollution and Lay Epidemiology in China', in *The China Quarterly*, 214, pp. 302–320.

Pia, Andrea (forthcoming, 2016). '"We follow reason, not the law": disavowing the law in rural China'. *Political and Legal Anthropology Review.*

Weller, Robert (2006). *Discovering Nature: Globalization and Environmental Culture in China and Taiwan.* Cambridge: Cambridge University Press.

Reference

Chakrabarty, Dipesh (2009). "The Climate of History: Four Theses", in *Eurozine,* October 30, 2009: [online]. Available at http://www.eurozine.com/articles/2009-10-30-chakrabarty-en.html. (Accessed on February 23, 2015).

Chapter 9

Ritual and Belief

One of the oldest and most central topics of anthropology, ritual is still a subject of definitional and theoretical disputation. Ritual is always a sequence of actions whose order must be obeyed, including much attention to detail and frequent repetition, so that every performance, even when variations can be observed over time, is reckoned to be a repetition of the last time it was performed. Further, rituals are performed for a purpose, whether that be in the course of a liturgy in a sacred place sacralising the performers and their audience, an offering to deities or ancestors or propitiations against maleficent forces to secure health or safety of human and agrarian fertility or success in examinations or in business, or to give thanks for any of these, or else to perform a rite of passage, for instance into marriage.

Should ritual be understood according to the meaning of the objects used, the actions or gestures of their use, and the sequence itself? Or is the explanation according to meaning secondary to the ritual itself, which is set off from other kinds of act by the sheer length and strictness of the order of acts? Is it just the setting off that matters, and the meanings and explanations always partial and disputable? What is the relation of ritual to myth, the stories by which we live? Does ritual imply belief, or is belief, or the statement of belief, itself a ritual? In other words does ritual imply knowledge, as does belief?

The objects, actions and sequence of rituals do refer to myths. But are the telling of myths and the performance of rituals two quite different orderings of the flow and chances of life? In any case study of ritual requires us to enquire how rituals relate to myths in different combinations, loosely or tightly. Because the actions and objects in ritual and myth are symbolic, with multiple meanings, it has been argued that ritual can resolve inherent contradictions, or disruptions of social life by the fact that it is both ordering and ambivalent. Ritual is purifying and sanctifying, yet also ambivalent.

What kind of knowledge do rituals convey? Is it knowledge of propriety, for instance, as in greetings and forms of address? Rituals refer to a transcendental order that surrounds mundane life. Is that true even of the rituals of greeting that make no direct reference to it, as for instance death rituals do make?

In any case, rituals of all kinds are a discipline in which performances, not just by ritual experts but also by those who ask the experts to lead or perform them, are ways of learning to do things properly, including respect for ritual order. They are therefore ways of fashioning social and moral personality.

When you have in dynastic China, a tradition that places the conduct of rite (something that includes manners as well as offerings to ancestors) at the center of civilization and rule, and included in that tradition is the idea that ritual orders life, it seems to give answers to some of these questions. And when that was followed by republican governments that attempted to banish a whole field of ritual for effect that they called "superstition" in promoting scientific civilization, the history and ethnography of China offers case studies to test and modify the anthropology not only of ritual and belief but also of secularism.

9.1 Government by Rite

For most of the centuries of Chinese imperial orthodoxy (from the Han dynasty to the present day) Confucius' as distinct from other strands of Chinese political philosophy was singled out. Within that stress on Confucius was a stress on observation of Li — manners and rites — supplemented by the Legalist philosophy of rewards and punishments. Observation of Li was of course supported by the sanction of military force and the promulgation of laws. But priority was given to Li, which is the cultivation of good relations, the proprieties of differentiated association as the anthropologist Fei called them — or the role ethics (as Roger Ames elaborated philosophically) of father–son, but more generally parent-child including mother–son, mother–daughter, mother–daughter-in-law, husband–wife, elder–younger siblings, ruler-subject, and friends — extending outward to host–guest relations, and their celebration in calendrical and life-cycle rituals. These rituals include addressing and naming by titles the powers and principles that make up the universe, the honoring of ancestors, sages and heroes, military protectors, honest officials, good judges, virtuous widows, and upright elders.

Government by Rite was an official discourse as is governance by the micro-disciplines of individual self-regulation, which is the discursive formation of the disciplinary regime that emerged in 18th century Europe according to Michel Foucault. Both contain ideologies that make a given politics and its hierarchies look natural — within an accepted sense of reality. Government by Rite implicitly teaches an ideology of scales and steps in a hierarchy of respect.

The current mainland Chinese regime now governs according to another discourse of hierarchy up to a single unifying Party leadership, named variously 'market socialism' or 'socialism with Chinese characteristics', but mixing Chinese spirituality (namely, the Party as inheritor and projector of a long tradition) with material improvements in livelihood. The sage Confucius is now invoked as a nationalist emblem of distinctiveness.

So let us take up some more general anthropological theories of ritual as conveying ideology.

9.2 Ritual and Ideology

In his book *Ritual, History and Power* (1989), two chapters stand out in which Maurice Bloch expounds his theory of ritual as transmission of ideology. In the first, 'Symbols, song, dance and features of articulation', he shows that ritual is quite unlike any other form of communication or articulation in that it is so formal. Unlike ordinary language, ritual is purely formal and not propositional. The force of ritual is neither explanatory nor descriptive, it is emotive and illocutionary. Putting performers through a ritual involves them in a drama including singing and dancing, in which their bodies are involved wholly, not just in speech, joined with others, coordinated in the same performance. That is rituals' emotive force. Because rituals mark occasions, such as the preparation of a child that launches its readiness for adulthood they achieve their aim simply by being performed, by a statement that it is done. The doing of ritual to its completion confers the status as an act. That is ritual's illocutionary force.

In the second of the two chapters, 'From cognition to ideology', Bloch takes up the three stage theory of rites of passage first elaborated by Arnold van Gennep and further developed by Victor Turner, in which the passage is from one status to a new one through a middle phase that is outside both, betwixt and between, a threshold that breaks from all order and role. Bloch re-describes these stages, bringing out the violence of the assault the ritual mounts on the everyday experience of practical cognition, in the first stage by a slant or exaggeration of the source of life or dangers to it, in the second by an assault on even that exaggeration so that the participants are taken beyond time, place, and role. The third phase is the transition from that chaos when ritual constructs an image of order and authority, which is a recreation of the encompassing world and a giving of life. This according to Bloch is the dramatic sequence, highly emotive, of all ritual but in particular of rites of passage.

Following Bloch, we could describe even a short ritual of greeting as implying though not acting out chaos, which is to say that if not completed the underlying order would be destroyed and need to be re-asserted. But the main point in this chapter is that ritual teaches what it establishes in the third stage, an image of authority and of obedience to it, as the source of life. More critical is his point that this is ideological because it both depends on and denies much of what ordinary practical cognition and experience of life teaches us. It denies by its selection of status and role for a commanding authority and a hierarchy of those who have power and resources to exert the violence by which the hierarchy is established and maintained and induces compliance by ritual violence, which is acceptance of a current reality in which the power structure authorized is what we depend on for our lives.

Bell makes full use of Bloch's theory in her book (1992) *Ritual theory, ritual practice.* In particular, she elaborates the emotive force of ritual and the politics of seeking authority through ritual.

Her book is a general survey, summary and enquiry into all anthropological writing on ritual, into which she occasionally brings her own area expertize in China. Along with so many other anthropologists in all spheres of enquiry, Bell prefers a noun that refers to process rather than to an object, ritual. She prefers "ritualization". It is not just a process, but also a strategy, and she therefore asks the question what does ritualization do? She rejects the functionalist answer that it must reproduce social solidarity. She turns our attention to the making of the distinction between sacred and profane and the effect of performances in producing ritual agents without assuming that they correspond to the social order of the profane. She asks why do people turn to ritual, what ritual does, and how does it do it.

In the chapter "The ritual body", she gives the answer to why people turn to ritual: to 'forge an experience of redemptive harmony' (p. 116). "Redemptive" means to claim a return on what is owed both by and to the person acceding and submitting to a ritual when addressing ritual objects — the gods and ancestors, the universe of Heavenly encompassment — namely according to an ideal of justice and of just reward. Two situations together induce a resort to ritual. One is when relationships of power are being negotiated and when a basis for them is sought beside and beyond direct force or a particular position of authority. The other is when such authority is claimed to be socially redemptive, as she adds, in such a way that it is also personally redemptive; to be personally redemptive, as desired, it must also be socially redemptive.

Her answer to what ritual does is as Bloch says by its performance, not its explicable meaning. But she extends this through a theory of ritual as disciplinary formation of its agents. Her theory of the formation of ritual agents relies heavily and explicitly on Bourdieu's concepts of *doxa* and *habitus.* Habitus is what is learned as habitual practice and supports a particular hierarchical social system. Ritual is the learning of such a practice by submitting to the ritual, so more than by habit it is done by a decision to accede to a ritual. Learning and participating in ritual is a practical experience of a model situation or sequence of schemes of a basic number of differentiations (which Bell calls oppositions) such as male–female, inner–outer, right–left, up–down. They are learned in practice and the way they are related to each other acts as an instrument for knowing and appropriating the world. Here she is close to the Confucian orthodoxy of learning by and from exemplary propriety. Learning through ritual moulds dispositions that are effective in a world set out in the way ritual sets it out. In short, ritual provides an experience of totality and coherence. But it is the coherence of a current *hegemony*. Here she adds a concept taken from the Italian Marxist theorist and activist Antonio Gramsci. Hegemony is a system of dominance that is always at issue, through the potential of forming an alternative hegemony of what is understood in practice.

Emphasizing this idea of a challenge to hegemony more explicitly than does Bell, let us refer as she does to Bourdieu. To Bourdieu (*Pascalian Meditations* 2000: p. 172), the alternative to a current hegemony requires not just the making explicit of the implicit assumptions (beliefs) of an existing common sense. There must also be a counter-training, an alternative ritual. 'While making things explicit can help, only a thoroughgoing process of counter-training, involving repeated exercises, can, like an athlete's training, durably transform habitus.' Nevertheless, it can and does happen, though maybe not in such an innovative manner. One such means, if we follow Bell, might be through transformations of ritual or through the very juxtaposing of the world as seen through ritual with the world as seen after the installation of a new and secular ruling ideology, its political rituals and its officials.

In any event, as Bell stresses, ritual is already a playing out of oppositions in an encompassing system. The experience of an encompassing and hierarchical system is achieved by the order of actions, including bowing, presenting gifts or offerings, rhetorical speech, song, the revealing of otherwise hidden objects, manipulation of objects, inhaling and eating, expelling and burning. The ordering performance makes basic couples of opposites in such a way that they are not simply complementary, but are in an asymmetrical opposition. One side is more powerful or dominant or morally superior to the other, and each couple informs the other couples, possibly through an overarching couple or one of them leading to an ultimate origin such as inner as distinct from outer, hidden as distinct from apparent.

So ritual is to be distinguished from

a) other social practices, through reference to and experience of or intimation of an ultimate reality and a timeless tradition. Bell writes 'Ritualization does not *resolve* a social contradiction. Rather it catches up into itself all the experienced and conventional conflicts and oppositions of social life, juxtaposing and homologizing them into a loose and provisional systematicity' (pp. 105–106). It creates a context for other social practices and thus acts on them. It is a practical learning to be, an ontological practice, by the making of a place and by the positioning of bodies in relation to each other. It creates ritualized agents who act as recreators and emenders of ritual as if they were doing what has always been done, holding the ritual as a model for and of other social practices.
b) By being a long and set order, ritual is as rhetoric is to other forms of statement; it is not a propositional statement of belief; it is not a narrative sequence like a history. It may be explicated by the telling of a story, but the story does not capture ritual, which is a socially and personally redemptive drama, but not a theater play. And in being a-logical it is not a structure of oppositions and their resolutions in a paradigmatic order of classification. It is instead a constant deferral of resolution through a sequential interleaving of oppositions (e.g. of fleshly life and everlasting life) hinting at an ultimate and higher unity and harmony.

This is entirely compatible with, and indeed it seems to us to rely on, Bloch's theory of ritual as a learning of ideology, a conquest by the transcendent (the encompassing space and time) of the locations and bodies of vitality.

But since words, songs and pictures are used in rituals, such as Chinese death rituals, it cannot be said that stories are merely added to the hierarchical order enacted in ritual. The order can be seen and names of positions in it heard in the songs and the scriptures intoned. They celebrate virtue, purity and transformative and authoritative powers, even though they are not explicitly ideological. Here Chinese case studies challenge

Bell and Bloch so that we may need to at least modify their separation of myth from ritual.

First, though, because of Bloch's and Bell's emphasis on ritual practice, we must deal with the vexed distinction between orthodoxy, insistence on doctrinal belief, and orthopraxy, insistence on correct practice.

9.3 Belief and Ritual Practice: Orthodoxy and Orthopraxy

Doxa = opinion and doctrine;
ortho = that which is considered to be correct, authorized;
hetero = from the perspective of an authorized truth of opinion, untrue, or confused or in error.

We are dealing with questions of authority and authorization. But orthodoxy also means a doctrinal assertion of truth, as in religious ritual. The usual definitions of "religion" hinge on "faith" or "belief" in something. "Faith" is a loyalty to that thing and the hope that it will be revealed or experienced. "Belief" has three senses. One is a declared truth — 'I believe in…'. It can be a profession of faith in something; for instance, as in the Catholic catechism 'I believe in the Holy Trinity..' Another is a necessary assumption that can be inferred from statements and practices, for instance that beings exist in some sense after they have died, when the same person knows that the dead don't eat, has a clear and practical concept of biological death, but nevertheless offers food to a dead person, an ancestor. The third is a cognitively learned and relied upon knowledge, which can be made explicit by a statement that 'I believe it to be true that…' (avian flu is deadly). Only the third comes close to what Bloch means by propositional statements, based on experience and practical cognition and trust in empirical expertize. Belief is now very often a reference to trust in a scientific truth. In earlier times, trust had to be placed in other authorities, less open to dispute and empirical tests for the truth: in China, the texts of a sage-king era; in medieval Europe, Papal authority.

From a later book by Bell (1997), we find an illuminating discussion of orthodoxy and orthopraxy. In Chapter 6 'Ritual density' she makes a wise point that orthodoxy and orthopraxy are not hard and fast types, but tendencies in religious ritual and law. Within Islam for instance, there is equal emphasis on the profession of belief in one God and His prophet and the obedience of laws that govern a moral life.

In China, texts of divine or sage revelation including Daoist scriptures and Buddhist sutras are chanted and accompanied by music in temple rituals and funerals. Reciting of scriptures is part of ritual expertise, which also includes the playing of music. This expertise is a practical knowledge learned to the point that it is habitual. The Daoist, who also recites scriptures, performs rituals in a state of mind in which other things enter his mind, including the images of a prescribed meditation but also an adaptation to the surroundings and to out-of-body experience through which he draws in his audience of partial performers and listeners.

Besides recited scriptures, there are texts of guidance and prescription and vernacular advice on how to conduct oneself in gift exchange, or written guides to proper conduct, including how to write letters, compose eulogies, and conduct funerals and weddings. But the texts recited or used at various points refer to deities, the nature of the cosmos and of death and life after death, which can well be described as either a sense of being in the world, or as a belief and they are part of ritual practice.

A controversy in the study of Chinese death rituals surrounds this issue. Watson (1987) claims that a certain basic set of rituals defines Chineseness (an identity created through standardized death rituals), in the same way that conservative Jewish communities create a sense of communal self through obedience to ritual with relatively little emphasis on belief. Obviously death rituals in China convey and are performed in conformity to a "belief" that ancestors should be commemorated. The distinction between orthopraxy and orthodoxy hinges on the place and effect of textual references and verbal address within rituals. How are these different from the professions of belief in Catholic and Islamic rituals?

Bear in mind Maurice Bloch's and many other theorists' argument that ritual is rhetorical action, and that verbal explication, however expert, is secondary interpretation. Ritual is performative and the function of texts within it is also performative, rather than interpretative. Everyone, including Bourdieu writing about the embodiment of ritual, and Watson himself, says that ritual conveys a cosmology. Religious texts and prescriptive texts (oral or written transmission prescribing rituals) convey a cosmology in China, as everywhere. But Watson contrasts standardization of doctrine (inner belief) and variation in ritual practice with standardization of ritual practice and variation of its interpretation.

There is variation in ritual practice. There is also variation in interpretation of Chinese death rituals by its practitioners. But the point made by both Watson, the anthropologist, and Rawski the historian (1997) is that variation is around a set of common practises. In addition there is variation of interpretation, but all use common means of explication that uses yin-yang and five-phase cosmology, continuation of an elder into ancestorhood, and the idea of a body and many souls that separate at death. Principally there are standard sets of death ritual in practice: (a) the Daoist or Buddhist rites for the salvation of the soul; (b) the burial of the body in a grave; (c) the eulogies and offerings to the deceased; (d) the turning of the deceased into an ancestor and the installation of an ancestral tablet.

The question of ideology turns on how these commonalities were inaugurated and how they were sustained. In other words, ideology becomes apparent when we pay attention to the prescriptive texts, rather than those used in rituals. Watson seems to be more impressed by the simple fact that evidence from provinces all over imperial China and on into the present day show that the practice of core sets and sequences of rituals are the same. He does not ask how this came about. In fact we need to question his notion of "Chineseness". For imperial China, neither the prescriptive texts nor the scriptures recited in rituals would have used an ethnic category, they would instead have invoked correct ritual as an attribute of civilization.

9.4 So, are We Actually Talking about the Influence of Writing and a State?

Some texts such as sutras are part of ritual while other texts are prescriptive, such as the Record of Rites (Li Ji). In some religions the texts of revelation are both liturgical and prescriptive; in Islam and Catholicism, there is a rite of professing faith and obedience to God and his Prophet or his Son.

In China, texts such as the Record of Rites (Li Ji) prescribe ritual and surround it with an interpretative vocabulary that amounts to a cosmology, but not an explicit set of beliefs in relation to which there is a ritual for professing faith. And they are not used in ritual. Evelyn Rawski argues that these prescriptive texts explain the commonality of practice and basic-assumption beliefs. They prescribe ritual as an ordering of appropriate inner states, including grief, and as the way to prevent disorder (*luan*) and that means reinforcement of hierarchy — what Bloch calls ideology and Bell hegemony.

The key period of transition — the Song (960–1279) — to which Rawski dates the concerted propagation of prescription and standardization of rites from the political center was a state that also conducted reform of marriage and funeral custom through printed texts and the cultivation of local elites through recruitment to rule through written examinations. Later dynasties devised a political ritual of what were called "Rural pacts", including lectures by local literati overseen by the assigned "magistrate", political office holder for both political (taxation) and legal functions, and a proclamation of what were called 'the sacred edicts' (*shengji*) of emperors, and the promotion of models of virtue and error in official temple ceremonies. All this was preceded by the printed propagation of a classic of learning and moral reform in the Southern Song dynasty (12th century): Zhu Xi's Jia Li (Family Rites).

Evelyn Rawski assimilates to this centrally organized dissemination of knowledge the transmission of other texts and expertizes of vernacular literacy: those of *fengshui* (the Chinese art of siting graves and buildings) and of Buddhist and Daoist family-apprenticeship traditions with their ritual handbooks and oral transmission of how to use them.

In an earlier work, Bell (1988) gives a Daoist example of standardization, but this is not just prescription, it is also of scriptures used in rituals. Daoist orthodoxy based on the fifth century edition of the Lingbao scriptures by Master Lu Xiuxing, establishes the rites to be performed by the descendents of Zhang Daoling and the masters they ordinated. They are the classics of what is still now the most popular school of Daoism, known as the Zhengyi school. The Lingbao scriptures subscribed to an imperial cosmology and the temporality of its realization. Daoist masters aim to be perfected persons and to join the company of sages. But they do so by adding a set of Heavens prior to the universe of the Three Powers, the Sancai that pivot around the emperor ruling over all beneath Heaven (Tianxia). By meditation and active ritual Daoist adepts return to the prior heavens in order to renew the Sancai themselves. By adding a prior set of Heavens (Tian) and by ritual discipline of meditation returning to it, they set themselves above the emperor.

In these scriptures, there is equal emphasis on rite and text. But the texts of the Lingbao scriptures edited by Master Lu are not just guides to ritual performance and scriptures to be sung in Daoist rites. Their disposition on the altar table of a Daoist sacred enclosure in a rite of sacrificial purification (*zhai*) is the central mediation between the prior and the posterior Heavens. This central rite makes the scriptures in their efficacity available to all, not the privilege of either an aristocracy or a scholar elite. It was and still is offered as a service of merit by ordained Daoists, performing sacrifice for the renewal not of the whole empire but of the territory centered on a new or a refurbished temple. Daoist masters prepare in addition for their clients at territorial festivals, a body of writing, including announcements, petitions, orders or talismans, a large number of texts that are sacrificed, transported to the gods and higher celestial beings by burning. These are texts with content, but not statements of dogma. They are sacred offerings, but not the sanctified book of a single creator, as in the Abrahamic religions in which loyalty or faith in the word of that creator is a part of their rituals.

Returning now not to the texts recited in rituals, but to the prescriptive texts that show the moral pedagogy or ideology of performing rituals correctly, they are historical in imperial China in two senses. (1) They occur as a standardization at a certain time and in a certain politics and economics. (2) They establish and propagate a canon of texts and of commentaries on them, renewed in each dynastic cycle after the Song dynasty. They include the timing of rites through the imperial court's publication of annual calendars and astronomic observations. The Song opening of civil service exams to commoners meant their elites learned the canonized selection of texts and some more observational ('lower') literature in the curriculum. To enable this, block printing was widespread by the 10th century. They learned from within and were themselves responsible for forming well-defined hierarchies of higher and lower arts and sciences.

Of the three possible kinds of texts associated closely with ritual: prescriptive texts, revealed texts recited in ritual, and revealed texts prescribing doctrine, faith and belief that become part of religious ritual, the third seems to be missing in China until the introduction of Islam and Christianity.

Except for the last, consent to taking part in rituals is compatible with having very different beliefs about what they do and what a participant believes to be true. On the other hand, habitual participation in rituals does mean, as Bell suggests all rituals do, learning a disposition towards a world beyond life and death. And rituals include the reciting of scriptures and address to gods whose stories are told in the rites.

9.5 Liberal Modernity, Ritual and the Cult of Sincerity

In their book *Ritual and its Consequences* (2008), Seligman, Weller, Puett, and Simon contrast a pair of dispositions, that of ritual and sincerity. Weller and Puett, are anthropologists and historians of China, but they use their knowledge of China, as did Catherine Bell to good effect in comparison with knowledge of other ritual traditions to produce a general theory of ritual. Interestingly, it is not critically different from either Bloch's or Bell's though they refer to them only marginally. Their main new contention is the contrast of ritual with sincerity, which they say is perennial, citing for instance the rise of Buddhist self-cultivation as a response of sincerity to the Hindi rituals of the time. But the rise of the Puritan cult of sincerity and of authenticity has informed liberal modernity and the autonomy of the individual to such an extent that its disposition has for the past 300 years determined our conception of religion as an affair of personal conscience and the performance of ritual as magic or superstition, following Max Weber's project of comparative universal religions.

Chapters 1 and 4 of their book are the core of their argument. In Chapter 1 they develop their theory of ritual as what they call "subjunctive", that is the performance of a social order in prescribed action that all participants know is not congruous with the everyday world and their experience of it but is an ideal, performed "as if" (the subjunctive) it does exist and could exist. In ritual social order, a way of classifying reality, is, as Bell pointed, also full of ambiguity, creating distinctions, but also blurring them in an integrated whole. It cultivates in its actors a longing for that sense of the whole, which may be posited as a past — as it usually is in accompanying myth and scripture — but also as a future that is never adequately realized. Nevertheless, the disposition ritual cultivates informs the audience or practitioners of rituals so that, for instance in such simple rites as saying please and thank you, we give form to everyday relations of fragmentation, of new situations, of potential coercion, and perform an ideal pattern or ornament which makes them more predictable and tolerable. This view is both neutral and benign whereas for Bell and Bloch ritual is always a resource of authority and authorization, sanctioned by violence in a way similar to and parallel to law, in particular for Bell, for whom ritual is a way of accommodating rival political interpretations of authority.

The subjunctive is the same as what Bloch calls "ideology" but Seligman *et al* view everyday as constantly changing from situation to situation. In their epistemological philosophy the everyday has no order other than what is provided to it by ritual. They include in this description of the mundane the division of labor created by industrial capitalism and indeed, by extension, any economic order, which Bloch simply describes as transactional. We leave open to readers whether it is right to describe the experience of the mundane as fragmented without ritual patterning or ornamentation.

Chapter 4 takes up the opposite idealizing disposition: sincerity. Two responses to the cult of sincerity, secularized in 'liberal modernity' as they name our current era, are ritual and religious fundamentalism and ethical self-realization, which can be a resort to the disciplines of personal prayer or meditation. Both refuse the mere performativity of ritual and its inherent ambiguities and multiple possibilities of interpretation. But equally both strive for an impossible ideal, which is always compromized and therefore to some extent always hypocritical. The purely secular revolutionary transformation of life and social relations is utopian, even as a long-term program in their view. On the other hand, you may understand the repetition of the policies and texts of a revolutionary program, such as that of the French revolution, or of Maoist China's revolution, as political rituals since they too are prescribed and performed as a sequence of actions that can be and were interpreted in many ways.

9.6 Maoist Political Ritual

During the era of the greatest flourishing of Maoist political rituals it was not possible to conduct anthropological fieldwork in the mainland of

China, but it was possible to interview people who fled from China, mainly from the Pearl River Delta, to Hong Kong. Obviously they were self-selected as those so thoroughly disillusioned with the campaigns of that period and their parts in them that they took the risk of fleeing across the water and over the border. Three anthropologically inclined sociologists, Chan, Unger, and Madsen were able to undertake something close to an ethnography by interviewing 26 people in Hong Kong from the same small Pearl River delta village, which they call Chen village, compiling some 3,000 pages of transcripts and interview notes (Madsen, 1984: p. 10) covering the history of the village from 1964 to 1982. In addition to their joint book, Richard Madsen on his own wrote and had published in the same year, 1984, a study of the period of the greatest intensity of political rituals in two campaigns, the Socialist Education Movement and the Cultural Revolution. As a trained Catholic missionary, a member of the Maryknoll Fathers, who abandoned the mission in favor of a doctoral degree in sociology at Harvard, he was well tuned to the institutions of moral formation within a political and ideological movement and to interpreting them in religious terms. But he willingly exposed himself to what the interviews might reveal to him and to sympathize with a sense of the worth of the Communist Revolution that they still endorsed.

Before coming to the political rituals of the campaigns, Madsen describes what he calls the "moral tradition" that had evolved by 1964. It was a mixture of collectivism and local lineage loyalty. The same mix has been observed in other villages (for instance by Ruf, 1998. *Cadres and Kin: making a socialist village in West China 1921–1991*, Stanford University Press), in which the class identification based on property in land and its redistribution followed by the formation of teams and brigades for collective work was laid over the unchanged residential pattern of local lineages and their branches. Even after the landlords and rich peasants who had been the leaders of the local lineages had been removed, the central lineage branch still had the more extensive patronage networks of the better off, sustaining what villagers after the Great Leap famine of 1959–1961 treasured as a return to "humanity" (rendao), while what had been the poorer local lineage branches were still poorer and with less extensive, or almost no networks of patronage.

Into this mix, in 1964 a work-team from the higher level of the Party entered to live with the poorest and inject a new socialist spirit with attacks on backsliding local cadres. Their method after a period of interrogation of local cadres and gathering of complaints against them was to institute the political ritual of struggle meetings, in which the cadres faced their accusers, made the confessions that they had already made in interrogations, and apologized. These meetings were emotionally highly charged, with resentful denunciations of favoritism, giving new life to class categories and to the social order of the revolution to create socialism and eventually reach an order of complete social justice. These were rituals with an ideology of change and revolutionary transformation of self and society, and so more than just an ideal or polite social ordering of everyday realities.

Then a further injection of revolutionary fervor and a new set of the same kind of rituals were instituted when the village, as every other village in China, became host to volunteer youth from city neighborhoods and middle schools. They had volunteered to live and work in the countryside, without a prospect of return to the city, as a way of proving themselves, in both senses of proof: being forged in the hardship and ardor of the socialist transformation of villages for the good of the whole of China and the more mundane sense of proving their revolutionary credentials for their personal records, as kept for everyone in the PRC.

The sent-down youth brigade farmed its allocated land ineffectively, but very effectively started the regular meetings, every lunchtime and evening, of production teams to study Mao thought. These had a formula that can well be described as ritual and like ritual they conveyed a world perspective full of feeling and moral purpose. First they celebrated the mythical person of Mao, then they added the mythic stories of revolutionary virtue in the persons of three heroes — collected in the easy-to-read anthology since called the 'little red book'. And then they sought to apply these, with the addition of the leading article of that day's People's Daily and its revolutionary anti-imperialist and anti-revisionist line, to the achievements since 1949 in Chen village. This celebration was reinforced by a revival of speaking bitterness (jiang ku), first instituted during land redistribution, in which older men and women spoke of the hardship and violence they had suffered before Liberation (1949) and everyone ate a meal of bitter herbs. The sent-down youth turned the stories of the three heroes into songs to be sung by the whole of each production team, a completely new musical tradition. Meetings ended with praise for those who had worked hard and well and self-criticisms by those who had been lazy. The meetings promoted a sense of the village and its teams as a big family, as before but now as part of a countrywide public good. A village-wide network of loudspeakers also broadcast revolutionary songs and announcements of praise to named team members for good, hard work. Disillusion came about, particularly among the sent-down youth who were Madsen's main informants, when some were not rewarded for their self-sacrificial efforts, and formed factions, and when villagers could see that they did not live up to the example of Mao and the other heroes.

Reinterpretation of the myths in terms of local exemplars and disputes over them, as well as repeated changes of line revealed the clay feet, as Madsen puts it, of the ritual's idol Mao. But the ideas of social justice, the slogans accompanying them and the songs celebrating their victory are still used and enjoyed in protests and parks all over China. In other words, these rituals of action and promise were at variance with the everyday reality of work and personal rivalries. Like all rituals they overlaid everyday with an ideal that was to some extent ambivalent, open to reinterpretation and to rival claims for authority and recognition. They differed from the rituals of dynastic government and the mainly, but not entirely suppressed rituals of continuity and protection addressed to ancestors and gods, and from life-cycle and death rituals in that they were secular, with recent and living heroes, and the ideal promoted by them was a realisable future. They could be described as utopian, but it is difficult to say whether they are ritual or anti-ritual disciplines or reactions of "sincerity".

9.7 Funerals Post-Mao

In describing how funerals are performed in 'Moonshadow village', in Mei county, Guangdong province in the 1990s, Oxfeld (2010) takes up the issue of orthopraxy and orthodoxy and the changes that have occurred under the PRC such that new ideologies are now juxtaposed with the continuation of funeral rites.

A key point concerning these changes is that secular ceremonies, started in the era of Mao, are continued in work units in cities, honoring the deceased both as a comrade and as a member of a family. But in the countryside, even though such ceremonies are familiar to villagers, funeral rituals consisting in the former common practice have been re-instituted after their suppression as waste and superstition. Oxfeld argues on the basis of villagers' own statements that they feel morally obliged to perform these rituals, which acknowledge an unrepayable debt to their parents and their parents' parents, in the male line. An important ritual segment of these death rituals is led by a master of ceremonies to pay homage to the deceased and takes place in the rebuilt lineage hall. Another segment, for the care of the soul in its journey through purgatory and toward reincarnation, is performed by Buddhist ritual experts reciting scriptures and performing the rescue of the soul at a specially constructed altar. There is a procession with the coffin to bury the body or cremate it (and eventually bury the ash urn). Becoming an ancestor is vividly contrasted with becoming a hungry ghost, a person who has died but not been given these death rituals.

Even Maoist cadres have engaged ritual experts to perform these rituals because, as one told Oxfeld, though he did not believe in gods or an afterlife 'to commemorate your roots is not the same as worshipping gods' (p. 131). In other words, his interpretation of the same rituals is not the same as someone who does believe in gods and ghosts. Another non-believer who nevertheless placed offerings at the graves of her late husband and his father despite saying that to do so was "superstitious" said she conformed because 'people say you should' (p. 132). Here as elsewhere, acceding to ritual practice is not out of belief, but out of a sense of community and conformity. You could say this is pure orthopraxy, yet it also retains an element of moral obligation that alludes to a common sense of ancestry.

Beyond conformity it is important to add the enjoyment of extravagance and of creating a lively occasion — in the more dramatic parts of the ritual of the soul's rescue, the burning of the soul house and consumer goods made of paper and cane or bamboo, and in the feasting and gambling that takes place between and during the scripture reciting ritual. The performance of this rescue of the soul, the lay ritual of eulogy, the guests invited to take part in it, the size of the procession, and the feasting and gambling are witnessed as measures of wealth and social status. They are the most social aspects of funeral rituals, complementing the rituals of offering to purgatorial deities and of placating ghosts. They are acts of hospitality (which will be the subject of the next chapter) and they incur the censorship of officials — now as in the past — for their excess. Yet the whole point in funeral (and temple) ritual is hospitable generosity or excess in acknowledgment of an infinite debt and gratitude. 'Otherwise people will say you are unfilial' (p. 139).

Chau (2006: p. 129–137) describes a more abbreviated but complete set of revived death rituals at the other, northern end of China. His account stresses the way the event is organized as a complex operation, coordinated by a director making sure everything is well coordinated and performed because of the dangers to reputation if it is not done well and in accordance with expectations, even though it is shorter and lacks the Buddhist and Daoist ritual experts of former years. His emphasis on hosting and hospitality will be considered in detail in the next chapter.

Here we can conclude that the old importance of manners, rites and relationships of respect still exists, but it coexists with other discourses and ideologies and the formative results of Maoist political rituals. On one hand, since it is true that these death rituals are transmitted and coexist with the transmission and performance of quite different hierarchies and ideologies, it is arguable that rituals support not some explicit ideology or doctrine, but are flexibly reinterpretable according to changed circumstances. On the other hand, rituals of domestic and collective life might continue to convey a specifiable hierarchy of patrilineal ancestors and territorial protector gods, or of newer ideals of collective social justice. The issue then is how they coexist with the national narrative of history in which the Party is leading China into its future. Even though the most deliberately and often performed rituals of revolutionary transformation are no longer performed, their effects in slogans and songs remain and the rituals of for instance the annual celebrations of the founding of the Party, or of the founding of the PRC, are equally secular and future oriented.

From the examples of Chinese death rituals and their history, we can conclude that they are ideological as Bloch claims for all ritual, even when participants are not aware of the history of their institution and their prescription. They also show that they transmit an hierarchical order of authority, as both Bloch and Bell claim for all ritual practice. But they raise serious questions about the claim that ritual is just correct performance, since Chinese death rituals include scriptures, songs, pictorial representations and dance dramas that enact a world of ancestors, deities, demons, and ghosts. In other words, orthopraxy includes words, images, and other representations, even if it does not include professions of dogmatic faith.

Seminar Questions

Do Chinese rituals convey 'belief'?

How might they be interpreted as either hegemonic or as counter-hegemonic in the present day?

Do Chinese examples of secular or political ritual offer ways of distinguishing it from religious or traditional ritual?

Readings

Bell, Catherine (1992). *Ritual Theory, Ritual Practice.* Oxford University Press: Oxford, pp. 182–223.

Bell, Catherine (1997). *Ritual: perspectives and dimensions.* Oxford University Press (Chapter 6 'Ritual density' — particularly the section on "orthodoxy and orthopraxy" pp. 191–197).

Bell, Catherine (1988). 'Ritualisation of texts and textualisation of ritual in the codification of Taoist liturgy', *History of Religions,* 27(4), pp. 366–392.

Bloch, Maurice (1989). *Ritual, History and Power; selected papers in anthropology.* Monographs in Anthropology 58. The Athlone Press: London. (chapters 2 "Symbols, song, dance and features of articulation: Is religion an extreme form of traditional authority?" and 5 "From cognition to ideology", pp. 19–45 and 106–136).

Chau, Adam (2006). *Miraculous Response; doing popular religion in contemporary China.* Stanford: Stanford University Press: Stanford, pp. 129–137.

Madsen, Richard (1984). *Morality and Power in a Chinese Village.* University of California Press: Berkeley and London Press (Chapters 2–5).

Oxfeld, Ellen (2004). 'When you drink water, think of its source: morality, status, and reinvention in rural Chinese funerals', in *The Journal of East Asian Studies,* 64(4), pp. 961–990.

Oxfield, Ellen (2010). *Drink Water, but Remember the Source; moral discourse in a Chinese village.* University of California Press: California (Chapter 4 'Everlasting Debts').

Rawski, Evelyn S. (1987). 'A historian's approach to Chinese death ritual', in James L.Watson and Evelyn Rawski (eds.) *Death Ritual in Late Imperial and Modern China.* University of California Press: California, pp. 20–36.

Ruf, Gregory (1998). *Cadres and Kin: making a socialist village in West China 1921–1991.* Stanford University Press.

Seligman, Adam B., Weller, Robert P., Puett, Michel J., and Simon, Bennet (2008). *Ritual and its Consequences: An Essay on the Limits of Sincerity.* Oxford University Press: Oxford and New York (Chapters 1 and 4).

Watson, James L. (1987). 'The structure of Chinese funerary rites: elementary forms, ritual sequence, and the primacy of performance', in Watson and Evelyn Rawski (eds.) *Death Ritual in Late Imperial and Modern China.* University of California Press: California, pp. 3–19.

Chapter 10

Hospitality

'Hospitality' suggests that every human culture includes reaching out to fellow humans, according to its own conception of humanity. But as we shall see, the main features of hospitality are that it entails profoundly unequal relationships and is full of ambivalences, not a simple recognition of common humanity. Hospitality is a relation between a "sovereign", who is master of a space, moving up in scale from a home to a polity, and a visitor. In other words, it is a relationship of the generosity of an insider to an outsider, however defined.

This chapter will first expound the idea of hospitality as a basis of civilization, including civility and good manners. It will then take up the anthropology of hospitality, before moving on to imperial Chinese guest rituals and anthropologists' studies of Chinese conceptions and practices of hospitality, in order to see how they illuminate the anthropology of hospitality.

10.1 The Constraint to Share and Be Generous: The Basis of Civilization

Generosity requires self-constraint. Self-constraint according to rules and norms, self-constraint represents the minimal definition of "civilization." Every known culture demands self-constraint and can therefore be deemed a civilization. Egalitarian societies of hunters and foragers, such as the Hadza in East Africa, exercise constraint on selfishness, which children are taught, to oblige them to share food and other possessions.

Similarly, every society has rules about appropriate giving, and acceptance and return of gifts, as Marcel Mauss' most famous book *The Gift* had established. Those who breach these rules are, in the terms of their own civilization, considered to be less than human or, in other words, uncivilized or barbarian.

As Matei Candea and Giovanni Da Col, the editors of the special issue of *JRAI: The return to hospitality: strangers, guests, and ambiguous encounters*, point out in their introductory article (2012), hospitality could well have been a theme as classic as that of the gift in anthropology. Indeed, hospitality could be considered a master concept, including the exchange of gifts, among which feasts figure most prominently in practice. Feasting is one of the major means of redistribution in a gift economy, with gifts upwards to chiefs and the feast as a return gift.

At base, hospitality is about feeding and sheltering. The most basic gift is food, from the simplest and least formal feeding to the most elaborate and ceremonious banqueting in the premises of the host's home or hall. So, for the hunter in egalitarian bands, the sharing of the spoils obeys rules of who gets what cut, as it is shared. There is a grading of the sharing of food, from the daily to the occasional, from the most domestic sharers of home outwards to other increasingly less frequent and less intimate sharers of food in terms of kinship and friendship distance. These are the relations of reciprocity set out by Sahlins (1965). But in that early work, they appear to be in fixed categories of (a) generalized exchange (among kin), (b) reciprocal (with affines), (c) immediate trade, and (d) negative exchange raid and war. In reality, they are more dynamic — the establishing and maintaining of relations, or the loosening and cooling of relations as well as the reduction or the increase of social distance. This rather simple framework is elaborated in the more hierarchical societies where there are the added dimensions of hypergamy or hypogamy (marriage up or down the social hierarchy for a woman) and spheres of exchange — from the most valuable of valuables and their circulation down to the basic ingredients of food and clothing, and the relations of caste, class and authority through patronage and redistribution — of gift upwards in exchange for favor downwards.

The most potent myths and rules of hospitality, at their most ambivalent, are concerned with hospitality at the greatest social distance — the feeding and shelter to be offered to strangers who could be beggars, wanderers, travelers, itinerant traders, religious mendicants, all those most alarming, but also necessary to settled agrarian societies and their states.

If, on the other hand, strangers are also raiders and warriors, hospitality to them is a peace-making ceremony. Then it is not a single stranger hosted by a sovereign at home, but a coming together of equal sovereigns 'as one stomach', a stomach that is white and unbesmirched by secrets of envy, as the people in the region of the Omo river in Ethiopia would say (Strecker, 1999).

10.2 Altruism: The Impossible Gift on the Ultimate Scale of Humanity

Scaling up to the biggest scope, the rules of hospitality seem to entail ideas of universality and fellow humanity beyond the belongings of kinship, tribe, civilization and nation: the recognition of fellowship with one who is also completely different but still human.

In the philosophy of otherness, from Kant's *Perpetual Peace* (1795) to Derrida's *Of Hospitality* (2000), we are in the realm of the impossible gift, the altruism of giving oneself or one's sense of self to the recognition of any Other. This is the highest scale of the Eurocentric universe of monotheism, in which the absolute Other is the Creator of humanity and the universe as an all-encompassing and transcendent of the merely mortal. In the moral philosophy of Kant and the reflections on it by Derrida, it is given a secular interpretation. In Derrida's work, this involves bringing to the fore the etymology of the word 'hospitality' as a combination of the words in Latin for guest and for master, highlighting the ideal of recognition of the other as a readiness to *give up sovereignty* to the other (Candea and De Col, 2012: p. 54). The equivalent but opposite would be the selling of one's soul to the Devil, or to Mephistopheles in the Faust legend. In both, the Good and the Wicked Other, the giving of sovereignty is to entertain and give oneself up to an all-powerful Other.

At less than universal scales, we come to the actual practice of hospitality not as the giving up, but as the retention of sovereignty. Mastery of a home can be scaled up to mastery of a lineage, or further to a kingdom, empire, or nation. Indeed, the ideologies of rule, of empires as of nations, usually use the idea of home, be it of domestic economy or of family feeling, to conjure up a doctrine of protection by and loyalty to a state and its economic policies. Similarly, 'the stranger' is a shifter in scales of identification with higher levels of collectivity. The stranger is to be entertained and at the same time kept at a distance and watched. This is the standard practice of hospitality.

10.3 An Anthropological Study of Hospitality

Pride in hospitality is a feature of all cultures, more so in Arab and other Mediterranean societies. Shryock (2012) writes of a Bedouin people in Jordan, but he makes it quite clear that they share a common heritage with the stories of hospitality transmitted in Graeco-Roman traditions and in the Abrahamic biblical traditions. The central point he makes is that hospitality is a show of confidant sovereignty, on every scale from a Bedouin household to the kingdom of Jordan. The extension of sovereignty as expansive and protective generosity to visitors by invitation or by chance is the ideal and it is put on show in rites of hospitality. Even so, as he points out, it is an essentially unequal relationship, in which the sovereign pride of saying generously 'my house is your house' is, in fact, staged in a special part of the house, to which the guest is confined, not just spatially but also following the rules of proper guest conduct, so that the other side of the truth of generosity is that, as these Bedouin say, 'the guest is prisoner of the host'.

The discourse that highlights this ideal takes the form of stories about bad hosts and bad guests. One set of stories summarized by Shryock concerns the ascendance of a lineage to the governorship of an area under the Ottoman Empire and then the kingdom of Jordan. They are stories of the politics of hospitality, whereas the ideal is that hospitality be above politics. Banquets are complements to battlegrounds: they are stories of offense to hospitality, rivalry to be sovereign hosts and so of refusing to be guests (which is to cede sovereignty), and of hosts slaying guests lured by their hospitality.

Shryock points out that Kant recognized this essential asymmetry of sovereign host and obedient guest in his condition for perpetual peace, by prescribing that visitors (traders, diplomats and travelers, essential for the exchange between sovereign republics in a world federation of republics) keep moving and not claim to belong to the visited republic (in the days before mass labor migration). Derrida, on the other hand, recognized the asymmetry of hospitality as a challenge to sovereignty in the name of a higher justice of hospitality, which is not the practice of actual hospitality, but to which you could say "hospitality" is an appeal, the inference of a world without sovereigns.

Shryock also points out that the tradition of keeping the stranger at bay in the contemporary world is a function of the hospitality industry, in which the same pride of heritage and of provision for guests is commercially expressed. Mass media, tourism, and ritual as cultural performance create audience participants as consumers of entertainment and nostalgia and also become the means of keeping the visitor at a distance from the ritual and feasting of actual kin and other networks.

10.4 Imperial Chinese Guest Ritual

Chinese rituals of hospitality offer a completely different scenario of sovereignty, in which the guest is a superior and encompassing sovereign in relation to the sovereign host. Therefore, Chinese hospitality enacts a complex interplay of sovereignty in terms of mastery over a given space.

On vessels of the period known as the Shang in the second millennium BC, sacrificial bronze containers and heaters of millet-based alcohol, steamed millets and cooked meats were inscribed on their inside surfaces. Many of these inscriptions mention one of the rites using such vessels, called the Bin or the guest ritual. Here the guest was either an ancestor, or one of the spirits that can bring rain or drought. Through ancestors, human nobles and kings could approach the supreme deity Di (who according to some scholars may be a collective term for all supreme ancestors). This is hospitality to a guest who is superior, in which the hospitality of food and drink could be described as a host offering a tribute to a guest in a reversal of or a transfer of sovereignty upwards.

After the unification of the kingdoms that had formed a federation or were at war with each other, the guest rituals of Han and subsequent imperial dynasties included the imperial host in his capital receiving, feasting, and giving valuables to the representatives of sovereigns on and beyond the border regions of the empire, who brought tribute and gifts to the emperor. A version of the same unequal relation of reciprocity was enacted in the journeys of imperial emissaries to the empire's border regions, in which the burden of imperial hospitality had to be borne by the tributary guests, showcasing another case of a reversal or transfer of sovereignty upwards.

A lower-level version of this practice occurred as recently as the 20th century, as Mueggler (2001: Chapter 4) describes. One of the minority communities, categorized by Chinese officials as Yi, the Lolop'o (as they describe themselves) of Zhizuo in the far north of Yunnan province, selected the household of a couple who had lived well and was sufficiently able to raise the funds for the proper conduct of the rites honoring ancestors and preserving the fertility of the valley. In similar ways, households were and are selected all over China under different titles and in different ways as leaders of the rituals of local territorial communities. But in Zhizuo, the leading household for a year is required not only to conduct these rites, but also to be the host to the 'stream of soldiers, officials, police, merchants and other influential visitors' (p. 105) who passed through Zhizuo, an example of the lowest level and scale of hosting higher leaders and their underlings. It was a pattern repeated up through to the highest levels below the emperor's and the republic's central government, until the People's Republic put an end to such tributary relationships in China.

With more powerful guests, the "guest" ritual of tribute and gracious hospitality could become a contest of sovereignty and ultimately of conquest. Imperial Chinese dealings with those on and over its border regions, called Yi, which is a generic term for those who were not fully assimilated into civilization in China, could consist in relations of trade and marriage as well as tribute. But on another border, the horsemen and their tribal federations in the north, all the way through to the Qing, could see the tributary and trading relations with the agrarian Chinese as giving in to their demands. Imperial weakness could turn into a new dynasty of conquerors, as indeed evident in how the Manchu conquest became the Qing dynasty.

For the English-reading world, the most famous case of hospitality as a contest of sovereignties was the British trade and diplomatic embassy from King George III in 1793 to the Qing Qianlong emperor. It was led by Lord Macartney who relayed pleas to remove imperial restrictions on trade with Britain and other European powers. The guest ritual of tributaries demanded an obeisance, called the kowtow, involving nine times sinking to the knees with forehead on the floor, but Macartney insisted this embassy was from a sovereign to a sovereign, a relation of equals, and that he would not accept the kowtow requirement. The emperor compromized and allowed him simply to genuflect before him on his platform, as he would before his own sovereign (Hevia, 1995). However, in his imperial (sacred) edict to Macartney after the audience, the emperor treated the embassy as a friendly tribute mission and made no trade concessions (Hevia, 1995). The subsequent history of this relationship culminates in the unequal treaties and the plunder and sacking by European powers of the imperial gardens and their palaces in all the styles of the world with China at its center, including European palaces built with the help of European architects. These gardens were an enactment of the centrality of the imperial dynasty in the world that came to the court with gifts and the styles of building and clothing and other manners. One of the justifications of the European plunder and of the treaties that forced open so-called treaty ports was the doctrine of free trade and to acquire compensation for the confiscation of opium brought into China by British and Indian merchants. But another was precisely over the translation of Yi, the category of tributary guest people. The British enforced acceptance of a treaty in which the translation of Yi was 'barbarian' and therefore an insult to them (Liu, 2004).

These Chinese cases reinforce the anthropology of hospitality, which treats it as an asymmetrical relationship that threatens to break down into a contest of sovereignties. But in addition, they present the case of being host to a superior being, the emperor or ancestors or a supreme deity, which opens up the question of which of the two is the sovereign and which the host is. Later in this chapter, this question will be elaborated, but first let us look at some more detailed anthropologies of Chinese hospitality.

10.5 Chinese Anthropologies of Hospitality

Stafford's (2000) ethnography of villages ("Angang" in Taiwan and "dragon-head" in north-eastern China) is deployed to develop a universal theme of separation, but inevitably it is also about the hosting of guests. Greeting and seeing off guests in various degrees of social distance is the subject of Chapter 2 of Stafford's book. Two points should be noted. One is that guests include spiritual, invisible beings: ancestors (representative of the host and other families), ghosts (the forgotten ancestors or the abandoned, who have no descendants to be their hosts, in the surrounding territory) and gods (the guardians and protectors of that territory). The second is that those who are closest domestically and familially have the least etiquette of polite treatment in their comings and goings — they are not 'guests'. Instead of being guests, they would rather be co-hosts, or act for one of their number who was the nominal host.

Stafford, like Shryock, pays particular attention to scaled-up hospitality, including not only the hosting of important visitors, who represent a superior scale including gods and ancestors, but also the politics of sovereign hospitality. The imperial guest ritual is now transformed ––think of receptions in the Great Hall of the People, or other standard fare of diplomacy and public news presentation in which subtle alterations of etiquette signal the state of the relation from the host's, or from the guest's point of view, views that express different intentions that may be in conflict. The differences between them continue to be contests of sovereignty, the host seeking to assert its sovereignty by displaying an etiquette of generosity and formality and the guest wanting its sovereignty recognized as an equal, reciprocal partner rather than as an inferior. This is hospitality as a relation among sovereigns, just as the peace ceremony in Ethiopia mentioned above was.

According to Stafford, not treating the closest as guests, is as much a norm of conduct as guest ritual is. Both hide a tension. The guest ritual gives overt expression to (or demands the performance of) feelings of joy at greeting and regret at parting, whereas the non-guest conduct of familiarity and intimacy excludes the emotional expression despite the fact that strong emotions are inevitably involved. Those emotions might be mixed or not reciprocated, but the idealized relation of intimacy and nurture in the reproduction of family relations extending to ancestors is maintained.

We could add that the making of friendship is often ritualized as the arrangement of regular occasions to eat and drink together as a group, in which the event is co-hosted rather than treating anyone as guest. This is the relation of individuals as close sovereigns.

But note that the formality of relations of hospitality are never those of fixed relations, but a medium for jockeying for favors and prestige even among those who profess to be equals, seated at a round banqueting table. Toasting and the skill of speaking and engendering a joint sense of fellowship are ways of gaining authority at a banquet.

In the last pages of Chapter 2, Stafford turns to close relations of friendship and their extraordinarily sentimental, even romantic expressions as a matter of form. He dwells on the 'overcoming of separation through memory' (p. 68), which is through tokens, such as photographs formally posed together, but also letters and poems sent to each other in times of separation, all of which are called *liu ge jinian*, 'leaving a reminder behind', using the same word *liu* used to describe the detaining of a departing guest in the ritual of parting.

In the last chapter of his book, Stafford observes the use of poems on the separation and hoped-for reunion of friends in expressions of the separation and hoped-for reunion of Taiwan with the Mainland, on both sides. This scaled-up expression of co-hospitality is, of course, also a contest of sovereignties expressed in terms of a current tension and a desired peace.

On hospitality to guests who are more powerful, resourceful or with authority over the host, we can refer to Yan's *The Flow of Gifts*, where he stresses the gift upwards, which may be a banquet to which the superior is invited as recognition of the authority and/or protection of a superior. Of course, the reciprocation is the granting of access to 'what he has in his gift,' as the British expression goes. In this gift are permissions, access to credit, protection against other powerful people or just the prestige lent by his presence. Refusal of the superior to accept an invitation to a banquet by an inferior is to limit or cut off that gift relation.

Gift relations and hospitality in China were and remain hierarchical, though the terms (and the politics) of hierarchy have radically changed. The contest of sovereignty that characterizes hospitality may, in the light of anthropological studies in China, be re-worded as a jockeying for positions of relative superiority, using the authority of a current host and the authority of the rituals of hospitality and reciprocity themselves. This cannot be true just of China, but the elaboration of gift exchange and hospitality in China allows us to add this to the general anthropology of hospitality.

We are yet to explore further dimensions of the ambivalence of hospitality, evident elsewhere as well as in China, as we approach what might be called negative hospitality, or a burden on hospitality that threatens to become negative reciprocity.

10.6 Guest as a Parasite; Host as a Poisoner

Let us take a cue from Bloch (2005), where he describes how hospitality to a stranger among the Zafimaniry of Madagascar involves taking him into the host's home and finding a term of kinship by which to address him, in other words to treat him not as stranger, but as kin and therefore of the same body of kinship that shares food. To eat together is to share the substance of life together and become consubstantial. Everywhere, eating and drinking alcohol together is also an act of proclaiming equality along with oneness, while at the same time there is a partially disguised and disavowed inequality between the host and the guest evident in the ranks of seating orders. In addition, the Zafimaniry also fear that food offered will be poisoned. This is the shadow side of making strangers close kin by the sharing of food. The fear of poisoning conveys the fact that separation, by which the eaters have become strangers to each other, also means actual or potential rivalry and conflict, inferred from kin who might poison.

Similarly, in many African cultures, *witchcraft* emanates from close kin. The stomach is not just the bond of consubstantiality. It is also potentially the seat of witchcraft.

In the volume edited by Candea and Da Col (2012), there are other examples of such acute ambivalence, a guest becoming a parasitic threat, while also being a claimant to generous charity; or a host who is not just generous, but poisonous.

From the Dechen in the Tibetan highlands, Giovanni Da Col (2012) describes a fear that the host has been inhabited by a parasitic poison god who preys on the field of fortune of his or her guests, getting into them and their energy field from the inside and gobbling them up, turning them into their own outsides: 'the nemesis of hospitality, reciprocity, and reproductive kinship' (p. 179). It is a striking image for the similar fear that an insecure native has about his country being taken over by migrants, in which he becomes estranged in his own land.

The parasite is the complementary opposite of both guest and host, of the whole reciprocal relationship of hospitable recognition. Exorcism and ostracism, or just avoidance, are the separating and distancing remedies for parasitism, and they too are opposites of hospitality.

Two current depictions of a stranger bring out this ambivalence. They are the stranger as a fugitive and the guest as a parasite, exploiting the host's generosity, a counterpart to the honored guest from a superior level, who can be an impossible burden on the domestic economy. Think of the opposing discourses of offering asylum and controlling immigration. On the one side, asylum is offered as an act of hospitality to fugitives from oppression. On the other side, a migrant population (usually because of its marks of strangeness) is a target of those who claim they are an impossible burden on the domestic economy. Migrants, even if they are so-called "economic" migrants, seekers of adventure and new opportunities, come from relatively deprived situations and sometimes enter as smuggled goods into the well-named 'host' nation. They flee extremes of exploitation. In the end, neither the threatened chauvinist inhospitality, nor the generously principled asylum host to the deprived and the oppressed, can prevail in their own terms. Actual hospitality compromizes between the two ends of this ambivalence.

Having explored the full range of ambivalence surrounding hospitality with the help of anthropological studies in China, we can finally turn to the most asymmetrical of hospitalities, to a greatly superior being and a greatly feared parasite or pest.

10.7 Hosting Gods, Ghosts and Other Guests

Worshipping gods is to play host to them, offering them food, but a god stands for an encompassing authority. Territorial protector gods obviously encompass all those who live in that territory. Chau's book (2006) is about the temple of one such territorial protector, the Black Dragon King (Hei Longwang) of Longwanggou and neighboring villages in northern Shaanxi province. His book covers the religiosity of the people living there and the politics of the local elite and the local state involving the temple's manager Boss Wang. But Chau's central concern is with the ritual, particularly the festivals for the God, as putting on an event and hospitality. In Chapter 2, he expands on the tasks, skills and organization involved in what he calls 'hosting' and 'event production.'

'Worshippers volunteer at temple festivals and say they are "helping out" the deity in staging the festival' (p. 126). Chau seeks to balance the emphasis on liturgical aspects of ritual in previous studies by looking into the social organization of the ritual, particularly of funerals and festivals, which are large-scale events. As the local people call it, *ban shi'r* (to put on an event) is to play host, fulfilling a social and a ritual obligation, always involving a feast and offerings to spirits (the ancestors, the gods, and ghosts) and exorcism and propitiation of demons to avoid trouble. The social obligations are to reciprocate and maintain networks of social relations and to reproduce and if possible to expand the sovereignty (i.e. to reaffirm and enlarge the reputation) of the host.

The festival is a huge feat of organization and expense. It is hosted on a large scale of reciprocities. The ritual liturgical element in the festival is far less than in the funeral that Chau describes, which lacks either Buddhist, or Daoist ritual experts who had been active in pre-Communist years and are now part of the funeral elsewhere in other parts of northern China (Jones, 2010). Perhaps it is for this reason that Chau stresses the social so much as to qualify the ritual as "theoretical" when he writes that 'theoretically the host would be the deity itself' (p. 137), when it is clear that (as Stafford points out) hosting the deity is a peculiar relationship of inducing his descent to the temple for the festival as an honored guest. Is he turned into a host as suggested by the curious expressions (quoted on p. 138) that the holders of the event are 'helping out the venerable Dragon King to produce the event' and that 'people depend on gods and gods depend on people' in the same way that a guest such as the emperor, or his emissary is also then the host?

Two other directions of hospitality must be added. One is the charitable hospitality to the ghosts, the spirits of the dead who have not become ancestors and are wandering, tormented and potentially tormenting, posing a danger to the living. In both funerals and in god festivals, the Daoist and Buddhist ritualists of northern (and other parts of) China by their ritual gestures and the reading of scriptures convert great tables full of offerings (later to be eaten at feasts in the hosts' homes) into food for these wandering spirits so that they will not harm the inhabitants of the god's territory, inviting them to eat first and then sending them back again as inferior guests.

The other direction of hospitality is, of course, the feasting and the occasion, which can include procession and music and theater, creating what Chau's Shaanxi villagers call 'red and fiery' (*honghuo*), which in other parts of China is called 'hot and noisy' (*renao*) sociality. In Chapter 8, Chau goes into extensive detail on all the entertaining activities surrounding an occasion of feasting in which every household is a host and the whole territory becomes a stage for guests to come and enjoy themselves with the hosts. This is hospitality that successive governments of China, imperial and republican, have denounced as excessive, but that recurs despite them, for pleasure and pride in the locality — a more horizontal, but still asymmetrical direction of hospitality, in which the guests reciprocate on another occasion as hosts with their own local pride and solidarity.

Anthropological studies of Chinese hospitality, such as by Chau, Stafford, Mueggler and Da Col, have shown the full extent of the asymmetries and ambivalences of hospitality. They range from the guest who is treated as a host, to the host who is feared as a threat to life. They illustrate rival sovereignties in competing to put on 'red hot' social occasions or in jockeying for position and reputation by speeches and toasting at feasts. Fear of failure to be a successful host is exemplified in the substitution of sovereignty by conquest in the fateful history of the guest ritual in imperial China. Could these extreme asymmetries be peculiar to Chinese hospitality or typical of very hierarchical civilizations?

Seminar Questions

Do the ethics of hospitality change as the scale of reference broadens: compare Chinese with European or any other instances?

How do Chinese etiquette and 'hosting' illustrate some of the ambivalences of hospitality?

Readings

Bloch, Maurice (2005). 'Commensality and poisoning', in his *Essays on cultural transmission*, Berg: Oxford, pp. 45–59.

Candea, Matei and Da Col, Giovanni (eds.) (2012). Special issue of *JRAI The return to hospitality: strangers, guests, and ambiguous encounters* (Introduction).

Chau, Adam (2006). *Miraculous Response: doing popular religion in contemporary China.* Stanford University Press: Stanford (chapter 8 'Red-hot sociality' pp. 147–168).

Da Col, Giovanni (2012). 'The poisoner and the parasite: cosmoeconomics, fear, and hospitality among Dechen Tibetans', in Candea and Da Col (eds.) pp. 175–195.

Mueggler, Eric (2001). *The Age of Wild Ghosts; memory, violence, and place in southwest China*: University of California Press: Berkeley and London (chapter 4 'The valley house' pp. 95–126).

Sahlins, Marshall (1965). 'On the sociology of primitive exchange', in M. Banton (ed.) *The Relevance of Models for Social Anthropology.* Monographs of the ASA no. 1, Tavistock: London, pp. 139–236.

Shryock, Andrew (2012). 'Breaking hospitality apart: bad hosts, bad guests, and the problem of sovereignty', in *JRAI special issue: the return to hospitality: strangers, guests, and ambiguous encounters* (eds.) Candea and Da Col.

Stafford, Charles (2000). *Separation and Reunion in Modern China.* Cambridge University Press: Cambridge (Chapter 2 'The etiquette of parting and return' pp. 55–69).

Strecker, Iwo (1999). 'The temptations of war and the struggle for peace among the Hamar of south Ethiopia', in Elwert, Georg, Feuchtwang, Stephan and Norbert, Dieter (eds.) Dynamics of Violence; processes of escalation and de-escalation in violent group conflicts. Supplement No 1 of *Sociologus*, Duncker & Humblot: Berlin, pp. 227–259.

References

Hevia, James L. (1995). *Cherishing Men from Afar; Qing guest ritual and the Macartney embassy of 1793*, Duke University Press: Durham.

Jones, Stephen (2010). *In Search of the Folk Daoists of North China*, Ashgate: Farnham.

Liu, Lydia (2004). *The Clash of Empires; the invention of China in modern world making*, Harvard University Press: Cambridge Mass. and London.

Yan, Yunxiang (1996). *The Flow of Gifts: Reciprocity and Social Networks in a Chinese Village.* Stanford University Press: Stanford.

Chapter 11

The Stranger-King and the Outside of an Imperial Civilization

Hospitality, as we have seen, is always about the opening up of the host's sovereignty to the visitors. In discussing hospitality, the term 'stranger' includes not just the lone wanderer who may be dangerous or someone infinitely more powerful, who appears in a disguise of lowliness. We have added to this the representative of sovereignty on a higher scale, which includes a lower sovereignty, one example of which is the noble or the king and his entourage visiting and becoming a burden of hospitality on his host-subjects. Now we propose to expand this idea using the suggestion that sovereigns on this large scale are by nature strangers.

The chapter will first expound the theme and conception of the stranger-king and then illustrate to what extent it illuminates Chinese history and anthropology. This analysis of Chinese civilization offers insights into the relationship of sovereignty between self and other through the activities of centring by the state. We will trace these centring processes at two scales: first, the relationship between the dynastic empire and its tributary peripheries; second, through bringing in their affinal kin and offspring. In line with arguments made in the previous chapters, the interconnections between state ideology, ritual and myth refract in the historical and ethnographic examples from China, offering insights into centring processes in anthropological studies of civilization and cosmocracy.

11.1 The Theme of the Stranger-King

Heusch (1962, 1982) first elaborated the distinctions between claims to autochthony, which means being, belonging and claiming authority through native lines of descent and having ownership of the land, and the lineages of chiefs, kings and emperors whose origins were outside their domains in a large number of west and central African chiefdoms and kingdoms or mercantile empires.

Marshall Sahlins has elaborated this relationship between autochthonous and external authority in a number of publications, including the one in 2012 in which he starts out from Firth's study of chiefs among the Tikopia, an Austronesian people. Sahlins claims he has found it all over the Austronesian world, in east and southeast Asia, in the Graeco-Roman world and in the Americas. On the basis of the stranger-king theme, Sahlins generalizes (2015) about all forms of hierarchy and state preceding the states of capitalist economies originating in and globally spread from post-Reformation Europe.

For most of human history, he argues, control over life and fertility and primarily control of wealth in people, rather than in land and other means of production, was held by those who could claim to be the mediators of cosmological powers that give and also endanger life, while the land and other means of production were the property of those with ancestral claims to them. To this, we should add the other kind of autochthonous claim, namely the possession of earth cults or their equivalents. The rulers in what became the first states were those who could by conquest convince or had already convinced their subjects that they were mediators to more powerful, superior ancestors and larger-scale powers than those of local earth cults. Such rulers were treated as divine or semi-divine at the same time as being human bodies. Similarly their subjects and their lands and animals, for hunting or for cultivation, were spirit-guardians and physical bodies.

In contrast, the dual nature of human beings starting from Greek philosophy, but culminating in the myths of economic maximizing rationality, are dual in a different way. They have calculating and regulating minds, which are also the source and function of the state and its bureaucracies, and bestial or animal bodies whose wants need to be formed and subjectified by state, labor and market disciplines.

Plainly, this crude, if substantial dichotomy, hides a great deal of variation and a number of questions about, for instance, the difference between medieval Christian and Greek and Roman states, let alone the great differences that exist among hunter foragers and between them and the mercantile, pastoral and agrarian empires and states that succeeded the invention of agriculture and the domestication of animals. But it does highlight the anthropology of cosmocratic rule, namely the authority of those who claimed and were recognized to be life-givers and life-takers.

At least in some respects, China can be included in this conception of a state and its sovereignty. The claim to be descended from Heaven was made in the title of the Chinese emperor, Tianzi — son of heaven. Heaven is not just outside, but in scale encompasses the earth on which his subjects live so that the empire is the universe, called All Under Heaven (Tianxia). The emperor was thus not only a fellow human, but also one who, as the descendant and chief mediator between earth and the heaven, encompassed all his subjects, regulating their calendar and ensuring the cosmological sources of fertility, in short, granting them life. He was alone formally allowed to address Heaven, and when his subjects did — as error, or as usurpation of his privilege — this was a known sign of disorder in the empire and universe. Who was host, when he visited his subjects or tributary princedoms — them or him? He is the encompassing sovereign as a guest who gives not as tribute, but as host.

This 'ideology' is but one instance of rulers claiming they are givers of life, not the women and men who actually give and sustain life. Bloch, as already discussed in Chapter 9 (see also his 1992 *Prey into Hunter; the politics of religious experience*, Cambridge University Press) has detected as the theme of every rite of passage and succession the ideological reconquest of life that endorses a current ruling order. This in a way makes rulers strangers by their removal from the flesh and the earth. But that alone is not enough to characterize them as stranger-kings.

For that, the first condition is the opposition of two kinds of authority, as Sahlins says, that which is derived from autochthony and that which is derived from external origins. Typically the latter is, as Sahlins points out, claimed by an affinal link to succession to rule through autochthonous wife givers or takers in their relations of hospitality and tribute, gift-giving and marriage with lineages outside their territory, or by conquest when such relations of trade and gift turn to war. Or else the claim to succession comes from one who has been banished and the very reasons for his banishment (the commission of unnatural acts of incest or murder) are taken as signs of his immunity to moral norms and therefore his transcendence of them, proven by actual success in mustering wealth, or forces for conquest. Often the sovereign was a complete outsider, for instance a merchant or a pastoral leader who had organized tribes into a force that could control trade and had established relations of trade and marriage with the agrarian settled monarch, nobility or elite.

Such were the descendants of the nomads called the Xiongnu, confederacies of tribes that in western Eurasia were called Huns, who after pacts with the Chinese emperors of the Han dynasty, including the giving of Chinese princesses to them in marriage, promised not to war with the Chinese empire. Finally, after the division of the Han empire, they took the capital city Luoyang, led by a man who had been a slave of the Chinese. He had no other claim to succession than conquest. But the great merit of the stranger-king model is that it draws our attention not just to relations of hierarchy and the history of a state from its inside, but to the way an inside is conceived through the making and maintaining of boundaries with an outside and on how that outside is conceived from the inside. We thus need to see the Chinese imperial state and its imagery as a relation to an outside.

11.2 Heteronomy

> "The union with the Other gives rise to the society as a self-producing totality—and the permanent contradiction that this autonomy is a function of heteronomy."
>
> (Sahlins, 2012: p. 8)

For Sahlins, no culture is complete; it is always defined in relation to an outside other, which is an actual other, outside the territory of a culture, possibly a traditional enemy, but also conceived as having access to resources and powers not in the control of the culture viewed from inside. In short, every culture is defined as an inside, differentiated and self-defined against its outside and other. The stranger-king syndrome is a very widespread way, in which this inside/outside incompletion is manifest. Here we must distinguish between scales of territorial insides because it can be said of the followers of every local set of traditions that they distinguish themselves by differentiation from neighboring, but similar local traditions. There is vagueness in the use by Sahlins of the word "culture" such that it can refer to small local differentiation as well as far larger-scale self-differentiation.

Because of existing marriage and trading and other relations among cultural insides and their outsides, some similarities must be assumed to exist, but, on the other hand, since we are thinking about rulers claiming sovereignty, we must be referring to as large a scale as the territory of a state, even though it might well share a conception of the encompassing world with neighboring tribes or states.

"China" was identified by the name of a dynasty, which is to say with royal ancestral descent. We can call its rule a cosmocracy because it was equated with an encompassing cosmology whose capital was the political capital of an empire, surrounded by large border regions and tributary states that partially shared the same cosmology. Within its spread, there were several lower scales of ancestral and territorial self-differentiation.

One of the ways to appreciate reference to an often vague encompassing outside is to consider the forms and mechanics of dealing with chance and contingency. Every civilization and its cultures includes institutions of divination, fortune telling or witchcraft detection, to answer questions of 'why me, why then, why here' beyond the empirically grounded causal explanations of injury, illness, prosperity, success or well-being. These are questions whose answers mobilize conceptions of fate, destiny, providence, luck, and bad luck or the location and nature of envy. There are countless and newly invented means and expertize for finding the answers — astrological, geomantic, with playing cards or by seeking the guidance of divinities through various mediums, including shamans, but also possibly by dice or in China divination blocks. They persist in the present day of every polity and its capitalist economy. But they refer to an encompassment beyond and therefore in one sense outside mundane life, but not to a wild outside.

The physical outside, where cultural or civilizational difference on a large scale as well as conquest can be envisaged, can also be a resource of precisely the powers of life-giving and death-dealing in the encompassing universe. The cosmological outside linked to the political outside according to the stranger-king model is "wild" — bush, mountainous, steppe land, desert, wilderness or 'beyond the reef', as Sahlins quotes from Malinowski's ethnography of the seagoing Trobriand islanders. Through going outside, access is gained to a society's or culture's gods, ancestors, ghosts and demons, who control the external conditions of life, harm and death that humans cannot control.

Was there an equivalent beyond the borders of the Chinese cosmocracy?

11.3 The Outside of Tianxia — All Under Heaven

Where Sahlins works from a center to its outside other, always stressing the importance of the outside and incompletion of the apparent but deceptive self-sameness of the inside, Wang Mingming (2012), writing about the Chinese idea of the world as *All Under Heaven*, keeps coming back to and stressing the center while enquiring about its outer regions. They make an interesting pair. They are not incompatible. But Wang Mingming's exposition is a China-centered anthropology, or rather a history of Chinese conceptions of the world and of the others from its center as self. Even when he is bringing in his reading of anthropology general and non-Chinese anthropologists of China, he is expounding Chinese-language sources for a Chinese anthropology of Chinese civilization. He praises the French social historian Marcel Granet of the early 20th century, who was a student of the famous anthropologist, Marcel Mauss, for doing this research. Thus he presents the importance of the center and indeed the whole process of centring what is outside and what comes from outside.

In the Chinese conception of the encompassing universe, the outside others were in mountains, or isles that were closer to heaven than was the emperor and to which the emperor would travel to renew his cosmological powers, or to seek immortality. Others outside were closer to earth or to the subterranean, ghosts, demons, and monsters — part-human, part-animal, which presented powerful chimera. These are certainly an outside of superior powers that are outside ordinary human control.

For two millennia before the formation of a single administered empire in 221 BCE, similar sacrifices and cosmographies were celebrated from several centers of rule. Larger spheres of rule over such rulers by one of them, though not yet as a unified empire shifted their center from east to west and back, indicating a centring in reference to other similar centers with the hegemonic center shifting among them.

Is this the same as what Sahlins calls heteronomy? The answer seems to be in the affirmative. Wang suggests that the third pre-imperial center, the Zhou 'asserted its centrality by means of infusing itself both vertically and horizontally with the "beyond" — not only with the "above" — which often countered its own ideology of centricity' (p. 344).

On the one hand, kings and their sub-kingdoms ordered the wilderness while journeying on pilgrimages to powerfully high and resourceful approaches to heaven within the wilderness. On the other hand, the further outside other, such as the people named the Qiang who were held captive and made slaves and then rose in revolt, were coming in from outside, with their own civilization. Indeed, all imperial dynasties of China had such distant outsiders with whom they warred, traded and exchanged gifts of hospitality. As Wang points out, Chinese rulers in the later Zhou period (the warring states and spring and autumn periods) borrowed from such others their clothing, means of transport (including horses) and styles of fighting. Knowledge of these outsiders was sometimes disparaging and sometimes admiring, but when linked to the encompassing heaven whose centring was the inside, it was a bringing in from the outside.

Centring remains the focus. It entails a long-standing conception of hierarchy, linking heaven, humanity and earth, not separating humanity from gods who command, or are whimsical or arbitrary interferers in human affairs as in the Greek/Roman conception, nor as Creator from creation as with the monotheistic religions. This same long period of 500 BCE to 200 CE, which has been called the "axial" age (producing all over the world philosophies and religions, not just Hellenic philosophy) in China produced 'the hundred schools of thought'. But they did not question this hierarchical and organic universe. It continued into the unified empire, administered not as fief-like kingdoms, but by an administration of garrisons and districts of representatives of the center. The conception of an organic and centered universe was re-elaborated and consolidated into a system of rites and sacred mountains, as Wang Mingming describes (and see also Henderson, 1984).

Into this frame entered the detailed empirical observations of travelers from China — Buddhists bringing or seeking enlightenment and scriptures from India, merchants, and diplomatic representatives of the emperor — in texts that are China's own ethnological tradition, equivalent to the European travellers and historians from the Greek historians onwards. This knowledge, as Wang describes it, was imperialist though in a different conception of empire than that which prevailed in the Mediterranean and the rest of Europe and certainly quite different from the later pre-modern and modern empires of the European monarchies and then nations. Rather it remained a centered order whose counterpart is a state of chaos, outside or, at times, inside, that needs to be re-ordered.

'The exchange between China as the center of the world and the peripheries of other countries was defined in terms of the son of heaven's obligation to pay greater gifts to the tribal chieftains, who were, in turn, the sons of their emperor "father",' writes Wang. 'Hierarchy was the defining characteristic of this Sino-centric world system. It was projected in a civilizing line departing from the central zone and extending into the zones of the "savages". The latter were the peripheries that produced materials and fancy products to be extracted by the center' (p. 364).

We would have to conclude from Wang that at the scale of the imperial cosmocracy some of the features of the stranger-king do apply to China, principally the idea of an outside wilderness that is both chaotic and a resource, including access to higher encompassing powers and exchange relations with rival sovereignties that often invaded and ruled over the imperial administration of China. But two other features of the stranger-king are absent. One is definition against the outside. Instead, there is the hierarchical relation to the celestial encompassment and its forces of order and judgement, from which rulers and/or their subjects can stray into chaos, when there will be rivalry to claim the mandate to return to order. Knowledge of the outside other is brought into the center of civilization and its centring order.

The other feature of the stranger-king syndrome is the dual authority of the autochthonous and their access to land and the immanent powers of earth as distinct from the external authority derived from encompassing powers and external sources. It is only partially to be found in China. For many centuries, China was ruled by ethnic others, who kept their rituals and forms of military organization, but also confirmed the celestial axis and its cosmology as their own legitimation. In addition, within the empire, although every place was farmed by people who considered themselves to be rooted by the graves of their ancestors, nearly everywhere they traced their lines beyond those graves to another place from which they had migrated. Perhaps, this is similar locally to a conquest of the remaining population and its claims. But the earth shrines that existed everywhere and the larger territorial protector shrines such as the temple of the Black Dragon King described by Chau (see Chapter 10) were not a separate authority from conquering or resettling dominant lineages, neither those for the empire as a whole nor those for each grassroots place.

Now let us look at one kingdom in the great border region of tributaries of the imperial cosmocratic center.

11.4 Ethnography of a Border Region

In the southwest of China, in the great border region stretching from the northwest southwards and including many influences of neighboring civilizations, such as the Tibetan, is an autonomous region of the Bai people centered on the town of Dali. The Bai had so assimilated, or should we say appropriated and made their own, the centered civilization of China that when they were studied in the 1940s by the anthropologist Francis Hsu — pushed out along with many other academics and the Nationalist government itself by the Japanese occupation of coastal and central China — he presented them as a classic of Chinese kinship (1948 *Under the Ancestors' Shadow*). Incidentally, the Bai and Dali had already been the subject of an excellent ethnography by C.P. Fitzgerald, which was published seven years before in 1941, in which the language and other distinctive features of Bai — whom he called Min Chia — are well described.

Now, the Bai are administered as an autonomous minority prefecture of the PRC. Another Chinese anthropologist, Liang Yongjia, has been studying their history and their current existence, paying close attention to their part-culture, and their hybrid self-identification. Liang (2011) has made creative use of the stranger-king model in this study and then gone on to examine (2013) what has become of this in the current era when one of their festivals has become a tourist attraction and a celebrated show of cultural heritage.

Liang (2011) refers to one of Sahlins' earlier publications (2008) where he distinguishes between stranger-kings and cosmocracies as two different instances of sovereign alterity. The stranger-king is an affinal outsider who breaks taboos of what is considered to define the human and thus proves his power and claims the authority to rule whereas the cosmocratic ruler is outside by attributes of virtue and sanctity that transcend the local in being universal. From examining the written records of the kingdoms of Nanzhao and Dali, home of the Bai, from the 7th to 13th centuries, Liang finds traits of both stranger-king and cosmocracy in the legitimating myths of their independence or autonomy. They are also the myths enacted in the Bai annual round of festivals, the greatest of which has also become a current tourist attraction.

Liang makes much of the distinction between the two kinds of sovereign alterity because both apply in his case study, saying that this proves that sovereignty does not have to be either of one type or of the other, as Sahlins seems to have claimed, though his later publications do not. In any case, the fact that they do both apply to the same histories indicates that we should indeed consider them as occurring together, just as we found in the case of the Chinese imperial cosmocracy that it also relied on bringing strangers and their attributes, skills and gifts in from the outside and often to the throne. Let us first look at the legitimating historical myths of the founding of the Nanzhao, and then at a more narrative history of the relationship between these kingdoms and their neighboring sovereign powers, including that of the Chinese emperor.

Two myths and variants of each tell of the stranger-king who is the founder of the enlarged Nanzhao and its successor Dali kingdom. The daughter of the divine emperor, carrying the title love-the-people emperor in the temple deifying him in present-day Dali, after being scolded by her father, runs off into the wild south where she is threatened by a serpent and rescued by a hunter, to whom she bestows her virginity that night out of gratitude. Waking in the morning, she finds that her lover is excessively ugly, but commits herself to him nonetheless. The emperor sends his son to find her and bring her back, but he is lost and dies on his mission. The emperor is full of grief and becomes furious. Eventually the hunter becomes, or was already, a chief of the wild southern region and plies the Nanzhao emperor with gifts. His ugly face, signified by his dark colour, indicates the monstrosity of the outsider. The gifts indicate willingness to be in a tributary relationship with the Nanzhao empire. After some years, the emperor is reconciled with his unruly daughter and invites her home. She comes but her ugly consort, fearing he will not be accepted, stays away but then follows her in hiding, fearing that she will not return to him. In the end, the emperor accepts his ugly son-in-law as a guest and the guest becomes host when the emperor dies, the son-in-law takes over the now expanded Nanzhao kingdom, including the wild south.

In the other body of stranger-king myths, the monstrosity of betrayal of hospitality replaces the monstrosity of ugliness. The founder of the Nanzhao unifies his five brothers' kingdoms with his own and invites his brothers to his court to a feast in a pagoda shrine hall. He absents himself from the feast and sets the wooden pagoda on fire with an offering of paper — spirit money. The brothers are burned to a char, beyond identification except for one, whose wife had given him an iron bracelet to wear. She rakes the hot ashes with her bare hands, locates the bracelet and recovers his ashes. In the pilgrimage to the temple deifying her in the present day, sutra-chanting groups of old women blacken their fingers as part of the ritual. When the monstrous king tries to seduce her, she kills herself, whereas the other four spouses of his brothers become his wives. So, the monster king becomes the founder of an expanded Nanzhao kingdom.

These are myths stressing the wild monstrosity of the stranger who comes from the outside as guest, or in the second set imposes himself as betrayer of hospitality and propriety, which indicates a monstrous breech of civilization (humanity).

The same kings, once established and in a peaceful succession, also laid claim to another historical mythology, that of the virtuous and transcendent incarnation of the bodhisattva Avalokitesvara and as agnatic successors to the King Asoka who is reputed to have in his last years nurtured Buddhism soon after the transcendence of Gautama Buddha. These are similar to the myths that sanctify kings that have spread throughout southeast Asia and have their own tributary chiefdoms against which they also go to war. In this tradition, the king/emperor is first and last a recluse, semi-divine, both of the mundane world and beyond it, having the powers to ennoble the mountains and rivers that mark the world of his imperial universe on earth. His ancestry is on a larger scale than that of his subjects, whom he may also claim to be his kin. His is the alterity of transcendence and the larger, encompassing scale.

Another set of myths feature the incarnation and disguise of divinities. In one such, the bodhisattva appears as a mendicant monk and is fed graciously with the food that the emperor's mother and daughter are bringing to the emperor — a tale of virtuous hospitality to a stranger. In another, the emperor or his successor is the child of a princess who finds herself mysteriously pregnant after an encounter, not with an ugly hunter but with a log in a stream, which is a dragon god in disguise. In the first, the emperor is blessed through his mother or daughter, and in the second he becomes a royal through his mother and a dragon. They are sanctified through affinal relations with a transcendent outsider, rather than with a wild outsider and are presented as virtuous rather than monstrous sovereigns.

Note that the founding sovereign of the Nanzhao kingdom or empire has features of the cosmocracy of the larger Chinese empire, but also features of the Buddhist, Theravada sovereignty characteristic of southeast Asia. Chinese imperial sovereigns did occasionally, particularly in the Tang and in the last Qing dynasty, have pretensions to be an incarnation of another bodhisattva, Manjusri, not Avalokitesvara and not as a norm. This takes us into the more strictly historical and less mytho-historical narrative, where it must be noted that Nanzhao was a tributary kingdom of both the Tang imperial dynasty and the Tibetan Tubo kingdom. It was even more mixed, since the Nanzhao emperor had three titles. One was Tianzi — just as the Tang emperor and his predecessors were; another was the title of a Burmese king; and the third title was Indian, Maharaja. Edmund Leach in *Political Systems of Highland Burma* noted that the Nanzhao in more recent history had both Indic and Sinic features, and indeed the Bai people may well be related by language and history to the Shan that Leach had studied. In sum, the Nanzhao sovereigns were not only guest-tributaries of the Chinese dynastic empire, but also a center of a civilizational mixture of their own and as a center, they brought in their own wilder fringes, just as the civilizational center in dynastic China centered its wilder fringes, in many cases by conquest, such as by the Mongols who as the Yuan dynasty finally fully incorporated Dali, successor to Nanzhao into the empire proper with its center in Beijing.

We will return to Dali and its main festival as an illustrative study of the modern state in China, in the next chapter.

11.5 The Wild: Another View of the Center from the Margin

Scott (2009) equates states with civilizations and his book is about ways people have found to escape from the bonds of civilizational states. He argues with great conviction and good evidence that so-called primitive people, living in small-scale low hierarchies and self-governing communities are, in fact, what he calls 'state effects'. They are in a symbiotic relationship of interdependence with states and therefore with steeper hierarchical civilizations; they are fugitives from states or have developed means of preventing their communities becoming state hierarchies; and they have evolved means of resisting the incorporation into neighboring states. In other words, they are coterminous with states. His book is a view of steeply hierarchical civilizations from their outsides and principally the outsides of the endeavors of states to order and exploit their peripheries, coercing their populations into labor, often slave labor, taxing them and appropriating the resources of their land. What is seen in this view is a formation of strategies of escaping from and avoiding coercion. Local centers within such states of peasants and their local elites in agrarian empires, also try to keep the state away, as they did in China (a point made by Scott in his concluding chapter), but they have less room for geographical manoeuvre than the local communities in the peripheries of civilizational centers and their states.

Scott uses his scholarship — the reading of ethnographies, histories, some documents and some archaeological finds — to establish a very large region, which, following one of his sources (van Schendel), he calls Zomia. Zomia is one of the long-lasting and largest regions containing people who are escaping from and avoiding incorporation into states. Geographically, it is the mountainous region east of Bengal that reaches Vietnam much further east. It includes the highlands of Burma, Thailand,

and Laos and what are now the south-western provinces of the PRC: Sichuan, Yunnan, Guizhou, and Guangxi, and it includes the Bai of Dali and the chiefdoms that they incorporated. This was a major periphery and border region of civilization in China.

Zomia is a region of civilizational crossings and mixtures, from India, from China, from Arabia by sea, and many others, in which small states formed on rivers to control the trade and resources coming down and entering up the rivers, some expanding into valleys where settled agriculture was possible. For most of their history, they were states with a small radius of control, but a far larger scope of claims to civilization by what Scott calls 'cosmological bluster' (p. 32) influenced by the various larger civilizations and their spreads from larger centers in their neighborhood. But in the mountainous massif behind and between these states, large and small, there are 'wilder' higher areas where hunting, foraging, shifting cultivation and trading are the economic means for subsistence. Redistributive rituals of feasting by local charismatic leaders are a common feature of these relatively egalitarian upland communities. Traveling and trading linked but never unified these small sovereign localities. From their points of view, civilization might be adapted from their nearby small states, indeed they may have practiced the same rituals, but the practices of especially the larger and more powerful states were violent, dangerous, corrupt and to be avoided. What is more, the small states often collapsed. They were less stable than the tried and trusted forms of subsistence and redistributive rituals of the uplands.

In the uplands, there were fluctuations and variations of shallow hierarchy from an egalitarianism that legitimated the assassination of a leader ambitious to command and to take over the collective feasting rituals, to the slightly steeper hierarchies of local king-like village chiefs and their confederacies —an oscillation first theorized by Edmund Leach in his classic *Political Systems of Highland Burma.*

To the centers, this oscillation and the egalitarian resort to the highlands was "chaos", though it was ordered and the highlanders were cultured. They spoke many languages to maintain their relations, distant though they were, with neighboring states. And most of them told myths of having once had the accomplishment of their own writing but that it had been stolen by or lost to the people of the state civilizations. These myths indicate both aspiration to these civilizations and escape from them. Escape from states did not exclude taking up versions and mixes of the centered civilizations, their cosmologies, forms of divination and authorization of charismatic leaders.

11.6 Conclusion

In this chapter, we have examined whether the civilizational state, or cosmocracy, of dynastic China fits or forces modifications in the theory of the stranger-king as the wild and monstrous other and the transcendent sovereign other in a cosmocracy. One feature of the stranger-king syndrome elsewhere, particularly in Africa, does not fit well and that is the dichotomy between autochthonous earth cults and lineages on the one hand, and the external ancestry and lineages of rulers, on the other. We find the latter, but the former do not occur as a rival form of authority. For instance, in providing fertility and healing, local cults are overarched by dynastic mediation with heaven to provide the same, healing and the fertility of the land. But we have found that on the scale of imperial rule and its sense of itself as a center of the universe, Tianxia, there is an outside that was to the center, a relatively less civilized or outright wild other, by which the center defined itself as cultivated, but which was also, both mythologically and actually, a huge periphery of potent resources including access to the divine, on one hand, and invasion or conquest of the center, on the other. There may be other features that you think, once you have read the studies, do not fit. For instance, did Chinese emperors claim to have powers that were occult, forms of sorcery, as distinct from the powers to destroy what they took to be challenges to their positions as rulers?

The main Chinese lesson we draw from anthropological studies of the stranger-king and cosmocracy, both at the scale of the dynastic empire and at the scale of one of its tributaries in the periphery, is the activity of centring, the bringing into the center from the outside of influences from other civilizations as well as affinal kin and their offspring. Centring is what studies of civilization and cosmocracy in China bring as a theme to anthropology.

We have also found that what characterizes civilization in these Chinese examples is always a mixture, the result of this constant bringing of others into the center from outside. Even though every civilization represents itself as continuous and so, more or less, self-same, it has, we suggest, in fact been quite transformed over time, both from internal and from external forces and influences.

Seminar Questions

What are the key features of the contrast between sovereign alterity and local autochthony in the stranger-king syndrome according to de Heusch and to Sahlins?

How did the Chinese empire and civilization rely on its outer others?

Was the Chinese emperor a stranger king?

Readings

de Heusch, Luc (1962). 'Aspects de la sacralité du pouvoir en Afrique', in *Le pouvoir et le sacré.* (eds.) Luc de Heusch *et al.*, 139–158, Institut de Sociologie, Université Libre de Bruxelles: Bruxelles.

de Heusch, Luc (1982). *The drunken king, or the origin of the state.* Indiana University Press: Bloomington.

Liang Yongjia (2011). 'Stranger-kingship and cosmocracy; or Sahlins in Southwest China', *Asia Pacific Journal of Anthropology*, 12(3), pp. 236–254.

Liang Yongjia (2013). 'Superscription without encompassment: turning Gwer Sa La festival into intangible cultural heritage', in *China: An International Journal,* 11(2), pp. 58–76.

Sahlins, Marshall (2012). 'Alterity and Autochtony: Austronesian cosmographies of the marvellous', *Hau: Journal of Ethnographic Theory*, 2(1), pp. 337–383.

Scott, James (2009). *The Art of Not Being Governed; an Anarchist History of Upland Southeast Asia*, Yale University Press: New Haven and London (Chapter 1 'Hills, valleys and states: an introduction to Zomia' pp. 1–39).

Wang Mingming (2012). 'All under heaven (tianxia); cosmological perspectives and political ontologies in pre-modern China', *Hau: Journal of Ethnographic Theory,* 2(1) pp. 337–383.

References

Henderson, John B. (1984). *The Development and Decline of Chinese Cosmology.* Columbia University Press: New York.

Sahlins, Marshall (2008). 'The stranger-king, or elementary forms of the politics of life', *Indonesia and the Malay World,* 36 (105), pp. 177–199.

Chapter 12

The Anthropology of the Modern State in China

Until the 19th century, the most prosperous and productive regions of China, measured in terms of Gross domestic Product (GDP) per person and average income, matched the most prosperous areas of Europe (Goldstone, 2002). Despite exports being a small part of the Chinese market economy, China was the center of its own world system with exchange relations of hospitality (tribute, treaty, marriage) and trade that reached Europe and Africa as well as the Pacific and Indian Ocean shores, directly or indirectly. China had remarkably large-scale industrial regions, in iron smelting, in ceramics, in silk-weaving and others. Nevertheless, steam-powered industrial production was first developed not in China, but in northern Europe as a way of producing commodities for profitable sale including export and they were commodities of everyday use, not just luxury items.

Steam-powered industry was an engine for sustained growth and accumulation of capital unmatched by any other previous periods of economic growth. So it was that in economic, technical and military might industrial capitalism powered what had by then become a European international system. The states involved were not modern states, but absolute monarchies with powerful bureaucracies. They were princedoms, empires, such as the Austro-Hungarian and the Prussian, or multiregional states such as France and Spain, and the UK. In

England, where steam-powered industrial revolution first occurred, it came long after the formation of a constitutional monarchy that is still now the basis of the United Kingdom as a multinational state. Yet as self-sustained growth of industrial capitalism spread throughout the continent from England in the course of the 19th century, nationalisms also spread and eventually consolidated a new kind of historical mythology and the ideological formation of so-called "nation" states. Characteristic of these nationalisms and the self-justification of their states, where they successfully achieved their freedom to form a state, was a language of intimate fellowship, modeled on military comrade- or friend-ship and on family loyalty, which had for long been metaphors for service to and parental care from sovereigns, be they princes, kings or emperors but were now mobilized to self-definition as a people with a putative common descent.

The anthropologist Gellner (1983) proposed a theory of nationalism that it was a movement led by intellectuals, but appealing to a common, popular cultural base and its past, involving compilations of folk music, customs, and tales, incorporating them into art music and the other finer arts such as fiction, while at the same time promoting a standardized vernacular literacy and a scientific education through a single system of mass schooling. Nationalism of people includes regionally different people, presenting it as a unified whole and bringing about a self-consciousness of their ways of living a "culture." This induces a newly self-conscious mirroring of themselves that is also a displaying of themselves to others, other cultures.

A number of examples of the construction of nationalist mythology and culture was collected by Hobsbawm and Ranger in *The Invention of Tradition*, a book (1983) whose title has been much quoted. What is interesting about these "inventions" is the extent that they are constructed, out of what materials and whether those materials already existed or were themselves "invented."

Anthropology, cultural and social, was born out of these movements and had to undergo serious self-critiques in order not to simply replicate the idea of cultural wholes. A similar danger of replicating this culturalist self-consciousness is now most evident in the way anthropologists become involved in heritage projects, which are an extension of the original nationalist movements, but now with a strong economic rationale in promoting tourist income. Display for others and for self-mirrored by others lends itself to short-hand descriptions of the typical — of stereotypes of expectation by others of the cultural self; at their worst these are racist denigrations. They can also be positive, or romanticizing stereotypes. But they are always limiting and differ from preferred self-images and from practical knowledge of differences.

As Herzfeld (1997) has argued, there is no reason for anthropologists not to study such projects of cultural display, including the stereotypes by which people, both central and marginal, are described. The point of anthropological fieldwork would be to bring out the ways that language, architecture, official policy, and the extension of the agencies of a state, even within the offices of that state, are always double-speaking between aggressive and defensive uses of such stereotypes, or using them in different languages or registers of language so that the differences produce jokes and other forms of irony, or the differences are used as disguise, or as excuse for what is actually done. Rules disguise personalized relations; personalized relations use the language of electoral representation and a communal common good. Neither of them adequately characterizes what is actually done into a single unified and unchanging order, though that is the face they put up.

Close and small-scale studies of locations note how local people attempt to distance themselves from "the state" as they see "it". Similarly, close studies of functionaries in a branch of the state note their own distancing both from those they administer and from upper levels of the state. In either case, the same study must face both up, sideways to other localities or other state agencies, and down. "State" is itself a reification of what is in fact a heterogeneous set of apparatuses of law-making and of policy-making, with others implementing each of these by bureaucratic administration, a legislature, and a judiciary. It is often quite difficult to know where "the state" ends and so-called "society," or "civil society" begins. To bring out these ironies and this blurring is the contribution of anthropology to political science.

12.1 Some Benchmark Characteristics of Modern States

Whatever the dates and whatever the characteristics of the different people-states and their regions, they all have these things in common:

- They are all now part of a global system that is a planetary world system of industrial and finance capitalism.
- They each have a project of what all of them in their various languages and conceptions call modernization — which is oriented to a future that is presumed to be an advance.
- At the same time, they all refer to their own origins as that of those people in some antiquity of "tradition," which is an essential counterpart of "modernity."
- Administratively and militarily they are states with far greater scope, penetration, and physical force than any previous state had.
- They are units of a growing system of international law (of treaties and arbitration) and international organizations such as the International Monetary Fund, the World Bank, the World Trade Organization, the United Nations and its sub-organizations (such as the Postal Union, the International Labour Office and the World Health Organization), and the International Court of Justice.

Some nations, such as the Russian Federation and the PRC, were empires that became people-states. Most European empires became nations at the cores of their own maritime empires, until their so-called possessions became de-colonized nations. Other nations were never empires or colonies, but none were unaffected by the industrial-capitalist empires of the 19th and 20th centuries. Most of the international relations of nations in that time have been those of war and settlement by treaty. Military preparation for war and defense has been one of the main state-based promotions of research and development and of advances in industry by state contracts.

With this much in common, there is still a great deal of variation and one of the ways to see that variation is through regional studies such as that accomplished by Prasenjit Duara and his account of the nations that emerged in relations to each other in northern East Asia.

12.2 China's Formation as an East Asian State

Duara (2009), an anthropologically well informed historian, distinguishes popular nationalism from state nationalism. Of course the two are interlinked, but when a populist national movement achieves its aim of state power, it changes into having as its primary concern the sovereignty of the state and its immediate regional relations. The state establishes a more didactic relation to its subjects, even though it may also at times seek to mobilize them. State-nationalism can lead and come into tension with the popular nationalism that it provokes. One does not exclude the other.

Duara describes the new kind of historical narrative attendant on nationalism and its state wherever it occurs in the world as 'linear historical consciousness' (p. 22). He traces its first north East Asian exponents in Tokugawa Japan and Qing China in the 19th century. The new narrative fed into the movement for constitutional reforms of their monarchies by being the new vehicle for rethinking dynastic histories. In Korea, it capped already strong moves of its own dynasty in the direction of separate statehood instead of tributary relations with the Qing Empire. Already, centuries before, the Korean monarchy had established the institution of the vernacular language in written script as a resistance to Qing domination. All three countries experienced reforms led by elite intellectuals advising their states, not by appeals to a popular base.

By the 19th century, all were affected by the spread of European industrial capitalism, its products, and its military forces. And all picked up very soon after it was first published in England the evolutionary sociology of Herbert Spencer and its theory of racial struggles for survival in a war in which the fittest will survive, a purportedly natural process called Social Darwinism. Racial struggle in the case of Tokugawa Japan and Qing China was therefore, not just to resist European imperialism, but to rival it with their own and to compete with each other. Japan under the newly revived state of the emperor, the Meiji, dominated this rivalry to arm and industrialize, defeating the Russian empire in a short war in 1905 and immediately expanding its rule into Manchuria and Korea. It was not until the 20th century that anti-imperialist nationalist movements grew and became strong in both Japan and China, while Korean state-nationalism was already anti-imperialist. In China and even more so in Korea, nationalism focused on Japanese imperialism.

Both kinds of nationalism, state-imperial and popular anti-imperialist, continued together.

Despite resistance to Japanese imperialism, nationalist movements in China and Korea were heavily influenced by Japan's industrial modernization, its universities where many Chinese and Korean students studied, and by Japanese translations of European social science and philosophy into its own Chinese-character script, including neologisms for new concepts such as civilization, culture, nation and race, feudalism, and revolution. Race, in particular, had a singular influence on nationalism. Nation was translated by the combination of characters for people (min) and ancestral line or origin (zu). In China, this meant finding an original ancestor, the Yellow Emperor, or archaeologically the levels of human remains in which fossils of 'Peking Man' were found in the 1920s to the southwest of Beijing for the birth of a regional civilization or species of human being. This need for an originating ancestor seems to be a characteristic of East Asian nationalism not to be found as strongly in Europe or North America. In fact, Peking Man is *homo erectus*, not *homo sapiens*, and a genetic survey conducted by a geneticist in Fudan University proves that modern Chinese and Southeast and East Asians are descended from the later arrival of *homo sapiens*, both stemming from the long migration out of Africa (Alice Roberts 2010, *The Incredible Human Journey; the story of how we colonized the planet.* London, Berlin, New York: Bloomsbury, pp. 179–204).

The extent of foreign influence, ideas, and materials involved in a nation and its new/old sense of its internal self is always far greater than is acknowledged. Duara calls this tendency "misrecognition" and it extends to a misrecognition amounting to reinvention of their own histories. "Misrecognition" is also an underestimation of a nation's dependence on the international system for the recognition of its sovereignty, attributing it instead to its own efforts, stressing of course its freedom and independence. This "dialectic" of recognition (what a nationalism recognizes) and misrecognition (what a nationalism either disavows or underplays) is true of every nationalism, he says. Thus, Japan took up European Enlightenment ideals and made them its own by finding them in Eastern history and civilization, now inherited and advanced by a resurgent Japan that would bring them back to benighted China and Korea.

In the PRC, the Chinese multinational state that cultivates the Yellow Emperor as the ancestor of the dominant Han race-nation and Confucius as its perennial sage has, since the beginning of 1978 in opening to the world of market capitalism with economic reforms and the end of the anti-imperialist state nationalism of Mao, led to equivalent nationalisms among minority nationalities (see, for instance, Bilik, 2002). Duara concludes that other potential social movements, for environmental protection for instance, may feed new nationalist movements. But note that Harrison (2001) has emphasized state nationalism in China, calling it "state patriotism." Both the Guomindang and the Communist Party in the Mainland (the Communist Party still now, the Guomindang no longer in multiparty Taiwan) demand loyalty to the ruling party for the sake of China.

12.3 Not Fleeing but Keeping a Negotiable Distance: Local Cultures in the PRC

A nation-state, which we think is better designated a "people-state," is a territorial sovereignty marked much more sharply and kept more fiercely through border controls and military garrisons than those of the dynasties of empires with their very broad border zones, or regions. The PRC state of centrally recognized nationalities is a way of maintaining its border regions within the scope and order of the central state, by strictly limited indirect rule in autonomous regions. Most of those nationalities, including the Yi and the Miao, in fact contain many local cultures just as does the most populous nationality, the Han. Cultural policy in China is to recognize these local cultures, through such spectacles as the New Year evening celebration of the costumes and music of recognized minority nationalities on television, as intrinsic parts of the national culture, a strictly limited and stereotypical version of its cultures.

A good idea of the experience of the central state from the point of view of a local culture within the Yi national minority is provided by Mueggler's (2001) monograph about the Lolop'o in Zhizuo township in Chuxiong county, northern Yunnan province. The Lolop'o are one among the many loosely linked people oscillating between more and less hierarchical polities in Scott's Zomia (please refer to the chapter on the stranger king). Indeed, Yunnan province is part of Zomia. The PRC state categorizes them as Yi. In their more hierarchical variants some Yi, the Northern, had kept other Zomian people, the Miao in particular, but also some Han too, as captive slaves. The Lolop'o were less state-like and were never slaveholders, indeed they thought of Yi slaveholders as raw-meat-eating barbarians! The Lolop'o speak a language more like Lisu (another categorized minority) than any of the mutually unintelligible dialects of the other Yi. Records by Qing officials describe them as living in small confederations of villages along valleys (Mueggler, 2001; pp. 11–15), just as James Scott says of all Zomian peoples.

As noted in the chapter on hospitality, under the Qing state and the Republican state of the first decades after 1911, the Zhizuo Lolop'o were at the lowest level of indirect rule in which they kept their own shallow hierarchy of ritual, feasting, and good fortune, with communal land in trust to their ancestors, through an annual selection of a host, who was given the title ts'ici. Mueggler writes (p. 197) 'the ts'ici used hospitality to maintain the moral and social boundaries between inside and outside'.. 'the ts'ici system worked to exclude the state from its [the ts'ici's] sustaining vision of generative unity....the moral opposite of Han officialdom — the inside to the state's outside.'

In 1950, the ts'ici institution was gradually disabled when the state of the PRC extended into this area and conducted anti-counter-revolutionary executions, land redistribution followed by collectivization of land and work. The Lolop'o began to find new ways of using their own orally transmitted traditions to understand and deal with this new state as it penetrated every aspect of local life. Some Lolop'o now entered the Party and its state apparatuses. The state was among them, not outside. Locally born cadres attended the rituals and contributed toward them the materials for sacrifice. The ancestral trust lands whose produce paid for the expenses of the rituals of productive land and reproductive fertility, maintaining the flow of life through digestive tracts, fields and wombs, were maintained as collective despite land reform policies of dividing and redistributing them. They became part of a single collective of agricultural production. Cadres took over the ritual duties of the ts'ici, sponsoring rituals and the required ritual expertize for their performance, but at the same time, they curtailed them drastically.

Collectivization, or rather re-collectivization in this case, was a gradual, directed but also improvised process where the setting up of collectivized markets kept failing due to lack of administrative acumen. Recalling all this and the mysterious illnesses and deaths of cadres living on sacred grounds usurped by this new, penetrative state, people told Mueggler that they were due to the offence taken by their supreme spirit of productivity, Agàmismo.

The key event of collectivization, which thereafter formed the new way the state was envisaged, was the Great Leap Forward (GLF) campaign of 1958–1960. It was the formation of communes on a greater scale and a military organization of the labor for large-scale projects of terrace-straightening in preparation for mechanization of agriculture, of irrigation canals and reservoirs, and of small furnaces for the smelting of iron for steel and copper production. Women, children, and old men farmed the collectivized fields for close planting of rice to increase grain production and its procurement to feed workers in cities. Procurements were raised despite the resulting falls in productivity below the level of 1957 harvests. Famine and starvation ensued, 1959–1961. The dead were not properly buried and no rites were performed for them.

Mortuary rituals include a verbal play accompanying offerings as bribes to the officials of a bureaucracy of purgatory, as everywhere within Chinese civilization, keeping them at a distance and enabling souls to rise from purgatory and become spirits and ancestors through these rituals. Mueggler sees this as Lolop'o creating and holding a distance from the imperial state. For other parts of China, it would be more appropriate to see them as a negotiating distance from, but also, with the state. But then other parts of Lolop'o cosmology, such as the spirit Agàmismo, are embedded in their own land and are quite different from the protector deities of local territories in more central parts of China, who are dressed and addressed as if they were imperial officials but celebrated not only as fierce, but also fair, unlike actual officials. In any case, during this period of collectivization, the famine dead received no rituals.

For two decades after the GLF, smaller-scale communes and their subdivisions into brigades and teams were maintained. But around 1980, the collective land was divided amongst households and open markets were introduced and expanded quickly, again as everywhere else in China. At the same time, attacks on rituals as superstition were reduced. The

Lolop'o resumed their mortuary rituals. But now they were more like exorcism in addition to the former exorcism rituals to ward off fearsome demonic spirits. These rituals were dominant and frequent at the time Mueggler was there in the 1990s.

Through these rituals of exorcism, 'the state was likened to a spectral chain [of mediations in scale up to the center], a predatory bureaucracy of wild ghosts, dominated by the fury and resentment of the unmourned famine dead' (p. 162).

The victims of starvation during the GLF were wild ghosts whose hunger could never be permanently appeased; they just had to be provisionally held off, to alleviate illness, madness, or crop failures, by exorcism and the accompanying offerings. They were distinct from white and black ghosts. White ghosts were under the predatory command of black ghosts. Together white and black wild ghosts constituted a gaping mouth within the land, along streams and paths, in houses and in bodies of the living, 'a long chain of ghost officials, clear across the national landscape to Beijing' (p. 198). This new vision of the state as an embedded tormentor also conveys a longing to return to their former domestic and ancestral economy protected by the ts'ici.

Note the reversals: the self-professed civilizational center is wild and black; the state is still outside, but embedded within. The distance that had been kept by the ts'ici civilization of hospitality has been invaded by a wild state. But the rituals, which are partly those of Chinese purgatorial bureaucracy and partly Lolop'o, and the songs in which they still evoke their old domestic generative order are themselves a distancing from the dominant ideologies of the state and its versions of civilization.

12.4 Further Cases of Cultural Distancing and Cultural Incorporation

The Lolop'o were incorporated by recognition of their otherness as Yi. "Culture" was certainly used in this recognition, but it was the result of forcible incorporation into an extended state, which is what Mueggler's chapter illustrates. Now we have to see how culture was used in less fearful cases.

When writing about such people as the Lolop'o in southwestern China as escapees from civilizational states, Scott emphasized that his description of Zomia could no longer apply after they had all been incorporated — albeit some less completely than others — into modern states. Zomia was no longer a highland refuge from states. The PRC in particular extended into the highlands, as in the case of the Lolop'o. Consolidation of the sovereign territory is an ongoing project of market integration led by transport and communications networks and by the capacity for military border defense, as in every modern state. Now the small sovereignties of kin groups, villages, and their confederacies have been incorporated into sovereign territorial states with armed garrisons at their borders and constant armed incursions, as in Burma, to "tame" the wild — bringing them into their fiscal vision, forcing them to settle. In Burma, strategies of rebellion and resistance persist, but now use the discourses of ethnic identity and of indigenous peoples and their rights, appealing to a supportive civilizational discourse on what is now a global scale.

In other words, the peripheries of nation states now use strategies not to escape (which they cannot) but as far as possible to form self-governing communities on their own terms, using whatever opportunities the incorporating state offers them to pursue their historical experiences transmitted through their oral culture. Among such opportunities are minority politics and tourism, which use the previous image of wild and free mountain people to maintain a cultural and civilizational distance within the territory of a unifying state. One such image is that of the Peach Blossom Garden, Taohua Yuan, a magically cut off valley or land of mountains and valleys where old and benign ways of living a simpler and purer life have been preserved to the delight of the author who accidentally comes upon it. This is a view of the other from the literate heights of a civilizational traveler and it is still used for cultural tourist promotion in the PRC.

Another view from another kind of literature is that of farmers within Chinese civilization and its states, including the PRC and Taiwan. A favourite collection of stories remains that of the bandits of the lakes and marshes — the Shui Hu Zhuan. These are stories of rebellious and small charismatic bands from what was a border region to which the righteous escaped from a corrupt state. They are the inspiration for theater and for the ritual military troupes that accompany territorial gods, who are local protectors. (For more, read Sutton, 2003). They and the historical-mythological stories collected in two other collections, the Romance of the Three Kingdoms (Sanguo Yanyi), and the Stories of the Enfeoffing of the Gods (Fengshen Yanyi) are the subjects of theater and story-telling performances all over China, as well as being sources for the founding of temples to the god-heroes of the stories.

Sharing the same civilization, or what is now cultural heritage, but from two quite different angles, the highly literate and the lowly talk past each other, as we shall see.

12.5 The Bai of Dali and their Culture in the New Dispensation

First, let us return to the Bai of Dali as they were under the PRC, whose dynastic myth-history we recounted in the chapter on the stranger king. In recognition of Bai otherness by the state of the People's Republic, Dali is now the capital of an autonomous prefecture. What is entailed in this recognition?

Liang (2013) shows that it is a layer over the Bai people's own revival of the rituals that enact the myths of the Nanzhao and Dali kingdoms. He calls that layering "superscription," a term used by Duara (1988) for the institutions by which the imperial dynastic state recognized local cults and incorporated them in order to control them. But this new superscription brings them into another kind of history and its legitimating myths, which are those of an evolutionary sequence derived from the anthropology of Henry Morgan and Friedrich Engels and the progressive development of China as the people led by the Chinese Communist Party.

In this history, the festival of Gwer Sa La, which is a fire, torch, singing, and dancing festival that is the center-piece of an annual set of rites in Dali, is both primitive and modern. The superscription was literally the documentation of the festival for an application through the Beijing Ministry of Culture to UNESCO for national status as a monument of intangible cultural heritage. According to this document put together by prefectural and provincial governments, the festival celebrated primitive matriarchy, sexual freedom, and equality between the sexes, which was also modern in showing the humanity of that equality. Backing the application, government agents organized a performance of what they understood to be an acceptable and attractive celebration of song, costume, and dance for the annual Spring Festival shown by the official television broadcaster, Central Chinese TV. When the bid failed to convince UNESCO, the vice-minister of the central Ministry of Culture condemned these efforts as false folklore. But the tourist attraction of the festival remains.

The TV spectacle was not a documentary, but what the officials took to be an encapsulation, with Bai performers doing their bidding. If it had been a documentary, it would have meant the makers spending a year or several visits as did Liang Yongjia, observing first of all that Gwer Sa La is like the other festivals in the Bai Dali year, a pilgrimage and placing of offerings at temples, in this case the temple of the Emperor who Loves the People, founder of the Nanzhao kingdom, and two other temples. The principal pilgrims are groups of older women who in their retirement from childbirth have become Buddhist sutra-chanting groups, making merit for their village. There is one group in each village and the women bring with them their village host- or root-god (benzvit).

What the super scribers in their documentation called a 'primitive fertility cult' and a 'Bai Valentine's Day' does have sexual content, but it is not promiscuous as implied in the documentation and is still promised as a tourist attraction. Men duel in songs and dances with women singer-dancers and some do set up sexual liaisons that are extra-marital, but are equally committed and long term, meeting again only at the next Gwer Sa La festival. Men also compete with each other to light straw torches with which they run to their fields to enhance the crop. The older women pray for rain and the fertility of land and domestic animals; newly-wed women pray for childbirth — in one rite by throwing coins until they hit the penis of a boy statue of Sakyamuni Buddha. What to the PRC state super scribers is the romantic primitive 'unleashing of the freedom of life' to the Bai is a festival 'as old as mankind', in which they petition gods for plentiful agricultural irrigation, for human, animal and land fertility, and for success in business or in building a house, or in passing examinations.

The backward but romantic "primitive" image of a place and a spectacle of release from the restraints of civilization is typical of the representation of marginal cultures to the republican center not only in China, but in many other modernizing people-states. It is a lucrative image, generating income from tourists interested in the landscape, its animals and its remote people. It is a modernizing way of bringing into a unified state its internal others for its own tourists but also tourists from abroad, a "modern" centring of its civilization and that civilization's border regions. The outside is of other people-nations and their own claims to be centers of civilization, recognized as such but also as stranger-regions whose resources are bountiful to be exploited in trade and investment.

Entepreneur's from Bai and many other "minorities" as well as Han in Yunnan themselves go overseas, for instance, into Burma but also further afield, and bring or send back goods and images from their travels in these stranger-regions.

Writing of the grasslands of the Cameroons in West Africa, Rowlands (2011), shows how the building of museums in the palaces of the Fon kingdoms is an extension of the stranger-king syndrome in a globalized economy. For central and West Africans such as these, the countries of Europe or North America are the bush, hunting grounds full of dangers, but also of untold resources to bring home (they call themselves "bushfallers", falling out to hunt in the bush). In hunting, they put themselves at risk of the terrible fate of becoming the invisible and overexploited zombies, who are invisible to both the host countries and their own. The kings, called Fons, on the other hand were and are seen to display as their armature the things they have been brought by European colonizers and from more contemporary strangers' fields. Their display is a way of shoring up their kingdoms against collapse, the display having as its converse their hidden powers of access to the invisible and external world of death and to do harm as well as to protect their subjects from it. Culture for them has become a means of exerting their precarious power.

For the Bai, their "culture" too is a precarious shelter for their own continuation of a misrecognized ritual that they display for tourists. But they do not use symbols of the outside world as an armature in their rites. Instead, their armature is their display of what the others want to see, including foreigners.

Turn now to an even more assimilated but still remote place, recently re-designated a minority nationality tourist attraction, even though it had no special rituals.

12.6 The Villages of Bashan in Enshi

Steinmüller (2013) has extended Herzfeld's (1997) idea of cultural intimacy to describe the way villagers in Bashan, Enshi, Hubei province, distancing themselves from the local and the central state. It is a more ironic distance, less fearful than that of the Lolop'o, and it brings out how perhaps the Bai too experience the differences between their cultural performance for the state and the rituals they perform for themselves. Except that in the case of Enshi, villagers are far less willing to claim for themselves an ethnic, or minority nationality status.

In Chapter 1 of his book, Steinmüller uses Ardener's (1989) theory of remoteness to describe the relationship of these mountain villagers to the central state. Remoteness is of course the view from a center; the inhabitants of the "remote" place experience their relation to the center as a vulnerability to intrusion, including development projects, from which they try to defend themselves, but usually cannot. What is for those in more central places the everyday normality of a regulated existence, for the inhabitants of this vulnerable location is more often an event rather than a regularity, hence Ardener's description of the remote as being "event-dense"; they are constantly disturbed. But we would need to comment that the same can be said of the majority of city residents who are dislocated by property development projects (Feuchtwang *et al.*, 2016). It might be better to say that the administration of law, plan, and policy is represented as regular, and the rich who benefit from state-regulated industrial capitalism can experience that administration as protective and regular, but everyone else is disturbed in its implementation and form whatever distances and defenses they can to accommodate and alter it.

The examples Steinmüller gives of such events in the villages he studied are a development project to extend the growing of tea and to create for the place (and its people and products) a "special flavour" (*tese*). This involved, for instance, replacing a watchtower built on a hilltop during the Mao years of readiness for war with a huge red teapot, an advertisement for trade. The special flavor of the place was enhanced by its formation as a minority nationality area, of autonomous townships and the prefecture of Enshi for the Dong, Tujia and the Miao classified minorities. Formal recognition was given content by the officials of these new government levels by the construction of tourist sites where visitors can be entertained by songs and dances by locals trained by Dong performers from another province, Guizhou. The promotion of these performances and other ethnic or local specialties used terms taken from the Peach Blossom Garden, found in Qing dynasty gazetteers of the area, and the same romanticized and sexualized terms as were used by the government promoters of the Bai in Dali. At the same time, the government promoters congratulated themselves on lifting the "civilizational level" of what had been backward.

Steinmüller remarks on how the villagers presented themselves to him as an outsider from Europe and from the city in accommodating terms as "backward," poor, and remote. On the pervasiveness of this new discourse of civilization and how it differs from traditional civilization, see Feuchtwang (2012). In official discourse, this language of raising the level of civilization and of development is governmental beneficence.

One of the ironies of the vulnerable situation of villagers in Enshi is that officials had to look for members of the minorities. They could not rely on custom or language, because they all speak the local dialect of Mandarin. Instead they had to rely on the family names recorded in Qing gazateers as the Chinese names that the local Dong, Tujia and Miao minorities had taken. All of them consider their own history in terms of the patrilineal inheritance of these names in exactly the same way as do Chinese from all over China. Most intimately — it took several months before Steinmüller was told by people who had become his friends — they identify themselves according to the fate of their houses and the whole place in which they live, calculated according to almanacs and fengshui (Chinese geomancy) experts, considered backward here and all over China by the official and intellectual classes. This is how they perceived the local in their own way, as do locals in entirely Han places. Knowing and sharing this only with those they could trust in the face of government civilizing missions and tourist sites where they are identified as minority nationalities, they formed what Steinmüller calls, extending Herzfeld, a 'community of complicity'.

One of the big development projects in Enshi and elsewhere in China was the 2006–2011 'Construction of a Socialist New Countryside'. In Chapter 7, Steinmüller shows the ironies of its implementation in the villages he studied. These development projects were not only to turn subsistence crop land into "forests" — in which tea plantations could be counted — and encourage entrepreneurial farmers growing and trading organic tea. It also involved bringing into domestic use hygienic appliances and new housing, but with painted facades and with fences and balconies displaying the look of the left-behind minority specialty. In fact the rebuilt houses, partially financed by government funds but always also by the households themselves, were confined to the side of the road through the model village at the center of the area, on the route of all the visits from higher officials promoting the policy and nominally inspecting its thorough implementation. Out of public hearing, both officials and villagers abandoned the official discourse of development and a fair bureaucratic administration and called these developments 'face projects' (*mianzi gongcheng*). Here, then, a community of complicity was maintained both among local officials and the villagers. Both cadres and villagers tacitly admitted that the villagers who received government subsidies and helped them implement the policy and present the village in a good light had personal connections with each other. Villagers complained that the officials, who included the village committee whose members were no longer local farmers, but younger professionally trained cadres who did not live in the village, pocketed much of the funding that eventually trickled down after the upper reaches of government had taken their portions. But on the other hand they admitted to the effectiveness of currying personal relations through accepting the hospitality of the village head, who was local, and presenting her and others with gifts.

Not only does this illustrate the formation of communities of complicity, it also illustrates how the implementation of policy works. Those first subsidized allowed themselves, to their own advantage, to become effective agents of the policy, even though not themselves cadres or officials. Further, the formation of a model village and its housing was effective because villagers higher into the mountains rebuilt their houses in a similar style when they could afford the expenses.. They agreed to display themselves as having a local specialty.

At the grassroots, the few remaining cadres who are local also face neighbors in their implementation of policy, but most face only upwards in their career prospects. Pieke (2004), from fieldwork within the Chinese

Communist Party in Yunnan province, points out that the training of rural cadres has the barely hidden curriculum of forming connections, jostling for promotion and learning how to use ideology. The hidden curriculum makes them into another community of complicity.

The state is controlling, unifying, and extended but reliant on those who maintain a distance from it.

12.7 An Indisputably Han Local Study

Brandstädter (2003) writing of Meidao, a village in southern Fujian, which has become rich since the end of the Mao era, partly through connections with overseas relatives, describes a new configuration of power in which locally revived traditional institutions have incorporated local cadres and have become its effective government. It emerged out of the initial ruthless "chaos" of the first years of post-Mao economic reforms, of cadres' opportunism in alliance with emerging entrepreneurs. The new configurations of power are lineages and temples and their management committees. These committees comprised in equal numbers 'representatives of the new elite of successful businessmen, influential local cadres presently and formerly in office, overseas relatives, as well as the heads of the different lineage branches. Under the umbrella of the ancestral cult, the lineage thus united the members of different competing elites and bundled their resources together: the political power and bureaucratic connections of the old and present cadres, the economic power and transnational connections of the new economic elite, and the new/old ritual authority of lineage elders' (p. 97). She concludes that 'restored kinship and community institutions have come to organize the local state' (p. 102).

Many others have remarked on the same phenomenon in villages in other parts of south-eastern China and in Sichuan province, where there are elections and elected leaders or just Party secretaries that live in face-to-face relations with the ruled, such intermediate institutions can hold the political leader to account. Ancestral and other ritual communities can become grounds for the testing and nomination of elected village leaders in China (see, for instance, Tsai, 2007).

12.8 Conclusion

The state in the PRC, which includes the Chinese Communist Party, may be exceptional in its extension, by establishing a Party branch and a governmental committee in all administrative villages and urban neighborhoods. It is also less formally extended in officials' personal connections by which they recruit local people for the implementation of policies. But these studies also show that at the same time, there are opportunities for communities of complicity in which different and distanced senses of locality and local solidarity are maintained beneath the protection of cultural and development projects. This is one aspect of what anthropological studies of the modern state in China have been able to show. Another is the way that "culture", which was the self-conscious construction of nationalism, has become a doubled image. On one hand through the local government and the Ministry of Culture and tourist agencies culture is constructed in the name of preserving attractive local flavor. On the other hand, it is a continuation — which in the China of the succession to a period of suppression, is revival — that is now inevitably to some extent self-conscious, of institutions of hospitality, of divination, and of other rituals.

Seminar Questions

To what extent can the PRC state still be described from its grassroots as a stranger?

Is culture just a state invention of tradition?

Readings

Ardener, Edwin (1989). "'Remote areas" — some theoretical considerations', in Malcolm Chapman (ed.) Edwin Ardener: *The Voice of Prophecy and Other Essays*. Blackwell: Oxford, pp. 211–223.

Brandstädter, Susanne (2003). 'With Elias in China: civilising process, local restorations and power in contemporary rural China', *Anthropological Theory*, 3(1), pp. 87–105.

Duara, Prasenjit (2009). *The Global and the Regional in China's Nation Formation*. Routledge: London and New York.

Mueggler, Eric (2001). 'A spectral state', in *The Age of Wild Ghosts: Memory, Violence, and Place in Southwest China*. California University Press, pp. 159–198.

Pieke, Frank (2004). 'Contours of an anthropology of the Chinese state: political structure, agency and economic development in rural China', *Journal of the Royal Anthropological Institute N.S.*, 10, pp. 517–538.

Rowlands, Michael (2011). 'Of substances, palaces, and museums', *Journal of the Royal Anthropological Institute (N.S.)*, S21–S36.

References

Bilik, Naran (2002). 'The ethnicity of anthropology in China: discursive diversity and linguistic relativity', *Critique of Anthropology*, 22(2), pp. 133–148.

Duara, Prasenjit (1988). 'Superscribing symbols: the myth of Guandi, Chinese God of War' *Journal of Asian Studies*, 47(4), pp. 778–795.

Feuchtwang, Stephan, Zhang Hui and Morais, Paula (2016). 'The formation of governmental community and the closure of housing classes', chapter 13 in Gipouloux, Francois (ed.) *China's Urban Century*, Edward Elgar: London.

Feuchtwang, Stephan (2012). 'Civilisation and its discontents in contemporary China' Japan Focus July 2012. *The Asia Pacific Journal*: [online] http://japanfocus.org/-Stephan-Feuchtwang/3801.

Gellner, Ernest (1983). *Nations and Nationalism*. I Cornell University Press: Ithaca NY.

Goldstone, Jack A. (2002). 'Efflorescences and economic growth in world history: rethinking the "rise of the West" and the Industrial Revolution', *Journal of World History*, 13(2), pp. 323–389.

Harrison, Henrietta (2001). *China* (*Inventing the Nation*), Arnold: London (Chapter 4).

Herzfeld, Michael (1997). *Cultural Intimacy; Social Poetics in the Nation-state*, Routledge: London and New York.

Hobsbawm, Eric and Ranger, Terence (1983). *The Invention of Tradition*, Cambridge University Press: Cambridge.

Sutton, Donald (2003). *Steps of Perfection: Exorcistic Performance and Chinese Religion in 20th-century Taiwan*. Cambridge, Mass.: Harvard Asia Center Series; distributed by Harvard University Press.

Tsai, Lily L. (2007). *Accountability without Democracy; Solidary Groups and Public Goods Provision in Rural China*. Cambridge University Press: Cambridge.

Chapter 13

Conclusion

We hope that we have achieved two things in writing this book. One is a new way of studying the anthropology of China, namely one based on anthropology as much as on China. The other is to bring anthropological studies of China into the field of general anthropology. Each chapter has shown ways that anthropological studies of China contribute to, challenge, and entail modifications of the way each of the classical and more recent themes in mainstream anthropology that we have introduced are treated and understood. Anthropologists cannot afford to ignore the anthropology of China!

Chapter 2 offered the possibility that theories developed in the history of China, or of East Asia, ideas of the world and its centers and margins, or by anthropologists of China more recently, could become classical themes for more general anthropology, in the same way as caste and hierarchy have from the anthropology of India. So, for instance, Fei's own comparative idea of the traditional, rurally based conception of a system of differentiated moral subjects moving through asymmetrically ordered statuses (*chaxugeju*), from gendered child to ancestor, is compared and contrasted by him to the Christian and Euro–North-American individual belonging to a number of groups and categories. We can add that his conception of the Chinese moral subject offers a completely different idea of hierarchy, of self-cultivation, aspiration and social mobility to that of caste. In both cases, the spread of industrial capitalism, wage labor and its class system into these different status hierarchies, and the class relations that they ordered, raises the question whether the new class relations and a more individualistic moral subject destroy or transform or somehow re-set the old hierarchies. In both cases, some transmission of the older tradition is observable, so this is an ongoing topic for enquiry and comparison.

In Chapters 3 and 4, a key element of Chinese hierarchy, deference of female to male and of young to old, as well as of subject to ruler, was given its historical context. The patrilineal and patrilocal kinship system in China is learned and transmitted as a naturalized ideology through ritual, and through various institutions of marriage, lineage, and naming, and it is maintained in practices of forming and maintaining relationships. China's great written documentation of its history allows us to present the conditions in which a kinship system, similar to other patrilineal and patrilocal systems, was generalized for a whole population subject to the rule of a state, in this case an empire justified by an encompassing idea, of Tian, as the supreme physical, universal, and moral principles of order and change. For general anthropology, this raises the question of the origins and conditions for the existence of this and other kinship systems. China's modern state system of registration and conduct of population policy, not just its market economy and urbanization, is similarly ideological and has had a transformative effect on the transmitted kinship system, but has not eliminated it. Modernization is therefore too broad and too imprecise a theory to describe, let alone explain these changes. Both kinship and relatedness, as Chinese instances of these universal practices show, must be assumed to have their own more particular histories as ideologies.

Chapter 5's studies of the rich Chinese vocabulary of exchange and reciprocity, a lexicon of moral approval and condemnation, in which relations of trust and mistrust are voiced, offer a Chinese theme of the making of interpersonal relationships to the world of anthropology and the topic of social reproduction. But they enter into a general anthropology that is equally rich in concepts and distinctions, including the possibility of the social destructiveness of short-term monetary exchanges and contractual relations. What emerges from this encounter is a Chinese slant on the hierarchy of gift exchange, in which the recipient remains the superior because she or he is already established in a position of resourceful authority and prestige in state and market relations and receives the gift as a petition for patronage and favor. Again, this is suggestive for comparison with other systems of authority and prestige.

The spread of media conveying romantic ideals and narratives of love as self-cultivation into the Chinese ideological institutions of kinship and marriage create new stories through which young people understand their lives, seemingly confirming a universal distinction. As Chapter 6's studies show, Chinese conjugal relations could be understood by means of a shift from familiar and face-to-face settings in which love and affection emerged in the interstices of socially sanctioned arrangements towards an open-ness of romance through engagements with strangers and a proliferation of contacts. But population policy and transmitted senses of reciprocal obligations of intergenerational support and care here again modify the universal anthropological finding. And here too, the modification requires anthropologists to ask more historical and political questions about the commerce, consumerism, and media of romance, sex, and love.

Studies of food in China offer examples in Chapter 7 of an equally universal anthropological finding, that the formation of nations in a global system of states generates comparison of self and other, in self-conscious performances and preferences of production and consumption of food. Belonging has at its core the intergenerational transmission, through families, of "home" cooking, but at the same time an attraction to the exotic, whether through other cuisines or whatever is identified with being "modern". Peculiar to China is the macrobiotic cosmology of balance in which eating and the presentation of food is couched. This tradition interacts with the nutritional sciences that have spread globally. Each makes the other self-conscious, and this is true everywhere, as is the borrowing and concoction of new dishes for foreign consumption. Here, then, the anthropology of China offers fascinating local case studies but not necessarily a challenge to general anthropology.

Chapter 8's studies of human-environment interaction and activism in China seem to do the same: they offer intriguing local cases of the transformation of older traditions by the suffusion of the society: nature dichotomy that comes with the spread of biosciences and global politics. Even the art of siting (*fengshui*) and its cosmology, shared with food balance, has absorbed meteorology and concepts of "nature". But here, the studies of activism and protest against polluting industries and of local treatments of water and land disputes offer something more, suggestive for further comparative anthropology. They show a focal concern with ideas of the public good, social justice and the reduction of harm to humans within their environment, rather than the protection of a dehumanized realm of nature. State officials, their imposition of cold, inhuman law and development projects, from which they gain at the expense of human ill-health and dislocation, are the targets of local alliances of ritual institutions, locally trusted leaders and some officials in appeals to the moral leadership of the central state. Is this a uniquely modern Chinese tradition, or not?

With Chapter 9's studies of ritual and belief in China, we come from another perspective to the anthropology of ideology and encompassment, or cosmology, which was broached in Chapter 2 and the chapters on kinship, food and the environment. In this perspective, it is the institution of writing and the ritual recitation of written scriptures that Chinese studies thrust before anthropology. First it is the contrast of Chinese Daoist, Buddhist and redemptive society scriptures based on revelation against the scriptures of the monotheistic religions and their rituals of the profession of belief. But they convey as do all rituals, whether they include written scriptures or not, a structure of authoritative recognition of the social unit participating in them. This social unit can be a mourning household with its family line and social connections or a craft or trade or a territory, on the largest scale even the universe and its human centers, including the capital of the dynastic empire. Chinese rituals have been incorporated by comparative and synthesizing anthropologists into general theories of ritual already, as this chapter pointed out, when they argued against older functionalist theories of ritual as solidary rehearsals of an existing social order. But it is the contemporary legacy of the continued transmission of older rituals alongside the political rituals of more recent history, collectivist and nationalist idealizations of a secular future that prompts further anthropological thought.

Chapter 10 could be read as a culmination of the anthropology of gift and of food, Chapters 5 and 7, since hospitality, most often through gifts of food in banquets, brings into the sharpest focus how the treatment of strangers, of those not like self, of those who do not belong to the centered self and its rings of relationship and authority, is handled in a civilization. Into this relatively new subject of general anthropological theory, the long record of Chinese imperial rule, its guest ritual and tributary relationships brings a thought-provoking paradox. Hospitality, according to general anthropological theory, enacts a contest of sovereignty, in which the guest and stranger accept the sovereignty of the host's generosity. The paradox arises when the guest is of an order greater in scale, indeed encompassing the authority of the host. Who is then the host? Chinese cases of being host to imperial guests or of hosting gods present this paradox to general anthropology. The paradox cannot be uniquely Chinese. It is a complement of the gift-giver remaining inferior to the gift-receiver who is already in a position of great authority and prestige, presented in Chapter 5. Its complementary opposite is hospitable charity to beggars and ghosts, who may be feared, but do not present a strange or other sovereignty.

When in Chapter 11 we turned to anthropological theories of the state and in particular of pre-modern states through the model of the stranger-king, we found that guest rituals and the encompassing authority of Tian gave us another imperial contribution to anthropology. The complement to the stranger-king bringing in from outside the ritual charisma and affinal relationships to claim authoritative power over life and death, is the ritual and other processes of centring; that is to say, the gathering in from outside and creation of the centers of accumulation of ritual and other resources of the encompassing universe at all scales, rising from the house to the palace of the emperor. The outside is either or both the encompassing scale and the geographical outside from the perspective of the center. Centring must surely be added to the theory of the stranger-king.

Anthropological studies of the small-scale, the local and the marginal offer views up to the encompassing center, the state and its claims to moral authority, and at the same time bring to light strategies of maintaining autonomy within dependence, or of establishing a sovereign distance from a powerful civilizational state while maintaining its own civilization with neighbors. These, too, emerge in studies from out in the large fringe zones beyond and from localities under the Chinese civilizational state, and can be seen to perform their own rituals of centring and encompassment. Under the far more powerful and coercive state of modern China, in many ways typical of all other modern states, such local studies, examined in Chapter 12, shows us how cultural self-consciousness works, which local and international tourism, exoticism and diaspora had already revealed in the studies of food. Showing off the local for higher-scale recognition means accepting some or most of the terms of the newly coined 'cultural industries' and 'material and spiritual heritage' as a kind of mask under which claims to local belonging and senses of morality in its own transmitted discourses, fate calculations and festivals can be preserved. But this is only one instance of the juxtaposition of older transmissions, through ritual and other means of learning, with the newer institutions of state administration and their ideologies of the market, of socialism, or of loyalty to Party that is building the future of the people. The extraordinarily far-reaching powers of the modern Chinese Party-state may be exceptional in the imposition of policy and plan, but distancing is still possible by masking, by indifference, irony, scepticism and self-organization in large cities as well as in towns and villages.

Once again, these anthropological studies of specific contexts in China point to the importance of bringing into local accounts, the larger-scale and the powers and contested authority of the state and its administrative apparatuses. On the one hand, this is illuminated by the general anthropological elaboration of poetics and rhetoric, of irony in particular. On the other, readers may want to add the equally general anthropological elaboration of subjection to government and corporation, development, welfare and exploitation, to appraise local studies of the Chinese state.

If it is not already apparent, let us draw attention to what the anthropology of China brings to general anthropology most persistently. It pulls the following linked topics together: the formation and transformation of a large state; civilizational ideologies and encompassing justifications of authority; the historical record of long-term transformations, of continuity through change or *vice versa* of changes in what is held to be continuous and traditional from long before as well as under modern state authority and global capitalist flows; and how all of this becomes manifest in practices of learning (through rituals, exchanges, maintaining relationships, schooling, and experiences of being in a history). These form several distinct and not necessarily compatible repertoires of self-fashioning, moral judgment, and uncertainty.

That is what we conclude. But it is not definitive, except in laying claim to anthropological attention. Other readings of our chapters and their accompanying texts, and bringing to bear further relevant texts, are of course possible.

Index

A

abstraction, 9
affection, 113, 117
affinal, 75, 139, 229, 238, 241
affinal relations, 68
aiqing, 99
a large state, 268
alienation, 83
all under heaven, 30
altruism, 215
ancestors, 83, 199, 209, 220
ancestor worship, 55
ancestral hall, 48, 60
ancestral shrines, 54–55
ancestral tombs, 46
ancestral worship, 84
anthropocosmic, 177, 179
anthropocosmic worldview, 188
Anti-Rightist Campaign, 26
anti-structure, 43
Appadurai, Arjun, 122, 146–148, 150
Ardener, Edwin, 257
Asian societies, 16
Asian spices, 151
Astuti, Rita, 77
asylum, 223
asymmetrical opposition, 196
asymmetrical segmentation, 49
attachment, 108
authentic taste, 149
authority, 44–45, 194–195, 198, 204, 210, 221, 229, 241
autochthonous, 234, 241
autochthony, 228–229
autonomous subjectivity, 84
autonomy, 83, 108, 135, 267
axial, 233

B

balance, 167
Baltimore, 129
banquet, 221
Bedouin, 216
Belize, 146, 149–150
Bell, Catherine, 194–198, 201, 203–204, 210
belonging, 72, 265
Bilik, 249
birthday party, 155, 162

Bloch and Parry, 121–123, 134
Bloch, Maurice, 40–43, 45, 56, 61, 65, 67–68, 85, 120, 193–194, 197–199, 204, 209–210, 222, 229
Boas, Franz, 11
bodhisattva, 237–238
border region, 235, 240, 249, 253
Bourdieu, Pierre, 42, 144, 196, 199
Brandtstädter, Susanne, 137–139, 260
Bray, Francesca, 76
bridal lamentations, 84
Bruun, Ole, 186–187
Buddhism, 55, 177
bureaucracy, 50

C
Candea, Matei, 214
Candea and Da Col, 215, 222
canon, 202
Cantonese cuisine, 156–157
capitalism, 129, 137
Carsten, Janet, 72–75, 77–79
caste, 15–16, 18, 33, 147, 263
center as self, 232
centring, 227, 232–233, 241, 267
Chairman Mao, 128
Chakrabarty, 171
Chan and Zhang, 18
chaos, 129, 194, 234, 240
charitable estates, 59–60
charity, 35
Chau, Adam, 209, 224–225, 235
chaxugeju, 27, 30, 77, 263
Cheung, Sidney, 152
child, 41, 75
child development, 66
children, 65, 74, 77, 79–80, 90, 93–95, 161–162, 166, 181
child socialization, 82
Chinese Communist Party, 261
Chinese New Year, 67
Chinese Society of Sociology, 26
Christianity, 28
Chun, Allen, 48, 53, 55–58, 68
circumcision ritual, 43
city deity, 51
civilization, 227, 192, 213–215, 218, 231, 234–235, 237, 239–241, 251–252, 255–256, 258, 266
civilizational centers, 166, 238
civilizational distance, 253
civilizational state, 267
civilizational ideologies, 268
civilization of hospitality, 252
civil society, 35, 245
class status, 18
Clifford, James, 13
cognition, 40–41
coins, 124
Col, Da, 214
collective good, 185
collective property, 139
collectivism, 30, 205
colonial taste, 149
Columbian exchange, 151
commodities, 123
commodities markets, 125
commodity chains, 150
communal family, 58–60
communes, 33
community of complicity, 258–261
community solidarity, 127
companionship, 107
comparative, 23
comparative juxtapositions, 27
comparison, 9, 35–36
compassion, 34

compensation, 184
completion, 84
concubinage, 107
concubines, 77
Confucian, 177–178
Confucian family, 55
Confucianism, 28
Confucian virtue, 49
Confucius, 32, 192–193
conjugal relations, 265
connection, 72
consumerism, 34
contest of sovereignty, 218–221, 267
cookbooks, 147–148
corporation, 47, 50, 54, 62
cosmocracy, 231, 234, 236, 238, 241
cosmocratic rule, 229
cosmopolitanism, 165
cottage industry households, 89
courts, 63
cuisine, 145, 148
Culinary Schools, 145
Cultural Revolution, 20
cultural self-consciousness, 267
culture, 244, 249, 253, 256, 261
cycle of care, 78–79
cycle of yang, 79
cycles, 78
cycles of reciprocity, 72
cycles of yang and laiwang, 80

D

Da Col, 222
Daoism, 177
dating, 107, 111, 113
daughter-in-law, 81, 83–84, 114
daughters, 83–84, 87, 114
David, Wu, 152
death rituals, 199–200, 209
demonic spirits, 252
Derrida, 215, 217
Descola and Pálsson, 173–175
Descola, Philippe, 173
desire for autonomy, 85
desires, 81–83, 104, 108
destiny, 66, 111, 231
development projects, 259
dietetic knowledge, 154–155
differential mode, 29
differential mode of association, 27, 32, 77
diffusionist paradigms, 151
distanced senses of locality, 261
distinctions, 147, 158, 166
divination, 231
dogma, 202, 210
Douglas, Mary, 144
Duara, Prasenjit, 246–249, 254
Durkheim', 42

E

earth shrines, 235
Ebrey, Patricia, 56–60, 64, 68
economic liberalization, 23
egalitarian, 46, 240
egalitarianism, 240
egocentric person, 29
elders, 44, 49, 64
elite networks, 135, 137
emotion, 99, 105–106, 108, 220
emotive force, 194
encompassing heaven, 233
encompassing order, 44
encompassing sovereign, 229
encompassing universe, 232
encompassing world, 231
encompassment, 30, 266
entrepreneurs, 135

environmental activism, 179–180
environmental degradation, 172
environmental ethics, 187
estate, 48–49, 54–55, 58–60
ethics, 34, 106, 117
ethnic minorities, 22, 25
ethnography, 11, 13–14, 16, 35–36
ethnology, 22
examination system, 62
exchange, 15
exotic, 148, 153, 157, 160, 162, 265
exploitation, 62
extravagance, 208

F

face, 130, 134, 155
face projects, 259
factions, 207
family, 48–49, 58, 68, 90, 181
family planning policy, 90–95, 104
family ritual orthodoxy, 53
family treasure, 126
Famine, 251
Fardon, Richard, 10–12, 36
Farrer, James, 110–113, 117
father, 84
Faust, 215
feasting, 214, 225
Fei, Xiaotong, 10, 23–24, 26, 30–32, 36, 46, 77, 130, 263
Fei's sociological theory of China, 26
female sexuality, 107
fengshui, 186–188, 201, 258, 265
fertility goddesses, 181
festival foods, 155
Feuchtwang, Stephan, 186, 257–258
filial duty, 115
filial nationalism, 114
filial piety, 34
Fitzgerald, C. P., 235
Fong, Vanessa, 113–115, 117
food, 214
food safety, 154
foreign snacks, 165
fox fairies, 107
Freedman, Maurice, 47–50, 68
friendship, 135
From the Soil, 24–25
funeral rituals, 208–209

G

ganqing, 99–100, 105–106
Gates, Hill, 61, 64–65, 68, 125, 127–128
Gellner, Ernest, 244
Gell, Alfred, 101–103, 111, 116–117
gender, 34, 45–46, 61, 63, 81, 96, 133
gender hierarchy, 65, 136
genealogical formation, 59
genealogies, 55–56, 59, 81
generation, 81, 154
generational cleavages, 156
generosity, 213, 216
gentry, 50, 56
ghosts, 209, 220
Giddens, Anthony, 32
Gillette, Maris Boyd, 164, 166
Gladney, Dru, 22
global, 146
globalizing processes, 144
global standardization, 160
God of Wealth, 128
gods, 220
Goldstone, Jack, 243
Goodman, David, 158, 160
Goody, Jack, 144, 147
Government control, 51
Granet, Marcel, 232
grasslands of the Cameroons, 256

graves, 57–58, 60, 81, 235
gravesites, 125
Great Leap Forward, 19–20, 251
Greenhalgh and Winckler, 21, 92
Greenhalgh, Susan, 21, 92–93, 96
Gregory, Chris, 122
guanxi, 129–135, 137
Gudeman, 122
guest ritual, 217, 219, 266
guests, 220
Guo, Yuhua, 153–156
Gwer Sa La, 254–255

H

habitus, 195–196
Hamilton, Gary, 24
Hamilton and Wang, 21–22, 25, 27
happiness, 31
Harrell, Stevan, 17–23
Harrison, Henrietta, 249
Harris, Marvin, 144
haute cuisine, 152
heaven, 33, 229
Hegemony, 196
Henderson, John, 233
heritage, 217, 245, 254, 268
Herzfeld, Michael, 245, 257
heteronomy, 233
Heusch, de Luc, 228
Hevia, James, 219
hierarchical differentiation, 28, 30
hierarchy, 45, 52, 63, 65, 68, 130–131, 140, 193–194, 201, 221, 228, 230, 233, 263–264
hierarchy and equality, 46
high cuisine, 147
historical knowledge, 66–67
history, 66–67
Hobsbawm, Eric, 244
Hong Kong, 22–23, 158, 161–163
household, 18
household-based cottage industry, 88
household registration, 18, 90, 92
household registration system, 20, 86, 103
household responsibility system, 20
Hsu, Francis, 235
Hui, 164–166
human, 174, 214
human-centered orientation, 180
human development, 174
human feelings, 129–130
humanity, 215
Hundred Flowers campaign, 26
hungry ghost, 208

I

ideology, 41, 43–45, 47, 60, 67–68, 85
illness causation, 183–184
illocutionary force, 194
immorality, 31
imperial cosmology, 201
India, 146, 148
industrial capitalism, 244, 247
inside/outside, 231
intergenerational love, 99, 113
intergenerational transmission, 154
interpersonal relationships, 264
inter-textuality, 14
intimacy, 109–112
irony, 268

J

Jankowiak, William, 107–108, 112, 116
Jesuits, 178
Jones, Stephen, 224
Judd, Ellen, 84–85, 87, 90, 96
Jing, Jun, 180–182

K

Kabyle, Berber, 42
Kant, Immanuel, 215–216
kinship, 71–74, 77–78
kinship rituals, 138
kinship system, 264
Kipnis, Andrew, 21, 105, 108
Klein, Jakob, 157
Kleinman, Arthur, 18
Kopytoff, Gregor, 122

L

laiwang cycles, 78
land, 54–55, 63–64, 125, 138, 228
land reform, 18
land use, 185
Langkawi, 75
language acquisition, 41
law, 185
Leach, Edmund, 238, 240
legitimation, 45
Li, Zhang,192
Liang, Yongjia, 235–236, 254–255
liminal, 44
Lindholm, Charles, 100, 116
lineage formation, 52
lineage paradigm, 47, 81
lineage(s), 15, 39, 47–50, 54, 58–61, 63–65, 68, 77, 83, 138–139, 205, 208, 228, 235, 260
Lingbao scriptures, 201–202
literacy, 244
local specialty, 259
local state, 260, 269
Lora-Wainwright, Anna, 183–184
love, 100, 103–104, 107–108, 112–114, 116–117, 155
luan, 129

M

Macartney, 219
Madsen, Richard, 205, 207
male friendship, 136
Malinowski, Bronisław, 11, 25, 73
Mao, 32, 206–207
Maoism, 18, 30–32, 65, 115, 154
Maoist, 24, 66
marital alliances, 46
marketing area, 52
marketing structures, 68
marketization, 62
markets, 50–51, 121
marriage, 100–105, 107, 109–113, 117, 125–126, 133
marriage alliances, 52
Martin, Emily, 123–125, 127–129, 134, 137
Marx, Karl, 121–122, 124, 129
Maryland, 123
matching, 103
matchmaking, 103, 133
Mauss, Marcel, 122, 214, 232
McDonald's, 160–163
mediation, 185–186, 199, 204
Meiji, 247
Merina, 41, 43, 45–46
merit, 133, 136
Miaoshan, 84
middle class, 147, 151, 159
migrant labor, 152
migrant networks, 89
migrants, 20, 88
military defense, 50
Mintz, Sidney, 145, 150–152, 157, 160–161, 163, 167
misrecognition, 248
misrecognized ritual, 256

modernization, 246, 264
modernity, 36
modern states, 253
money, 129
money symbolism, 125
monstrosity, 237
moral authority, 32–33, 185, 267
moral communities, 138–139
moral crisis, 33
moral decline, 134
moral economy, 137, 179
moral entitlement, 182
morality, 10, 24, 30–31, 121
moral judgment, 268
moral leadership, 266
moral norms, 230
moral person, 130
moral plenum, 185
moral subject, 263–264
moral vacuum, 186
Morgan, Lewis Henry, 21–22, 26
mortuary rituals, 251–252
mother, 84, 181
motherhood, 76–77
mourning grades, 49
Mueggler, Eric, 218, 249–252
music, 199
Muslim heritage, 164
Muslim worldview, 165
myths, 191–192, 207

N

Nanzhao, 236–238, 254–255
narratives of love, 265
national cuisine, 145–146, 148, 150
nationalism, 115, 244, 247–248
nationalist, 245
nationality, 22
native-place networks, 132
nativization, 23
nature, 73, 75–76, 174, 176, 178, 180, 265
nature and society, 173
nature–culture, 173–177, 179
negative hospitality, 222
neo-Confucian family values, 62
neo-Confucian ideology, 54–55, 59
neo-Confucians, 58
network, 28, 52, 88, 130
network society, 30
Nezha, 84
non-governmental organizations, 180
noodles and breads, 159
nurture, 79

O

only children, 114
order and change, 264
organizational mode of association, 27, 77
orthodoxy, 198, 207
orthopraxy, 207–208, 210
Osburg, John, 135–137
outside, 231–232
Oxfeld, Ellen, 207–208

P

Pálsson, Gísli, 173
paper money, 119, 125
parasite, 223
Park, Robert, 24
Parry and Bloch, 120
patriarchy, 48, 88
patriline, 96

patrilineage, 47
patrilineal continuity, 83
patriliny, 82
patriotism, 115
patronage, 136, 205, 214, 264
patron–client relationships, 135
Peach Blossom Garden, 253, 258
peasants, 19
people, 244
people-states, 246, 249
peripheries, 239–241, 253
personhood, 27
persons, 74–75
petition, 202, 255, 264
petitioners, 182
petty capitalism, 64
petty-capitalist, 62
petty-capitalist mode of production, 62
Pia, Andrea , 184
Pieke, Frank, 259
poison, 222
political protest, 182
political rituals, 196, 201, 204, 206, 266
popular protest, 180–181
population, 18, 91–92, 94
population policy, 21, 264–265
population quality, 93–94
Potter, Jack, 18, 105, 108
practices of learning, 268
premarital sex, 104
prescriptive texts, 200, 202
primogeniture, 63
privacy, 100, 109
property law, 63
propriety, 106
provincial cuisine, 159
psychology, 41
public good, 207, 265
Puett, Michael, 203
Puritan cult of sincerity, 203

Q

qi, 177, 186
Qing, 99
qingzhen, 165–166
qingzhen food, 164
qingzhen lifestyle, 164

R

race, 250
Ranger, Terence, 244
Rawski, Evelyn, 200–201
reciprocity, 78, 106, 129–131, 134, 214, 218
reconquest of life, 229
Reconstructing Rural China, 25
redemptive harmony, 195
regionalization, 10, 15, 17, 35
regions, 14
religion, 198
religious ritual, 202
religious worship, 16
remittances, 138
remoteness, 257
ren, 29
renqing, 129–130, 132, 134, 136
representation, 9
reproduction, 74–75, 96
reproductive technologies, 75
rites, 58, 60, 192, 201
rites of passage, 194
ritual, 29, 40, 43–44, 55–57, 68, 124, 128, 137–138, 261, 264
ritual handbooks, 201
ritualization, 195
ritual process, 44

ritual violence, 194
rival sovereignties, 234
Roberts, Alice, 248
Rofel, Lisa, 34
role ethics, 193
romance, 109, 221, 265
romantic love, 99–100, 102, 104, 110
romantic movements, 178
romantic passion, 107
romantic scripts, 107, 110
rotating credit associations, 126–127
Rowlands, Michael, 256
rule of law, 136
rural migrants, 92
rural-to-urban migration, 86
rural–urban continuum, 17

S

sacred, 195
sacrifice, 105, 114, 182, 202
Sahlins, 214, 228, 230, 232–233, 236
Sangren, Steven, 81–85, 96
Schneider, David, 74
schooling, 244
Scott, James, 239, 253
scripting, 102
scripts, 111–113, 117
scriptures, 199, 203, 208, 210, 266
secrecy, 102
secular, 196, 204, 207, 266
segregation, 164
self, 28, 32, 34, 99, 146, 150, 215, 227
self-affirmation, 147
self-constraint, 213
selfhood, 30, 120
selfishness, 31, 33
self-loss, 101
Seligman, Adam, 203–204
selves, 117
seniority, 45–46, 58, 63, 76, 83
sent-down youth, 206
sex, 34, 112–113, 116, 135
sex ratios, 95
sexuality, 100
Shan, 238
Shanxi food, 159
Shanxi identity, 158
Shirokogoroff, S.M., 24
Shryock, Andrew, 216–217, 220
Shui Hu Zhuan, 253
siblingship, 75
Simmel, Georg, 121, 124, 129
Simon, Bennett, 203
sincerity, 106, 203–204
Sino-centric world system, 234
Sinology, 16
Skinner, William, 18, 49–51, 68, 125
small sovereignties, 253
social class, 46
Social Darwinism, 247
social hierarchy, 158
sociality, 225
social justice, 209
social networking, 120, 135
social reproduction, 45, 82
society, 265
sociology, 25
songs, 207, 210
sons, 83–84
sovereign, 217, 221, 227, 230, 236
sovereign distance, 267
sovereign territory, 253
sovereignty, 215–218, 224, 231, 247–248
soy, 151
speaking bitterness, 206

special flavor, 257
Spencer, Herbert, 247
sphere, 174
spice trade, 153
spirit money, 127
spirituality, 193
Stafford, Charles, 65–67, 69, 78–80, 96, 116, 220–221, 224
standardization, 202
standard marketing community, 51
state(s), 40, 49–50, 53, 58, 61–64, 90–91, 93–94, 96, 132, 136, 172, 180, 201, 227–228, 239–240, 244–245, 252, 260, 264, 267
state authority, 128, 179
state hierarchies, 239
state laws, 185
state patriotism, 249
state socialism, 131
status, 133–134, 137–138
steam-powered industrial revolution, 244
steam-powered industry, 243
Steinmüller, Hans, 257–258
stereotypes, 245, 249
stranger, 223, 266
Strathern, Marilyn, 74
Strecker, Iwo, 215
struggle meetings, 206
subjunctive, 203
sugar, 150
superscription, 254
Sutton, Donald, 254
suzhi, 21
sworn brotherhood, 136

T

Taiwan, 22–23, 65, 78, 80–81, 123, 125, 128, 176–179
Taussig, 122
temple, 202, 260
temple associations, 139
temple festivals, 224
territorial communities, 218
territorial festivals, 202
territorial gods, 253
territorial protector gods, 209
territorial protector shrines, 235
territorial sovereignty, 249
Theravada sovereignty, 238
Thompson, Stuart, 76
tian, 177–178, 202, 267
tianxia, 30, 201, 229
Tianzi, 229
tourism, 253, 267
tourists, 256
tourist sites, 258
Traditional Chinese Medicine, 154
transactional cycles, 121
transnational, 149–150, 246
tributary, 62
tributary guests, 218
tributary mode of production, 62
trust, 32–33, 111, 121, 198, 264
Tsai, Lilly, 262
Tsai, Chang, 58
ts'ici, 250, 252
tuantigeju, 27
Tubo, 238
Turner, Victor, 43

U

Umeda, 101–102
UNESCO, 254–255
United Kingdom, 244
unity and diversity, 16–17
unplanned persons, 94
urban, 19
urbanization, 62

usury, 126–127
uterine family, 80

V
value, 134, 156
Vezo, 77–78
village communities, 17
village studies, 22
violence, 114, 194
virilocality, 82–83

W
wandering spirits, 225
Wang, Zheng, 24
Wang, Mingming, 232–234
war, 246
water resource, 185
Watson, James, 160–163, 199–200
Weber, Max, 203
webs, 29
weddings, 81
Weller, Robert, 176–180, 182–183, 203
wilderness, 234
wild ghosts, 252
Wilks, Richard, 146, 149–150
witchcraft, 222
Wolf, Margery, 80, 87
woman's autonomy, 126
women, 81, 89
women's kinship, 86–87
work, 72, 105
work points, 18
work units, 19, 33
world cuisine, 150, 152
world system, 243
writing, 240, 266
Writing Culture, 11, 13
Wu and Cheung, 153

X
Xiongnu, 230
Xi, Zhu, 57, 201

Y
yang cycles, 78
Yang, Mayfair, 116, 132, 134
Yan, Yunxiang, 11, 30–36, 108–112, 116–117, 130, 134, 221
Yi, 219
Yuhua, Guo, 153

Z
Zafimaniry, 222
Zhang, Li, 88–89, 96
ziran, 177–178, 188
Zomia, 239

www.ingramcontent.com/pod-product-compliance
Lightning Source LLC
Chambersburg PA
CBHW050632280326
41932CB00015B/2614

* 9 7 8 1 7 8 3 2 6 9 8 3 9 *